Blood Kin of Jesus

BLOOD KIN OF JESUS

James and the Lost Jewish Church

Kenneth Hanson, PhD

COUNCIL
OAK BOOKS

Tulsa / San Francisco

www.counciloakbooks.com

ISBN 978-1-57178-224-3

Interior design and illustrations by Melanie Haage

Library of Congress Cataloging-in-Publication Data

Hanson, Kenneth, 1953–

Blood kin of Jesus : James and the lost Jewish church / Kenneth Hanson.

   p. cm.

Includes bibliographical references and index.

ISBN 978-1-57178-224-3 (pbk. : alk. paper)

1. James, Brother of the Lord, Saint. 2. Church history—Primitive and early church, ca. 30–600. 3. Christianity—Origin. 4. Jesus Christ—Brethren. 5. Jesus Christ—Family. I. Title.

BS2454.J3H36 2009
232.9--dc22

2009024646

To my sons and heirs,
Jonathan and Pieter

contents

illustrations

PREFACE

THREE LONG DECADES AGO, AS A YOUNG HISTORY STUDENT, I trudged off to the Middle East with the stated objective of discovering the historical Jesus. What I encountered instead was an historical Jew, bound by the pious observance of the Torah, from its greatest commandments to its most intimate, yet pietistic precepts. In time I took up teaching duties in a program of Judaic Studies at a major university. Many have subsequently asked whatever may have possessed me to pursue such a radical direction and unusual career path. It is a fair question.

Growing up Methodist in suburban Chicago, I was always struck by the fact that as much time as I spent in the local house of worship, the Jesus I was exposed to — staring out from stained-glass windows with an otherworldly look on his face — didn't seem like a person I would particularly want to meet, much less get to know. He seemed strangely alien, even though the artist had clearly tried to depict him as a European Caucasian, with long straight hair and an equally long and wispy beard, and eyes that seemed a little bit too blue. The composite result was an effeminate looking man, who couldn't possibly have been "real," at least in the same sense as other historical figures I had learned about in school. He certainly seemed very holy, but not very approachable.

I never missed a week of Sunday school classes, but none of this exposure to Protestant Christianity ever introduced me to the world in which Jesus lived – a Jewish world, populated by pious Israelites, whose devotion to God was a perfect reflection of their fidelity to the Torah, the five books of Moses. My entire religious experience left me oddly discontented. If we were intent on following a man whose home was ancient Galilee, why was serious study of this region never even contemplated? Why was there no desire to know anything about his people, his own tribe of Judah, and his own family, all of whom seemed consigned to the shadows?

As I reached my teenage years, the Sunday school curriculum focused on the history and growth of the western church, tracing it all the way back to the apostle Paul and his missionary journeys across the Roman empire. Nary a word was spoken about the "mother church," the church in Jerusalem, and what ultimately became of it. Whatever happened to the disciples in the east, the Jewish disciples, who must have retained some connection with the faith of their ancestors – of Abraham, Isaac, Jacob and Moses? Most importantly, what became of Jesus' family members, who must without question have known him better than anyone else – his brothers, his sisters, and of course his mother?

As I entered my college years, I felt strangely drawn to the land of Israel itself. I majored in history, focusing on the ancient near east, and during my senior year I boarded my first international flight, bound for the city of Jerusalem. To say that Israel changed me would be a gross understatement. It completely altered my self-conception. It taught me a new language, an ancient tongue revived as "modern Hebrew." This in turn led me to the study of scores of ancient texts in their original idiom. In time the young Anglo-Saxon Protestant found himself regularly attending synagogues, learning to pray as Jesus prayed. I began to understand Jesus and his movement in a new way, no longer trapped by the bonds of religious dogma, but as an historical person and a phenomenon in the real world. In the end the Christian became a Jew, and this book is the result.

This book was originally conceived as a work of ten chapters, perhaps with the Ten Commandments in mind. But somehow ten chapters never materialized, which may have some significance in the mystical realm. After all, Beethoven produced nine symphonies, not ten. I therefore respectfully reserve the number ten for Moses, and this tome will remain at nine. It begs only to be read with an open mind. It is written for all, Jews and non-Jews alike, who simply desire to know. As the great Galilean himself reportedly said, "You shall know the truth…"

I

The First Family:
Who Were They?

HE GREAT TEACHER WAS NO MORE. THE MESSIAH HAD BEEN martyred. But it was not a glorious death, like a warrior who fell in some celebrated battle. No, this was ignominious humiliation, as a victim nailed to a Roman execution post. His band of disciples had fled in terror. His personal understudy had denied even knowing him. That should have been the end of it. One more rabble-rouser done in by the law of the empire.

As time went by there would be others like him. A crazed prophet would ascend from Egypt and lead a group of thirty thousand up the Mount of Olives, where he would, by supernatural power, command the walls of Jerusalem to fall down. Another messianic impostor named Theudas would claim to be able to part the Jordan River and lead the people across, like Joshua of old.[1] But the procurator Fadus would dispatch his cavalry and have the prophet's head "liberated" from his shoulders and brought back to Jerusalem.

In a time of grave internal crisis, when nationalistic hopes had been thwarted by sheer imperial might, messiahs were multiple. The ancient Jewish historian Josephus Flavius summed it up, describing an age of men maddened by false promises and soured by true miseries:

> Deceivers and impostors, under the pretense of divine inspiration fostering revolutionary changes, they persuaded the multitude to act like madmen, and led them out into the desert under the

belief that God would there give them tokens of deliverance.
(*The Jewish War*, book II, line 259)

The Romans of course had a way of dispensing with prophets and
pseudo-messiahs, and, with little coaxing required, dispersing their misguided disciples. Everyone expected a similar fate to befall the bewil-
dered followers of Galilee's contribution to messianic martyrdom, Jesus of
Nazareth. But that was not to be the fate of the "Jesus movement."

One of the most curious realities in history is the simple fact that after the humiliating death of its leader the movement not only survived, it
exploded – from Jerusalem, across Judea, across the Galilee and to lands
beyond. Its unexpected, unanticipated success defies elucidation, and from
that ancient era to our own day, perhaps the best explanation may be that
the Heirs of Jesus' ministry were firmly convinced of the miracle of resurrection. The idea that Jesus had died by crucifixion, was buried and subsequently came back to life was the one thing that gave them unity and
hope. Their faith was founded on the resurrection and the promise of new
life. Some modern scholars refer to ancient Christianity as nothing short
of a "resurrection cult." Whether the Master's resurrection was accepted
as fact or merely as an allegorical tale (after the manner of some modern

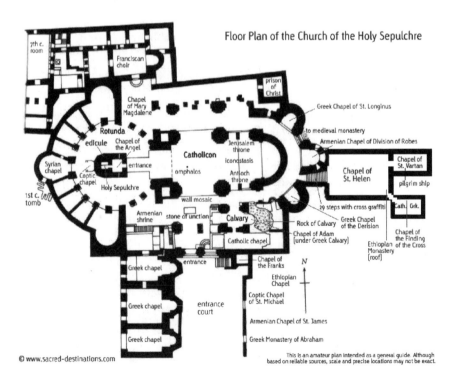

Floor Plan of the Church of the Holy Sepulchre

© www.sacred-destinations.com

This is an amateur plan intended as a general guide. Although
based on reliable sources, scale and precise locations may not be exact.

interpreters), one thing is clear: however strongly they quibbled, the earliest Christians could always agree on the essential meaning of resurrection – a new and abundant life in the here-and-now for all who would receive it.

And they knew where it happened, more or less exactly, in the Old City of Jerusalem. An ancient church, whose foundations were laid in the days of the empress Helena, mother of Rome's mighty Emperor Constantine, today sanctifies the spot, covering a rocky outcropping known in ancient Aramaic as Golgotha – the equivalent of the Hebrew *Golgolet* – meaning "Skull." Visitors to this dank and musty sanctuary of Romanesque architecture can even today venture into its subterranean vaults, descending into its underground substructure to behold first century tombs, situated exactly where we would expect to find the rock-hewn crypt of a pious Israelite named Joseph of Arimathea, who hastily lent his own sepulcher to the distraught family of a freshly executed Galilean preacher named Yeshua m'Natzeret – Jesus of Nazareth.

Galileans No More

Immediately following the dark day on which the Master was crucified, the focus of the story shifts from Yeshua himself to his band of disciples – twelve not-so-simple men from the Galilee plus a newcomer/ "intruder" named Saul (better known as Paul). They are the ones who will keep the divine message alive. They are the ones who will build the fledgling movement into a potent force to be reckoned with throughout the Roman empire. Little is said of the family members, who are all but ignored by the forward march of the New Testament narrative. It is up to us, millennia removed from Roman Judea, to ask who knew Yeshua better – his family or his friends? We almost forget the tension that must have been churning beneath the surface over leadership of the community, which came to be called the "Church." After all, the events in the wake of the crucifixion are so dramatic that all else pales by comparison.

Readers of the New Testament recall the traditional story, as recounted by the books of Luke and Acts. There were multiple reports, which spread like a desert wind, that the resurrected Yeshua had been seen. On one occasion two of Yeshua's disciples were traveling the road that led from Jerusalem to a small village about seven miles away called Emmaus, when a stranger appeared and discussed with them the events surrounding the execution of the Master. Later, he agreed to spend the night with them and sat down with them for supper, only to mysteriously vanish. They immediately recognized two things – that this was no stranger but the resurrected Master himself, and that, far from being a phantom body (as the Gnostic Christians would later teach), this was a real person, who broke bread and ate. When the two disciples hastened back to Jerusalem and related their incredible encounter to the others, Yeshua suddenly materialized again, even showing the wounds of crucifixion to prove his identity. This was no ghostly apparition. It was resurrection; it was reality. The "motto" in those days may well have been: No resurrection, no Messiah.

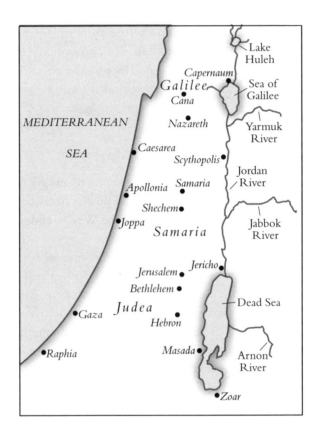

Yeshua was said to have appeared among his devoted followers one last time on the Mount of Olives, whereupon he physically ascended from that natural limestone ridge, due east of the city, into the heavens. His final directive was clear. They were not to return to the Galilee. They were not to leave Jerusalem at all, but to wait for a mysterious supernatural gift, imparted by the *Shekhinah*, subsequently known as the "Holy Spirit." Not surprisingly, the disciples headed back to the city, gathered together in a certain house, and deliberated over who would take the place of Yehuda (Judas), who had killed himself in the wake of the Master's death. This group was the nucleus of an ecclesiastical organization which needed leaders and a structure of authority, "inherited" from the Master himself. These bold actions resembled a similar development many centuries later in the heart of Europe, when ultra-Orthodox Hasidic Rebbes would establish what amounted to rabbinic "dynasties," carrying on the teachings of the great Kabbalistic sages such as the Baal Shem Tov. The disciples of these sages so venerated their masters that they were accused by their fellow Jews of "rabbi worship." Nonetheless, dynamic teachers need dynamic disciples who will establish dynamic organizations. It is the only way their "logos" – their divine utterance – will live on.

At the end of the deliberations in Jerusalem, a new disciple named Matthias was chosen to replace Judas. Then, fifty days after Passover, on the Feast of Shavuot ("Weeks") – called "Pentecost" in Greek – the disciple named Shimon – whom we have come to know as Peter – stood up in front of an enormous crowd and held forth in thunderous oratory. The results were astounding. A multitude of people, including a large company of Jews who were visiting from abroad on the occasion of the feast, were added to their number as followers of "the Way" – code language for the new Jesus movement.

As the Book of Acts tells the story, after this clarion call has been issued by this dedicated and well-organized society of believers, there is no question who is in charge. The disciples/ apostles advance the narrative; they act decisively. The immediate family members are relegated to the sidelines, all but forgotten. They have not, however, disappeared, and will resurface in due course, as conflict ignites over the movement's direction, character and very survival. In the meantime, we should ask ourselves a question that the New Testament narrative conveniently skirts: where are Yeshua's family members? His brothers? His sisters? And most importantly, where is his mother?

Miriam – the Distraught Mother

How can we ignore Miriam? She, who would be revered for centuries to come and beatified as the Holy Mother, at this point appears to mysteriously vanish from the story. One thing we know with certainty is that Miriam, like the new society of Yeshua's disciples, would never return to her home in the Galilee. She would remain in Jerusalem for the rest of her days. It is possible today to visit an impressive church on the natural ridge called Mount Zion, known as the Dormitian. It is the place where, according to long established Church tradition, Miriam died. The imposing stone edifice is today the defining landmark of the holy mountain, dwarfing the nearby tomb of King David, which sits in humble semi-obscurity.

Over time Miriam would receive at the hands of western Christendom a facelift and a name change. Mary, as she came to be called, would be virtually deified and completely divorced from her Jewishness. The Church realized early on that it could not completely de-Judaize Jesus (his ethnicity being too much a part of his fundamental character), so it settled for de-Judaizing Mary. We can nonetheless reconstruct at least some of the details of her life as a pious Jewish woman of ancient Israel. We start in her home town, listed by the New Testament as a place called Nazareth in an area known as "the Region," in Hebrew *ha-Galil* – the Galilee.

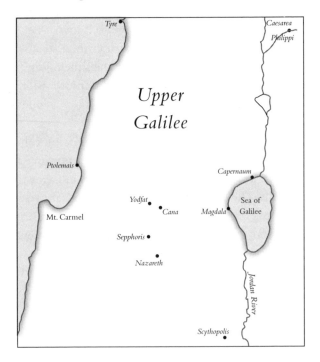

Neither Miriam nor any of her family, including her most famous son, can be understood without appreciating the character of this strategic and culturally baffling region. The one thing that can be said with certainty about the Galilee, the northern district of the ancient land of Israel, is that it completely defies modern stereotypes. It was by no means a pastoral menagerie of green pastures, quiet landscapes and babbling brooks. It was considered a troublesome region by all, including Jerusalemites and Judeans in general, who frequently denigrated their unruly neighbors to the north. At the time of Yeshua's birth, the entire area was ruled by an occupying army. As we in the United States became unpleasantly aware during our own country's occupation of Iraq, military occupation does not necessarily sit well with the native population, even under the best of circumstances. From the Roman point of view, these were far from the best of circumstances. This land was the furthest outpost of Roman rule, and it was almost useless to the Romans from an economic standpoint. It was not only remote, but much of it was barren. Nor were there material assets worth exploiting. Furthermore, unlike other Roman conquests, the native population, far from being docile peasants, were literate and had a highly developed military, religious and cultural background. They in fact regarded the mighty Romans as their intellectual inferiors.

To make matters worse, these arrogant natives not only despised the Romans, but they, like the present day Iraqis, had their own internal feuds — Pharisees versus Sadducees and so on. In addition, the topography of the area was cramped and difficult to traverse from a military standpoint. To make a final comparison with present-day Iraq, there was, after the death of the iron-fisted ruler Herod, a breakdown on the administrative side, with the country fragmenting into three largely autonomous regions: Judea in the south (ruled directly by Roman procurators and prefects), the territory east of the Jordan River (ruled by Herod Philip), and of course the Galilee (ruled by Herod Antipas). For all of these reasons, while Christians believe that it was the work of the Almighty that brought forth a messiah, the conditions at the time made God's work a lot easier.

Another analogy would be to compare the Galilee to America's southern states. The Galilee was to Judea as the "old South" was to the states located north of the Mason-Dixon line, namely, less sophisticated, less cosmopolitan, more provincial, yet teeming with independent-minded folk, motivated by religious faith, traditional values and a willingness to fight for the "just cause" – in other words: God, guns (in Galilee, swords) and guts. America's deep South birthed the Confederate rebels; the Galilee was the home base of a radical group of guerilla freedom fighters known as the Zealots. It should hardly surprise us that the Gospels refer to one of the twelve disciples as Simon the Zealot. It is also tempting to consider the name of the disciple known infamously as Judas Iscariot. Does Iscariot refer to the town where Judas was born? Or is it a cryptic reference to the most radical of all revolutionary groups of those days, the Sicarii, or "dagger men" – named after the *sicar* – the short dagger concealed within a man's cloak. The Galileans had coined a saying that well summarizes their sentiments: "God alone rules over His people." While avoiding any reference to imperial authorities, their intent was subversive nonetheless. No temporal authority would be recognized until divine rule was established once again over all of Israel.

But when it comes to understanding Miriam and her family, it is important to recognize that the Galilee was known for more than simply insurrection. For, inasmuch as its inhabitants were zealous for their freedom, they were also zealous for the Law. Scattered in pockets across the terraced hillsides were communities of staunch pietists known not for their military but their religious zeal. They spent their lives in the strict observance of the precepts of the Torah, seeking connection with the divine and an intimacy with the Deity that bordered on arrogance. They cleaved to God with purity of soul, focusing on divine compassion and loving-kindness, summed up in the Hebrew word *hesed*. In time they came to be known as a group by this very word – Hasidim – "compassionate" or "pious ones."[2] They were itinerant preachers who went from town to town, spreading their pietistic messages, with their own bands of disciples following along. Some were known for being able to bring rain during periods of drought. Others were known as miracle workers, imparting gifts of divine healing to those who suffered from illness and disease.

There is every reason to believe that Miriam was born and raised in such a pietistic environment, that her family was scrupulously observant of the Law in every respect. It was Miriam who made sure that her son Yeshua was circumcised according to religious precept on the eighth day and that he was not officially named until that moment (Luke 2:21). Thereafter, Miriam was careful to perform the purification ritual in Jerusalem (involving immersion in a ritual bath, or *mikveh*) following childbirth. It was Miriam and her husband Yosef (Joseph) who also made sure to perform the ritual known as *pidyon ha-ben* – "the redemption of the firstborn." According to Jewish law, every firstborn son belongs to God and must literally be bought back – in the case of Miriam and Yosef, through the sacrifice of a pair of doves or two young pigeons (Luke 2:22-24). This is not the behavior of ignorant peasantry – the stereotypical image of Jesus' family – but of learned Jews steeped in tradition.

We are told that Miriam, Yosef and family made a pilgrimage to

Jerusalem every year for the feast of Passover, which is again characteristic of scrupulously observant Israelites. Some years later the family was again in Jerusalem when Yeshua, who was now twelve years of age, turned up missing from the rest of the family. He was found in the Temple precincts, profoundly impressing the sages of the day with his detailed knowledge of the Torah (Luke 2:41-52). It was during this episode that young Yeshua made use of a kind of "code language" that identifies in the eyes of many contemporary scholars his true religious identity. He called the Temple "my Father's house." The traditional Israelite address to God was always in the plural, "Our Father." Only one ancient Jewish sect possessed the audacity to address God in the singular, as "My Father." They were the Pious – the Hasidim.[3] When Yeshua used this address in the Temple, Miriam did not recoil in shock, but rather "treasured these things in her heart," a clear indication of her own sympathy with the audacious approach of the Hasidic stream in ancient Judaism.

Miriam is soon left behind in the New Testament narrative, but we are told that as her son Yeshua grew to maturity he began to instruct people in a manner evocative of a Hasid. The nature of his teachings, the miracles attributed to him and his overall *modus operandi* have convinced not a few modern researchers that he was himself one of the Hasidim.[4] He was certainly aware of the radical, anti-Roman Zealots of Galilee, but his teachings evinced strong words of warning about following a revolutionary course. The ways of the Zealots would not bring about glorious liberation, but national catastrophe. It was a warning that would go largely unheeded; and perhaps the greatest irony of all is that he was charged with, and at the hands of the Roman prefect Pontius Pilatus executed for, insurrection.

After that dark day when Yehsua was executed, imagine the response, not just of his chosen disciples, but of his family members, including his mother, Miriam. The obvious thing to do would have been to get out of the city that had perpetrated this ghastly execution and go home to the Galilee as soon as possible. Had not Jesus given instructions from the cross? Looking down at Yohanan, known in English as John and to the world as the "Beloved Disciple," he said of Miriam, "This is your mother," as if to say, "Yohanan, you are to take care of my mother from now on." The text goes on to say that this disciple did indeed take her into his home. But where was home? Was it back in the Galilee – the home of Zebedee, who according to the Gospels was John's father? Apparently not. On the contrary, the New Testament book of Acts makes it plain that all of them, including history's most famous distraught mother, stayed on in Jerusalem. It was a decision that would change the course of world civilization.

The "Adopted" Son

Did Miriam disobey Yeshua's directive by remaining in the holy city? Some modern researchers have looked at this story again and have come to the startling conclusion that the "Beloved Disciple" is not to be confused with John the son of the Galilean named Zebedee, but that he was in fact a mysterious "thirteenth disciple." There are a number of peculiarities about this Yohanan that indicate that he was someone other than a Galilean fisherman. When Jesus was being interrogated before the High Priest Ciaphas prior to his ultimate sentence at the hands of the Roman prefect Pilatus, we are told that Shimon (Peter) remained "outside at the gate" while the Beloved Disciple went into the courtyard, being well known to the High Priest (John 18:15 ff.). The Beloved Disciple thereafter spoke to a servant girl on duty and ushered Shimon (Peter) in. The fact that Yohanan the Beloved knew the High Priest personally is a detail that has gone unnoticed by most readers of the text. Is it in any sense conceivable that the son of a Galilean fisherman would be personally acquainted with Jerusalem's great High Priest, whom Shimon (Peter) dared not even approach?

Another tantalizing clue presents itself at the site of the empty tomb, from which Jesus was believed to have risen. We are told that both Shimon and the Beloved Disciple were frantically running toward the tomb, which was reported to lie vacant by Mary Magdelene who had returned to anoint the body (John 20:1 ff.). The account relates that the Beloved Disciple reached the tomb first but halted at the entrance, deciding not to enter but allowing the impetuous Shimon to go in first. Only when Shimon incredulously declared that the burial chamber was in fact empty did the Beloved Disciple go in himself.

Why would the Beloved Disciple deliberately avoid entering a tomb? For the same reason that he would personally know the High Priest, namely that he was a member of the tribe of Levi and therefore a priest himself. In Jewish tradition Levites were forbidden to have contact with the dead, and to this day avoid walking through cemeteries. Only when the Beloved Disciple was assured by Shimon that the crypt was vacant did he lose the fear of ritually defiling himself and enter into the rock-hewn sepulcher.

With these clues to his identity, we cannot but hold out the tantalizing possibility that Yohanan the Beloved Disciple was in fact a mysterious thirteenth disciple, the one who laid his head on the Master's breast during the Last Supper, and the one to whom Yeshua entrusted his mother Miriam during his agony on the cross. If this Beloved Disciple were from a priestly family and had lived in Jerusalem long enough to be well acquainted with the High Priest Ciaphas, then he and his family must have possessed a residence in Jerusalem sufficiently well-appointed to make the Master's mother Miriam feel cared for. The narrative also makes clear that it wasn't only Yeshua's mother who remained in Jerusalem rather than returning to the Galilee; apparently all of the disciples chose to remain in the holy city.

Moreover, the quandary of where all of the disciples could have resided is resolved if we consider the wealth and status of the thirteenth disciple's priestly family. Without such a person among the followers of Jesus, what would they all have done? Would John the son of Zebedee have rushed out and found a Jerusalemite mortgage broker? Would all of the twelve have pooled their resources to make a down payment on a fine limestone dwelling? Or was the Beloved Disciple himself the heir to a lavish villa in Jerusalem, which would, on the miraculous reports of the Master's resurrection, become the locus of the new and most explosively powerful force in the history of world religion, *t'nuat Yeshua*, the "Jesus movement"?

The idea that Yohanan, this thirteenth disciple, was heir to an impressive residence in ancient Jerusalem's priestly quarter is not just a clever invention. Amazingly, it is today possible to visit several candidates for such a house, linked to a most surprising story of discovery. It began in the years after the 1967 Six Day War, when Jerusalem's old city fell to the modern nation of Israel. In those days the old Jewish Quarter lay in a state of ruin. In time it was decided to rebuild this area from the ground up, erecting new, limestone-faced buildings that preserve architectural continuity with the surrounding structures. But in the 1970s the ground-clearing operations began to unearth a series of long-buried chambers, with mosaic floors, painted faux marble walls and even an atrium pool still intact. The excavators had happened upon the remains of a palatial mansion from the first century of the Common Era, owned by the priestly family of Kathros.

This was the beginning of an archaeological frenzy to excavate an entire ancient Herodian quarter of the city, buried by centuries of rubble, even while new construction was being planned on the same ground overhead. A series of priestly residences have since been revealed, providing us with an intimate sense of what life was like in the city of Jerusalem in the days when the great Temple stood. Stone tables, water vessels and other utensils were still in place, and ritual immersion baths known as *mikvehs* were clearly visible, being a necessary adjunct to each priestly residence. This affluent ancient quarter had once been the domain of Jerusalem's elite priestly class. It was located due west of the Temple Mount and connected to it by an enormous bridge. The story of its ultimate demise is, however, also apparent in the archaeology. For as modern workers were clearing the site, they came upon human skeletal remains buried in ash, along with a spear and what would have been a remarkably preserved fresco, were it not covered with sooty singe marks – haunting evidence of pitched battle and intense burning.

The history books tell us that Jerusalem was surrounded by Roman legions in the year 70 of the Common Era, the year in which the great Temple was completely destroyed and the rest of the city put to the torch. But the Jewish rebels who fought the Romans would not surrender and fled from the Temple precincts into the priestly quarter, where hand-to-hand combat resulted in a Jewish bloodbath and a Roman victory. The massive limestone ashlars knocked down by the general Titus' enraged legionaries left this entire area covered by nearly forty feet of rubble, its grizzly secrets entombed for the next two millennia.

But what has this to do with our mysterious "thirteenth disciple"? If he were indeed a priest, then this newly excavated quarter is precisely the area of the city where his house would most likely have been located. The ancient Herodian Quarter is today open to visitors, and a small admission fee will take you into this subterranean world, well associated with the ancient priesthood, though few visitors realize that they may also be journeying to the very beginnings of Christianity in the days and weeks immediately following the execution of Jesus.

To have visited Jerusalem during the Passover season around the year 30 of the Common Era would have been to witness a city jammed to its ancient rafters with pilgrims from all over Israel and lands beyond. Accommodations were at a premium, and it is not unreasonable to imagine that Jesus, his disciples and his immediate family members would all have been present, in one of those villas owned by the family of Yohanan the Beloved. This may have been the famous "House of the Last Supper," rather than the traditional site on Mount Zion, which pilgrims are shown today and whose foundations clearly date from the Crusader period. This may also have been the home where the disciples were gathered when the resurrected Yeshua suddenly appeared to them and when "doubting Thomas" touched the Master's nail wounds. And Yeshua's appearance may have been enough to convince all of them to stay on in Jerusalem amidst the Saduccean priesthood that had demanded from Pilatus the Master's execution.

The disciples must have believed that there was a divinely ordained reason for remaining in Jerusalem. It was all part of the divine plan. Even Yeshua's brutal execution in this city was a divine appointment, which served to transplant this fledgling community of followers to the one city to which every Jewish eye looked, toward which every prayer was directed. Key among those early disciples was one of Yeshua's physical brothers, whose name is recalled not only in the New Testament, but by the contemporary Jewish historian Josephus Flavius. His name was Yaakov, or Jacob, anglicized to James.

Yaakov – the Emboldened Brother

We should bear in mind that from the very beginning there were two separate trends or traditions that characterized the early "Jesus movement." There was the apostolic trend, led by Shimon (Peter), Yeshua's protégé, and the somewhat distinct tradition of the family members, the "Heirs," led by Yeshua's spirited sibling, Yaakov. The one thing that can be said for certain regarding those two trends is that their leaders did not necessarily get along. What sort of person was Yaakov? What was the essence of his character? We are told in the Gospels that he was one of five brothers, including Yeshua, and at least two sisters – a minimum of seven siblings in the family of Miriam and her husband Yosef. According to the biblical narrative, they had all grown up in the Galilean village of Nazareth.

The name Nazareth comes from the Hebrew word *netzer*, meaning "shoot" or "branch," and it was linked by the New Testament writers to a passage from the prophet Isaiah (11:1): "A rod shall go forth from the stem of Jesse; a shoot (*netzer*) shall flower from his roots." It was a cryptic reference to a redemptive figure who it was believed would one day reestablish the vacant throne of King David – an anointed one, a Messiah. And so the Gospel account declares that Yeshua had fulfilled the ancient prophecy, "He shall be called a Nazarene" (Matthew 2:23). Of course this is not the exact text that appears in Isaiah, but it was such a "dead giveaway" to the Gospel writer, as he read it in the Hebrew, that he reworded the passage.

Unfortunately, nothing of first century Nazareth has been conclusively identified in archaeological excavations, save for an ancient wine press on its outskirts and this has led some to question whether the city existed at all in the first century of the Common Era. The so-called "Church Synagogue," believed by pilgrims to be the actual site visited by Yaakov, Yeshua and their family, is certainly from a later period. Nevertheless, hope that some trace of ancient Nazareth may yet be found has not been relinquished. Today, one may visit the remains of a Byzantine structure situated on a nearby hilltop, resting on un-excavated ruins that could indeed mark the spot of the first century synagogue known to the family of Miriam, Yosef and the seven siblings.

Wherever the ancient synagogue was located, one thing is clear. The function of this institution was not to serve as a place of prayer, a role associated with later synagogues down to modern times. On the contrary ancient synagogues served as a communal center, developed by the Pharisees as a place to study the sacred texts. Without question Yaakov, Yeshua and their brothers growing up in pious Galilee would have devoted the balance of their young lives to devouring the Torah and its precepts, learning the hundreds of commandments it embraced, as well as a lively tradition of Oral Law passed down from generation to generation, which could not be written down but had to be memorized, line upon line, precept upon precept. Everything we know about Yaakov and Yeshua's family demands that they were piously observant to this very degree.

While the Gospels record the life and teachings of Yeshua in considerable detail, we have relatively few details about Yaakov or the other brothers. But the moment we understand Yeshua as being part of the "stream" of the Hasidim, then Yaakov also comes into focus as a Hasid, one of the Pious.[5] Like Yeshua, he must have been steeped in the Torah from his youth, rigorously observant of Jewish law and determined in performing its precepts. While his famous brother took to wandering, he and his siblings remained in Nazareth, at least for a period of time.

But residence in Nazareth by no means implies a lack of sophistication or learning. Far from the popular image of illiterate and boorish peasants, Galileans were surprisingly cultured and cosmopolitan. There was a saying in the Roman world, "He who buys a Jewish slave has bought himself a master," and the Galilee spawned many a master of Torah. Just over the hill lay the prosperous, cosmopolitan city of Sepphoris. Un-excavated until recent decades, it has yielded a wealth of information that shows just how sophisticated Galileans really were. From prosperous homes, to mikvehs, to a Roman theater carved into the hillside, to an elaborate mosaic floor depicting a woman of unusual charm – dubbed the "Mona Lisa of the Galilee" – Sepphoris is an archaeological bonanza that has revolutionized our understanding of the northern region of Israel. Moreover, we cannot pretend to understand the people of Nazareth, including the family of Yeshua, without appreciating this prosperous city next door.

Sepphoris may in fact have given employment to Yeshua's family. Were they all carpenters, as the Gospels have led many to believe? Perhaps, though the Hebrew word for "carpenter" (*nagar*) actually means "joiner" and could equally refer to one who cut and joined limestone ashlars, like those used in nearby Sepphoris. Many Nazareans may have "commuted" on a regular basis to Sepphoris to earn their livelihoods. But far from living in pastoral tranquility, Yaakov, Yeshua and family had to put up with the cold reality of what the Galilee was becoming, a land smarting under the harshness of direct Roman rule and brimming with an increasing number of Zealots. For as devoted as the Hasidim were in their piety, the Freedom Fighters were zealous in their determination to be rid of the Roman yoke. They believed that the altar of liberty must be splashed periodically with the blood of martyrs. They would bend the knee only to God, not to some half-crazed Roman emperor a thousand miles away.

Yaakov and his fellow Hasidim doubtless saw the plight of the Jewish people differently. The course of the Zealots would lead not to splendid victory but national disaster. "Which is preferable?" they must have reasoned to themselves, "A single tyrant in Rome, a thousand miles away, or a thousand tyrants one mile away?" They must have believed that national revival would have to begin not at the point of a sword but in the heart and mind of every Israelite. For only when the people as a whole take on the yoke of the Kingdom of Heaven would the yoke of Rome fall off – by itself.

We first meet Yaakov during an incident recorded in the Gospels, when Yeshua, who by now had earned a reputation as a wandering teacher and healer, returned to Nazareth and spoke in the synagogue. The synagogue was a house of study, so the synagogue service consisted of a reading from the Torah followed by a passage from the prophets, coupled with an analytical examination or practical exegesis of those readings. Not surprisingly the locals were astounded at the level of sophistication in Yeshua's oration. Ancient Israelites had long argued over whether the most important value was Torah study or performing good deeds, and the Hasidim came down on the side of good deeds. But in Yeshua they had encountered a Hasid who was not only a performer of miracles, but was also a man of great learning.

"Isn't this the carpenter's son?" they asked rhetorically (Mark 6:3; Matthew 13:54–56). Actually the term "son of a carpenter" was sometimes used as a euphemism, to denote a prophet, and it is quite possible that the Gospels are merely reflecting the claims being made about him, that he spoke prophetically. Perhaps the crowd was sarcastically asking, "Who does he think he is, a prophet?" They went on to ask, "Isn't he the son of Miriam, and the brother of Yaakov and Yosef (Joseph) and Yehuda (Jude or Judas, not to be confused with Judas Iscariot) and Shimon (Simon, not to be confused with Simon Peter)? And don't his sisters live here with us?" The text says nothing more of the siblings, but is bold to relate that the locals were offended at the upstart Yeshua.

We also hear of Yaakov and the other brothers in John's Gospel (2:12), where we are told that they, along with Miriam, followed Yeshua down to Capernaum on the shore of the Sea of Galilee. Later, John tells us (7:2-5) that the brothers goaded Yeshua to leave the Galilee and travel to Judea so that everyone might see the wonders that he was performing. "If you do these things," they teased, "then reveal yourself to the world!" The text tellingly adds, "For his brothers did not believe in him." As we shall see, John's Gospel may well have exaggerated the claim that Yeshua's siblings doubted him. Certainly, they must all have been in Yeshua's court by the time he did go to Judea to be crucified and seen alive again. Yaakov in particular became a leader of the movement early on. He did in fact become the definitive head of the Jerusalem *kehilah*, the "Church."

What else do we know about this man, who remained "behind the scenes" but who was the leader of this movement from its inception? One often overlooked point is the fact that he was married. The apostle Paul (whose "authentic" Jewish name was Shaul) was, we will discover, no friend of Yaakov though he notes (in defending his own apostolic credentials) that the brother of Yeshua was married. He writes with regard to the "apostolic dynasty" that he was founding:

> Do we not possess sufficient authority to lead in matters concerning a sister of a wife, just as the Lord's brothers have, as well as Keifa (Shimon/ Peter)? (1 Corinthians 9:5, author's translation)

While Paul (Shaul) boasted of his celibacy (which would bring about a two-millennia long tradition of a celibate priesthood), he acknowledged that marriage was expected among his fellow Jews, and he gives us definitive evidence that all four of Yeshua's brothers, including Yaakov, had wives. Provided that these brothers were married, it is reasonable to conclude that they had children, perhaps many children, who would create their own dynasty as the "Heirs" of Yeshua. Why do we not know the names of their wives and the children who would carry on the definitive legacy of the Master? Because the writer/ editor of the narrative does not want us to know. Clearly, there is another agenda at work. It is an agenda aimed at blotting out as much as possible the fact that Yeshua even had brothers, much less that the seminal events that gave rise to the new movement were directed, orchestrated and presided over by one brother in particular, Yaakov.

Four Missing Brothers and a "Hijacked" Faith

The conspicuous silence of the New Testament narrative with regard to Yeshua's four brothers is broken only occasionally. This fact is all the more unusual given the stress the Bible places on genealogies and descendants. It is as though the Master's family is hidden between the lines of the text and we have to play detective to discover their whereabouts. One particular passage from the book of Acts comes into focus in the quest for the "Heirs." The traditional text reads:

> "And when they had come in, they went up into an upper room. There were Peter and James, and John and Andrew, Philip and Thomas, Bartholomew and Matthew, James *the son* of Alpheus and Simon Zealotes, and Judas *the brother* of James; these all were continuing with one accord in prayer and supplication, with *the* women and Mary the mother of Jesus, and **with his brothers**." (Acts 1:13-14)

The famous "upper room" was most likely the second story of Yohanan the Priest's elaborate villa in Jerusalem's Upper City, now pressed into service as the hub of the new movement. We have here a list of eleven of the disciples, as catalogued by Luke's Gospel (Luke 6:12-16), excluding Judas Iscariot, who had hanged himself. While there are not one but two disciples named James (as well as a certain Judas, who is listed as James' brother), neither may be identified with Yaakov, Yeshua's brother. What we find is a statement that might best be called gratuitous, mentioning "the women," "Mary," Yeshua's mother, and "his brothers." Whoever wrote and edited this account feels constrained at least to mention the Heirs, the family of Jesus, as a "footnote" to the narrative, but he will not even mention the brothers' names, especially not Yaakov, who we know from other sources was the de-facto leader of the movement. Instead, all the emphasis is placed on the apostolic leadership under the auspices of Shimon (Peter), another Yaakov (James the son of Zebedee) and the disciple named Yohanan (John, not to be confused with the thirteenth disciple, Yohanan the priest).

The eleven apostles, supplemented by Judas' replacement, Matthias, were conducting a massive public relations campaign on behalf of the movement, while its true shepherds, Yaakov and his brothers, with Mary at their side, have been obscured by a strong editorial hand – someone who wanted to forget the authentic legacy of the Heirs, as though the piously Jewish "Jesus movement" had never existed. This same writer/ editor wanted instead to trace this movement to the west. There can be only one reason for all of this obfuscation. The movement itself, now known as "the Way," was being "hijacked" by a new trend, embodied in a hitherto unknown follower named Shaul, whom history would come to know as Paul. It was through his dominating influence that the Jewish character and essence of the movement would be completely lost and forgotten. What would remain was thoroughly western, profoundly un-Jewish and alien to the Hasidic piety of Yeshua himself. Having separated itself from Judaism entirely, it would come to dominate the western half of the planet under a new name, Christianity.

At the same time, there is another way to view the official list of disciples present in Jerusalem (in the first chapter of Acts) and the lists represented in the Gospels. Notice how Luke's Gospel presents them:

> "He called His disciples. And He chose twelve of them, whom
> He also named apostles:
> 1) Simon, whom He also named Peter, and
> 2) Andrew his brother;
> 3) James and
> 4) John;
> 5) Philip and
> 6) Bartholomew;
> 7) **Matthew** and
> 8) Thomas;
> 9) **James the son of Alpheus**, and
> 10) **Simon** who was called Zelotes;
> 11) **Judas the brother of James**, and
> 12) Judas Iscariot, who also became the betrayer."
> (Luke 6: 12-16)

The disciple called James (Yaakov) the son of Alpheus is in Christian tradition also called James the less, and is occasionally identified with James (Yaakov) the Just – the brother of Yeshua. That would make them both sons of Mary (Miriam). But how could this be, given that Miriam's husband was Yosef (Joseph), not Alpheus? The answer is that after Yosef died, Miriam may well have had a second husband named Alpheus, known in John's Gospel as Clophas. The same Clophas (called Cleopas in Luke's Gospel) was one of the disciples on the road to Emmaus who encountered the resurrected Jesus, not knowing who he was:

> "And one of them, whose name was Cleopas, answered and said to Him, Are you only a stranger in Jerusalem and have not known the things which have occurred there in these days?" (Luke 24:18)

This Clophas is in other sources referred to as the brother of Joseph (Yosef), and it is notable that the Greek version of this name was in fact Alpheus. He would have taken Miriam to wife according to the precept of brother-in-law marriage mandated by the books of Moses. When a man died childless, it was his brother's responsibility to raise up children in his name. Moreover, the Hebrew root behind Clophas is *chalaph*, which means "to exchange" or "to replace." Had he been following the precept of the Torah, he would have replaced Yosef as Miriam's husband.[6]

Of course, according to Christian tradition it was not Joseph (Yosef) who was the father of Jesus (Yeshua), but the Holy Spirit. There was also a rumor that Yeshua was in truth the bastard child of a Roman soldier, a rumor vociferously denied by John's Gospel:

> "… born, not of blood, nor of *the* will of *the* flesh, nor of *the* will of man, but of God." (John 1:13)

Nevertheless, the case can be made that Yosef indeed died childless and that Yeshua's brothers and sisters were actually "half-siblings," by Clophas/Alpheus. As noted earlier, the names of the brothers are given to us by Mark's Gospel, which calls Yeshua: "… the brother of **James (Yaakov) and Joses (Yosef) and Judas (Yehuda) and Simon (Shimon)**" (Mark 6:3). This corresponds with what is related about the women at the foot of the cross:

> "… among whom was Mary Magdalene, and **Mary** the mother of **James** and **Joses**, and the mother of Zebedee's children."

(Mat. 27:56)

John's Gospel, however, does something curious. It lists Mary the mother of Yeshua separately from Mary the wife of Clophas:

> "And His mother stood by the cross of Jesus, and His mother's sister, **Mary the wife of Clopas**, and Mary Magdalene." (John 19:25)

The Gospel of John, being the last to be written (around the turn of the second century, CE) was already under the influence of a growing body of Christian theology that attempted to elevate Mary to semi-divine status and divorce her from "normal" sexuality.[7] In time she would not only be thoroughly de-Judaized, but venerated as the "ever-virgin" Mary. Notwithstanding John's slight editorializing, it should be evident that the mother of Yeshua and Miriam the wife of Clophas are one and the same.

It therefore appears that three of Yeshua's brothers – Yaakov (James), Shimon (Simon) and Yehuda (Judas) – were among the original twelve disciples. But what about the brother called Yosef (Joseph/ Joses)? Consider that in addition to James and Judas being called "sons of Alpheus," there is mention elsewhere of another "son of Alpheus," namely, the disciple named Matthew/ Levi:

> "He saw **Levi** *the son* **of Alpheus** sitting at the tax-office. And *He* said to him, Follow Me." (Mark 2:14)

Is it possible that Yosef (Joseph/ Joses) is the same as Levi/ Matthew? One possible scenario is that Clophas/ Alpheus fathered children by Miriam in accordance with the tradition of brother-in-law marriage, naming one of his sons Matthew/ Levi, but giving him another name, Yosef, in honor of his deceased brother, whom history knows as Joseph. Such a scenario should not surprise us, since multiple names were common in antiquity and since many Jews had both a Hebrew and a Greek name. Nor should it surprise us to find the names Matthew (Mattathias) and Levi, as well as Joseph, listed in the genealogy of Mary's betrothed husband, since it was common to bestow the name of one or more ancestors upon a newborn. Luke's Gospel declares that Yeshua was:

> "… son of **Joseph**, *son of* Heli, *son of* Matthat, *son of* **Levi**, *son of* Melchi, *son of* Janna, *son of* **Joseph**, *son of* **Mattathias** …" (Luke 3:23-25)

If all of this is true, the writer of the first chapter of Acts wants us to forget that Yeshua's brothers were among the original disciples, and he therefore lists them separately (Acts 1:14). But we should ask, what are the implications of Yeshua's four brothers being numbered with the twelve? What this means is that in the very beginning of the "Jesus movement," its two components, the apostolic trend and the dynastic trend (of the "Heirs"), were in fact one. And so it was during the formative period described in the book of Acts. But at some point, the so-called "apostles" to the west diverged from the family members. Thereafter, some later writer/ editor, who sided with Paul's apostolic movement and against the tradition carried on by the Heirs, simply edited the latter group out of the picture.

Perhaps it shouldn't surprise us that Yaakov, like Miriam, is ignored by the early chapters of the book of Acts. Readers are understandably riveted by the march of the narrative. Following Shimon's powerful address to the multitude on Shavuot, the Galilean disciples found new momentum. Shimon and Yohanan (John the son of Zebedee) went on to heal a lame man at the Temple, an act we would expect to find among the ancient miracle-working Hasidim and a clear indication that the early disciples did not abandon the sanctity of Jerusalem's Holy Hill. Nor do we have any indication that they were somehow disenchanted with the sacrificial system, for the massive Temple complex erected under the auspices of King Herod the Great was undoubtedly the geographic center of the movement.

Shimon and Yohanan (John) remain at the forefront of the narrative, which proceeds to tell us how they were threatened by the Sadducean priesthood but continued to speak boldly and publicly. Thereafter, Shimon called down divine judgment on Ananias and Sapphira who withheld a portion of the funds they had pledged to the growing community of disciples. More reports circulated of miracles and wonders at the hands of the apostles who, we are told, met regularly at the southern end of the Temple complex, a vast hall of Corinthian columns known as Solomon's Porch.

Conception Is Quiet

While Peter (Shimon) and Yohanan (John) are depicted preaching to the multitude, healing a lame man at the Temple, and speaking boldly before the Sadducee-dominated council, there is a subtle subtext to the story that speaks volumes. Less exciting but far more significant is a single verse that describes the lifestyle of the new movement:

"And all who believed were together and had all things common." (Acts 2:44)

At the risk of cliché, Peter (Shimon) and Yohanan (John) represented "sound and fury" but conception is quiet, often devoid of fanfare. The real strength of this new and burgeoning movement lay in its organizational structure. It was a society within a society that cared deeply about the needs of each individual. In this simple verse, the Greek of which seems to mimic the syntax of Hebrew, we are introduced to yet another designation for the ancient "Jesus movement": "believers" (Hebrew *ma'aminim*). "Belief" in Hebrew is not, as westerners imagine it, a state of mind. The Semitic root behind it is linked to the word "Amen," which is in turn linked to the word for "faith" (*emunah*), and it suggests steadfastness, being firm and unmovable. For ancient Jews, faith was not a matter of giving assent to creeds and doctrines, it was about persevering in "right"/"*kosher*" behavior. It is a serious mistake to transpose generations of Christian theology back on these early "believers" in Yeshua. For them, there was no such thing as theology. They had no sense of such hallowed Christian concepts as the trinity, Jesus as God incarnate, or anything of the sort. It wasn't the person of Yeshua who deserved worship, but the divine presence, immediate and active in their lives through dreams and visions, signs and miracles. These were the things spoken of by the prophet Joel, now invoked by Shimon as a "proof text" for what was going on during those early days. The message was nothing new. It was the kind of "connectedness" with God, championed by the early Hasidim and now given new meaning in the aftermath of what all were convinced was the miraculous resurrection of the Master.

When Yeshua had healed people or exorcised demons, he announced that the Kingdom of Heaven had come upon them. In the Jewish mind this was not something distant in the future, a harbinger of the end of the world. The Kingdom of Heaven consisted of the present-tense reign of God, filling the human soul. We might even think of it as an ancient form of mystical awareness, what Jews today call Kabbalah. There was a famous Hebrew maxim, "Whoever so much as recites the verse, 'Hear O Israel, the Lord our God is One,' submits to the yoke of the Kingdom of Heaven." This invisible realm had nothing to do with the hereafter; it had everything to do with the here and now. We might simply think of it as "the abundant life." "Repent!" declared Shimon to those gathered in the Temple. Just as "faith" is misunderstood by westerners, so is repentance. To the Jews repenting had not as much to do with a change of heart as with a change of behavior. As with faith it was defined by action, by remaining steadfast to the commandments of the books of Moses, the Torah. "Sin" consisted of specific transgressions of holy precept, both the written Torah and the Oral Law, which supplemented the written texts but was committed to memory. Nor was "sin" a state of mind. The word meant "to err," to take the wrong path. When a person turned around, chose the "*kosher*" way and began keeping the commandments, it was counted as repentance, and as a result doom would be exchanged for bounteous blessing in one's present life.

It was basically a pietistic, Hasidic message. For Shimon and his fellow "believers," Yeshua – who now for the first time was being unequivocally presented as the Anointed One, the Messiah – would send a divine unction, supernaturally, to empower the flock in their steadfast piety. He was the prophet "like Moses," predicted in the Torah itself. And his precepts were to be obeyed, just as those of Moses. The apostles didn't need to make explicit mention of "heaven" or "hell," since the Jews had long been teaching the concepts of reward and punishment in what they called "the world to come." But they also taught that all people, non-Jews as well as Jews, would be judged, not according to what they believed (especially with reference to the Messiah) but how they behaved. For Jews the standard was higher. They were to keep the 613 commandments of the Torah as faithfully as possible. For non-Jews it was a matter of keeping seven, common-sense precepts (such as refraining from bloodshed and from sexual immorality) known as the "laws of the sons of Noah."

In the aftermath of the healing of the paralytic at the Temple, the "salvation" message of Shimon and Yohanan was not about heaven and hell. It was about a generation of their fellow Israelites saving themselves from a nightmarish destruction about to descend on the nation. Shimon is quoted as saying, "And it shall be that every soul who will not hear that Prophet shall be destroyed from among the people." (Acts 3:23). While most westerners imagine this to be an exclusive judgment, that all those who fail to "convert" to the new "Christian" faith will be damned to hellfire, the ancient near-eastern mind was hardly so narrow. Instead, we need to consider the "subtext" of events transpiring in those days. By this point in history there had already arisen, like a specter in Israel's long night of foreign rule, a revolutionary movement hell-bent on liberating the land from Roman occupation. It took no great clairvoyance to appreciate what would be the end result of the Zealots' patriotic fervor, as they stirred up the countryside with their militant drumbeat. Their cause was in many ways just, trumpeting freedom from imperial tyranny, but their timing was inappropriate. The Hasidic way, Yeshua's way, was certainly not this way.

Modern readers want to know what the New Testament means when it speaks of being "saved," as though the term implies some sort of "hell insurance." Didn't Shimon declare, when he and Yohanan were being interrogated before the priestly council, "And there is salvation in no other One; for there is no other name under Heaven given among men by which we must be saved" (Acts 4:12). But again, we need to consider what the term meant in a Semitic, rather than Greek, context. The Hebrew root translated "save" is *yasha*, and it means to be rescued, delivered or even healed. It always refers to the here-and-now and never has to do with what westerners conceive as "going to heaven." The name Yeshua is in fact a derivation of this root, and it aptly describes the Master's mission during his three-year ministry. He was a Hasidic healer, not a preacher of damnation. As far as his apostolic followers were concerned, he was the definitive source of deliverance, rejuvenation and healing in the world. This was already somewhat of an extension of Yeshua's own teachings, which lack the exclusivity heralded by modern fundamentalists. Yeshua, for example, commended the ministry of Yohanan (John) the Baptizer, even though modern scholarship recognizes that the two men were on very different paths and that the Baptizer became seriously disenchanted with the Galilean prophet.

What we may be looking at in the speeches of Shimon, as recorded in Acts, is another example of a later editorial hand overwriting the text with an increasingly narrow world-view that was shared by one Jewish group in particular, the ultra-pious, ultra-exclusive Essenes, whose famous library is today known as the Dead Sea Scrolls. They were the one Jewish sect who were quick to condemn everyone who did not become a member of their elitist group. For Jews today, it is a hideously un-Jewish approach, and none lament the apparent disappearance of the Essenes. It is possible, however, as some scholars have suggested, that Christianity became in reality "Essenism that succeeded."[8]

In any case, one picture is clear from the early chapters of Acts. What began as a handful of traumatized disciples in the days after the Master's execution had exploded into a mixed multitude of Israelite Jews supplemented by Jews from abroad who had made pilgrimage to Jerusalem during the feast of Shavuot (Pentecost). Submitting to a purification ritual popularized by the Pharisees, known as the *mikveh* (today called "baptism"), many apparently chose to stay on in the holy city during the summer swelter. To remain in Jerusalem, as the original disciples had done, was a difficult and painful decision, involving substantial pangs of relocation. How would they support themselves? Where would they all live?

The shepherd and de-facto head of this assembly was neither Shimon

(Peter) nor Yohanan (John), but Yaakov. To this unsung hero of the Way fell the responsibility of bringing order to what would otherwise have been a chaotic rabble. He needed a model, a *modus operandi* for governing, and he found it partly among the Essenes, who had developed a community of their own along the shores of the Dead Sea, and partly among the faction generally vilified by later generations of Christians, the Pharisees. It seems that the Pharisees had developed, during the previous centuries, communally-oriented groups of disciples who called themselves *Haverim*, or "Friends." There are multiple parallels for such groups throughout history, including America's Quakers, the society of "Friends." But for ancient Jews, becoming a *Haver* ("Friend") meant withdrawing to some extent from the rest of society, living by a strict code of ritual purity, and devoting themselves to the most rigorous observance of Jewish law.[9] They developed a strong and close-knit community, mutually supportive and self-sustaining, in which they pooled their resources. They were particularly known (like the Essenes) for their communal meals, which gave them a sense of integrated unity. On the eve of the Sabbath (Friday night) they would come together at table to share their repast (having attained a high level of purity in the *mikveh*) and devote themselves to discussion of the Torah. Often a teacher or sage would lead the assembly, continuing the discussions throughout the night. Each group of this sort was known as a *Havurah*, or "fellowship." How curious, that none of the trappings of the institutional western Church were common among the early *ma'aminim* of Jerusalem. Instead, their organizational pattern bears a closer resemblance to modern Jewish *Havurah* groups, home gatherings that have become increasingly popular in contemporary Jewish congregations. Not surprisingly, the book of Acts tells us:

> "And they sold their possessions and goods and distributed them to all, according as anyone had need. And continuing with one accord in the temple, and breaking bread from house to house, they shared food with gladness and simplicity of heart, praising God and having favor with all the people." (Acts 2:45-47)

"Christianity is Jewish!" proclaimed one prominent Christian commentator. Considering the legacy of those early days, no statement could be closer to the truth.

Notes

1   The Josephus account reads: "It came to pass, while Cuspius Fadus was procurator of Judea, that a certain charlatan, whose name was Theudas, persuaded a great part of the people to take their effects with them, and follow him to the Jordan river; for he told them he was a prophet, and that he would, by his own command, divide the river, and afford them an easy passage over it. Many were deluded by his words. However, Fadus did not permit them to make any advantage of his wild attempt, but sent a troop of horsemen out against them. After falling upon them unexpectedly, they slew many of them, and took many of them alive. They also took Theudas alive, cut off his head, and carried it to Jerusalem." See Josephus, *Jewish Antiquities* 20.97-98.

2   See David Flusser, *Jewish Sources in Early Christianity* (New York: Adama Books, 1987), 33. See also S. Safrai and M. Stern, *The Jewish People in the First Century*, Vol. 2 (Philadelphia: Fortress Press, 1987), 798, 805. It is notable that at the outbreak of the Maccabean revolt, the Hasidim refused even to defend themselves on the Sabbath. See Sifre Deut. 203-4; T. Erubin 3:7; Midrash Tannaim, 123. They are said to have affixed tassels to their cloaks as soon as they had been cut to the minimum length (T.B. Menahoth 43a; Sifre Num. 115 (end). The Hasidim are also said to have forbidden marital relations on the Sabbath, and even from the preceding Wednesday. See T.B. Niddah 38a. See also Finkelstein, L, *MGWJ* 76 (1932): 525-534. It should be noted, however, that the "zealotic stand" of the Maccabean Hasidim has been challenged, along with Tcherikover's suggestion that they precipitated a revolt prior to the persecution of Antiochus IV Epiphanes. See S.L. Derfler, *The Hasmonean Revolt: Rebellioin or Revolution* (Lampeter, Dyfed, Wales: Edwin Mellen Press, 1989), 54-57. It has also been argued that while the Hasidim are said to have joined the Maccabean revolt, as evidenced by the reference in Daniel 11:34 ("They shall be helped with a little help"), their overriding attitude of passivity could hardly engender a powerful and unswerving dedication to the Hasmonean cause. This in turn may have led to the decline of the resistance movement after a relatively short period of time. See W.E. Rast, "Developments in Postexilic Judaism," *JOR* 50.1 (1970): 104. It is nonetheless interesting that in 2 Maccabees 14:6 Judah the Maccabee is described as leading the Hasidim. Moreover, the Dead Sea Scrolls (1 Qphab 8:9) seem to suggest that the Hasidim broke with the Hasmoneans, but only after offering initial support. See L.H. Feldman, Review of Efron, *Studies on the Hasmonean Period*, 1997, *JAOS* 114.1 (1994): 87-8.

3   The link between Jesus and the Hasidim is more compelling in light of the research that has revealed the latter were a phenomenon of the Galilee. See W.S Green, "Palestinian Holy Men: Charismatic Leadership and Rabbinic Tradition," *ANRW* 19.2 (1979): 619-47. Scholars have long noted Jesus' oft-used expression "My Father" (the equivalent of *Avi* in Hebrew) as opposed to the traditional address "Our Father" (*Avinu*). The Hasidim were in fact regarded as "sons of God." It is recorded that when Honi Ha-Me'agel had successfully brought rain, "Simeon b.

Shatah said to him, 'If you were not Honi, I should decree a ban of excommunication against you. But what am I going to do to you? For you importune before the Omnipresent, so he does what you want, like a son who importunes his father, so he does what he wants'." (Mishnah Taanit 3:8). It is also recorded that the Sages would send for a Hasid known as Yohanan the Withdrawn, dispatching children who would grab the hem of his garment, imploring, "Father, father, bring us rain." Yohanan would answer, "Master of the Universe, do it for the sake of those who do not discern between a father who brings rain and a father who does not bring rain" (Bab. Taanit 23b). See Flusser, 1987, 34.

4   Some place this sect in the early Hasmonean/ Maccabean period. See J. Kampen, *The Hasideans and the Origin of Pharisaism: A Study in 1 and 2 Maccabees* (Atlanta: Scholars Press, 1988). Kampen favors this early dating, charging that the writer of 1 Maccabees saw the Pharisees as descendants of the Hasideans, who are described as first among the scribes. D.R. Schwartz, however, agrees with Safrai, finding no evidence to place the *hasidim rishonim* in the Maccabean period. See D.R. Schwartz, Review of Kampen 1988, *JQR* 80.½ (1989): 187-9. See also E. Schurer, *History of the Jewish People in the Age of Jesus Christ*, Vol. 2 (Edinburgh: T&T Clark, 1986), 388-403.

5   With regard to purity among the Hasidim, Alon highlights "the Hasidic practice" of not uttering the Divine Name. See G. Alon, *Jews, Judaism, and the Classical World* (Jerusalem: Magnes Press, 1977). Moreover, its use (or even the use of a euphemism) was coupled with the requirement to be in a high state of ritual purity. See J. Efron, *Studies on the Hasmonean Period* (Leiden: E.J. Brill, 1997), 249, and E. Qimron, "The Damascus Covenant 15.1-2," *JQR* 81.102 (1990): 115-18. Qimron notes that the very mention of the Divine Name by a member of the Dead Sea sect was considered a serious transgression, the punishment for which was complete separation from the community. See Qimron, "Further Observations on the Laws of Oaths in the Damascus Document 15," *JQR* 85.1-2 (1994): 251-7. See also G. Vermes, *The Dead Sea Scrolls in English* (New York: Penguin Books, 1997), 37-8.

6   I am indebted in this analysis of Jesus' parents and his siblings to James Tabor, who breaks new ground in this discussion. See *The Jesus Dynasty: The Hidden History of Jesus, His Royal Family, and the Birth of Christianity* (New York: Simon & Schuster, 2007).

7   It has been unconvincingly alleged that the Gospel of John is strikingly similar in style to the Qumranic material, preserving material that was originally Aramaic or Hebrew. See F.M. Cross, *The Ancient Library of Qumran and Modern Biblical Studies* (New York: Greenwood Press, 1958), 161-2; K. Schubert, *The Dead Sea Community: the Background to the Dead Sea Scrolls* (New York: Greenwood Press, 1959), 152-3. F.C. Grant countered, branding such ideas an example of "the wish fathering the thought." See F.C. Grant, *The Gospels: Their Origin and Growth* (New York: Octagon Books, 1957), 175.

8   According to David Flusser, the initial stage of the Jesus movement derived from the character of Jesus' message, which he insists was largely rabbinic. A "second stratum" found expression in the *kerygma* of the hellenistic Christian communities and was largely influenced by the Essenes/ Dead Sea Sect. See D. Flusser, *Judaism and the Origins of Christianity* (Jerusalem: Magnes Press, 1988), xviii.

9   N. Golb and others note the influence on the Second Jewish Commonwealth of the ancient Haverim ("Friends") vis-à-vis the stringent maintenance of ritual purity. Golb points out that many features of 1QS are reminiscent of the concerns of the Haverim as described by rabbinic literature, including categories of purity involving bread, wine and clothing. See N. Golb, *Who Wrote the Dead Sea Scrolls: The Search for the Secret of Qumran* (New York: Scribner, 1995), 76-77.

2

The Great Tribe

S OME CHIEF EXECUTIVES ARE OUTSPOKEN AND CHARISMATIC while others are unobtrusive consolidators. History has its conquerors and its unifiers. In the east these two forces are known as the yang (the active, male impulse) and the yin (the more connective, female element). One lends balance and stability to the other.

When it comes to the Bible, there are prophets and priests. The great Israelite prophets such as Isaiah, Amos, Jeremiah and Ezekiel were strident voices of ethics and societal reform. "God has roared!" pronounced Amos. "Who cannot prophesy?" They were not so much "foretellers" as "forth-tellers," possessed by a radical spirit that challenged the status quo. But prophets alone were not sufficient to keep Israel afloat as a nation and as a people. The prophetic voice needed to be moderated by shepherds, and that was the task shouldered by a pragmatic priesthood. After the national catastrophe of Babylon's conquest of Israel in the sixth century BCE, the Israeli priests played a vital role, shepherding the exiled flock and bringing them back to Jerusalem. After seventy years of bitter exile, the Temple was rebuilt and a new age began. The de-facto leaders of the nation from that day forward were the new shepherd class, the priests. Unfortunately, compromisers and moderates, as good shepherds need to be, are seldom granted the recognition they deserve.

As we have already seen, the writer/editor of the book of Acts unquestionably hailed the "apostolic" branch of Yeshua's disciples as representing the future of the new movement (the Way) while downplaying the role of Yeshua's family. The disciples/ apostles, headed by Shimon (Peter), receive all the attention, acting in the "prophetic" role and actively expanding the ranks of the sect by the force of their own personalities. But it fell to another, unheralded group, the physical relatives and Heirs of Yeshua, to shepherd the movement and ground it in a solid foundation. The fact that one of the four brothers, Yaakov, was regarded as the "Good Shepherd" of the Way is independently attested by the Gospel of Thomas, one of the cache of Coptic papyri discovered accidentally in 1945 by an Egyptian farmer at a village called Nag Hammadi. Believed to be one of the earliest of all Christian texts, we find in it a passage in which the disciples ask Jesus to whom they should look for leadership after his departure. His response is that they should consult "James the Just, for whose sake heaven and earth came into being" (G. Thom. 12). This is quite an endorsement for an apostle who was systematically ignored by the first chapters of the book of Acts.

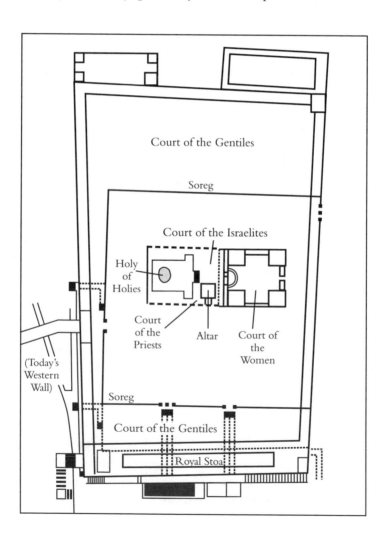

We should also recognize that whatever success was realized in those early days, it was in no small part to the credit of the Master's brother, Yaakov.

The prophet-priest paradigm has specific application to the early *ma'aminim*, for Yaakov's role can be seen as a binary counterpoint to that of Shimon (Peter). It was Shimon who acted as a "prophet" of the new movement, while Yaakov, as a shepherd of the flock, served in a "priestly" capacity as a steady hand and anchor. While not in the spotlight as prophets tended to be, the priest was nonetheless indispensable. While the initial chapters of the book of Acts are conspicuously silent with regard to Yaakov, we do have a good deal of testimony regarding him from the so-called "Church Fathers," the ecclesiastical pillars of Christianity, whose voluminous writings served as a groundwork for the whole faith. Two of these Church Fathers, Epiphanius and Jerome, have preserved a rather spectacular account regarding Yaakov, that at one point (or perhaps even more than once), he physically entered the innermost sanctuary of the Jerusalem Temple, the Holy of Holies. There, we are told, he made atonement to the point that "the skin of his knees became callused like a camel's."

Bear in mind, the very structure of the Temple was designed to restrict access. There was a vast court surrounding it, called the Court of the Gentiles, where non-Jews came to pay their respects to Israel's deity. But a low wall separated this court from the sacred precincts on which a stern warning was engraved denying non-Jews entry on pain of death. Next came the Court of Women, which served as a place of gathering for all Israelites, but which was in turn separated from the Court of Israel, into which only priests could venture. This is where the great altar for burnt offerings was situated, on which various animals were slaughtered and immolated on a daily basis for expiation of the people's transgressions. Beyond this was the Temple edifice itself, the doors of which were closed to all except a select number of priests who served inside on a rotating basis. At the far end of this gigantic hall, one final chamber was perpetually shrouded in darkness, shut off by an enormous curtain that could be penetrated only once a year on the Day of Atonement by the High Priest alone. This was the *Kodesh ha-Kodashim*, the Holy of Holies.

Some modern researchers have embraced the notion that Yaakov (or "James the Just") was in fact a priest and that he entered the Temple as a kind of "opposition High Priest."[1] Of course the Jewish priesthood had always been hereditary, descending through the tribe of Levi alone. Moreover, according to the Gospels, Yeshua's family was from the house of David (of the tribe of Judah), not Levi. Consequently, the very idea that Yaakov was of the priestly class seems at first glance to be a stretch. But what if Clophas – Miriam's second husband – was himself a priest? That would make all four of Yeshua's brothers priests. Is there any evidence of that? Recall that the disciple called Matthew (who we argued was one of the four brothers) was also called Levi. Suddenly, the idea that Yaakov was a priest becomes a distinct possibility.

Nonetheless, the suggestion that he might with impunity have entered the Holy of Holies sounds preposterous to a good many scholars who summarily dismiss the accounts of Epiphanius and Jerome as so much folklore.[2] Epiphanius goes on to describe Yaakov's appearance, saying that he wore the mitre of the High Priest. He is even said to have worn a linen garment, which was characteristic of the rank and file priesthood in those days. Perhaps there was some conflation of the early traditions about Yaakov and Yohanan (John) the Beloved Disciple, who, as we have seen, must indeed have been a priest and worn a white linen garment at all times. Some researchers have gone so far as to say that the two are one. This seems unlikely, given that the Beloved Disciple must have been a Jerusalemite with a fine home in the city where Miriam subsequently resided. It is nonetheless revealing that Yaakov was given the pseudonym "James the Just" not by the Gospel of Thomas alone, but by the early Church Fathers as well. This word "just" is expressed in Hebrew by the term *zadok*, which literally means "righteous" but which came to be applied specifically to priests. Ancient sources including the Dead Sea Scrolls refer frequently to the "Zadokite priesthood."

We should always bear in mind that eastern books were not written in a straightforward fashion palatable to the western mind, but were deliciously subtle, conveying concrete ideas in a deliberately non-linear fashion, with nuances and frequent exaggeration that confounds contemporary readers. Rather than dismissing the account of Epiphanius and Jerome as so much hyperbole, wouldn't it be better to look behind their accounts and imagine their deeper meaning, namely that Yaakov, whether or not he was a priest, was acting in a "priestly" role, to the point of taking upon himself the heavy burden of governing the growing sect? And that in the tradition of his martyred brother, he did it willingly and sacrificially, laying his own life on the line? This appears to have been his true "atoning" work.

Cult of Personality

One point often ignored by readers who gravitate to the story of the persecuted "believers" is that the general response of the local population was positive. Shimon, Yohanan and of course Yaakov may well have been

Jerusalem's latest celebrities. Whatever opposition they may have faced did not come from the general Israelite populace. The persecution, such as it was, came from the priestly/ Sadducean ranks, the same faction that had agitated for Yeshua's execution. The tragedy is that for most non-Jews, the stereotype persists to the present day that "the Jews rejected Jesus." It is an obscene distortion, which sadly lies directly behind two millennia of anti-Semitism. The priestly party, while wealthy and politically powerful, were small in number and by no means the darlings of the rank and file. The book of Acts is correct when it declares that the *ma'aminim* ("Believers") grew in favor with all the people. Moreover, winning the hearts and minds of the common folk did not come about by damning them all to hell unless they believed in Yeshua. Instead, they most likely looked to the ancient Hasidim, who were strict and demanding toward themselves but moderate and lenient toward others. It makes perfect sense that the followers of the Way were in fact a branch of the Hasidic movement, "populist" in tone and patronage. They were akin to the Pharisees, who were also "populist," drawing their support from the common people. The Hasidim never reached a majority status in the land of Israel, but to say that they were rejected would be a gross mistake.

How large did the new movement of Believers become in its earliest days? To place their numbers in the thousands, as the book of Acts does, may be somewhat of an exaggeration, especially given that so many of them came from abroad for the festival of Shavuot and many probably did return to their places of origin. But the book of Acts is probably correct in depicting the movement as sizable and on the rise. Shimon and Yohanan were the "front men," the "evangelists" of the day, while Yaakov presided over the daily administration of affairs. We should bear in mind that while the word "evangelist" conjures up notions of preaching to the Godless heathens, the evangelism of the Way never targeted non-Jews. Everyone who heard this "Hasidic" message was either a local Israelite or a Jew from some Gentile land. It is not unlike modern Hasidic Jews who actively "evangelize" fellow Jews, urging them to return to Torah observance and become "baal-teshuva" or "penitent ones." Never would ultra-Orthodox Jews target non-Jews for conversion. So it is today and so it was then.

In any case, there was a proliferation of sectarian groups among the Israelites in those days, including not only well-known sects such as Pharisees, Sadducees and Essenes, but such obscure cults as Boethusians (likely related to the Sadducees) and Morning Bathers, to whom Yohanan (Yohn) the Baptizer may well have been related. In fact we can say that there was no such thing as "Judaism" in the first century of the Common Era, but rather a multiple assortment of "Judaisms," of which the Way was a popular one. It would not remain monolithic, however, and it was only a matter of time until the movement would itself fracture into multiple expressions.

For now, it was springtime for the Way, which must have seemed like a lively alternative to the destructive path down which much of the nation was headed. We may conjecture that Yaakov's steady hand must have been guiding it, aided by his brothers Shimon, Yosef (Matthew) and Yehuda. Miriam and Clophas must also have remained as a living, symbolic presence of the Master. It is often the case that movements facing opposition and even persecution are strengthened, rather than weakened, by that opposition. This was certainly true of the Way. It also helps us understand the people's favorable reaction to the movement when their own autonomous legal council, the Sanhedrin, attempted to silence the growing numbers of ma'aminim. Shimon and Yohanan, having been thrown into prison for their activities, were, according to the narrative of Acts, released through angelic intervention, returning to the Temple Mount to teach the people. The account relates:

> And they called the Sanhedrin together, and all the elderhood of the sons of Israel, and sent to the prison to have them brought. But having come near, the officers did not find them in the prison. ... And when the high priest and the temple commander and the chief priests heard these things, they were bewildered.

... But one came ... saying, "Behold, the men whom you put in prison are standing in the temple and teaching the people." Then the commander went with the officers and brought them, not with force, for they feared the people, lest they should be stoned. (Acts 5:21-25)

The Jews had a long tradition of governing themselves, even during periods of foreign occupation. In the second century BCE they established a representative body known as the Great Assembly, which served as a political as well as a judicial body. It evolved into the Great Sanhedrin, on which sat seventy-one of the most prominent judges and sages in the land. Two members presided over the rest, the *Nasi*, or "President," who acted as chief justice, and the *Av Bet Din*, or "Father of the Court," who served as a kind of vice president.

While at least the priestly members of the Great Sanhedrin appear to have opposed the Way, there is a very good likelihood that the twelve disciples established a "Sanhedrin" of their own. Had not Yeshua given them this charge?:

"When the Son of man shall sit in the throne of His glory, you also shall sit on twelve thrones, judging the twelve tribes of Israel." (Matthew 19:28)

Most people read this verse in an eschatological context, believing that it refers to the "end of the world." But as we have seen, the contour of Hebrew thought was usually present-tense, and the disciples probably reasoned, "Why wait?" After all, the new movement clearly needed immediate guidance. Moreover, a strong case can be made that the leadership pattern involved plurality, not dictatorship. From the early days, when the prophet Samuel castigated the people for desiring a king, Jews had never been compliant subjects of dictators.

There was in fact a long established tradition in Pharisee circles of recognizing two popular sages in each generation who would teach the masses but who would also spar with each other on all manner of issues relating to daily life and behavior (Jewish Law, or *Halakhah* as it came to be called). These pre-rabbinic sages became an institution during the second century BCE, ruling the High Court (*Bet Din ha-Gadol*). They were known as the "Pairs" or the *Zugot*, of which five are to this day recognized as important figures in Jewish history. The fifth and final pair came to prominence during the first century BCE. One, named Shammai, represented the strict, conservative wing of the Pharisee party. The other is revered as the definitive voice of the liberal, moderate and ethical values that have characterized the Jewish faith ever since. His name was Hillel the Elder, and he is best known for formulating what the world recognizes as the "Golden Rule": "That which is hateful to yourself, do not do to your neighbor. That is the whole Torah; the rest is commentary." It is a maxim famously quoted by a somewhat later Israelite sage, Yeshua m'Natzeret: "Whatever you desire that men should do to you, do even so to them; for this is the Law and the Prophets" (Matthew 7:12).

We can in fact make a case that Yeshua, as an ancient Hasid, walked in the tradition of the *Zugot*, sometimes agreeing with Shammai, sometimes with Hillel. While he quoted Hillel, he sided with Shammai on such issues as divorce (only in cases of adultery) and opposing proselytism into Judaism ("Do not go into the way of the Gentiles," Matthew 10:5). Who would have been the other member of the "Pair," in Yeshua's generation? Most likely Yohanan (John) the Baptizer. And, as we might expect, they usually sparred with each other. The Baptizer was known for his apocalyptic mentality, expecting fiery judgment followed by a messianic age. Yeshua, by contrast, was much more focused on the "abundant life," the "Kingdom of Heaven," in the here and now. No wonder that the Baptizer ultimately sent messengers to Yeshua, asking, "Are you he that should come, or do we look for another?" (Luke 7:19). Of course Yeshua and Yohanan the Baptizer were not destined to be recognized as the sixth "Pair" (*Zug*), for the sect launched after them would inexorably be dragged westward, eventually to turn with fury against the Jewish nation and the Jewish people.

The pattern of plurality, however, continued. The Great Sanhedrin was itself governed by a "Pair," the *Nasi* and *Av Bet Din*, who mutually balanced each other.[3] Why should we then assume that the Way was governed by a single individual, Shimon (Peter)? Is it not more likely that Yaakov served as de-facto *Nasi*, "President" of the congregation, while Shimon filled the role of *Av Bet Din*, "Vice President"? We can also imagine that these two were true to form, sparring with each other on how to manage the burgeoning flock. Argument was, after all, an essential aspect of Jewish character.

An Unlikely Ally

Returning to the conflict between the *ma'aminim* and the Great Sanhedrin, we should pay attention to who the narrative says were at the time acting in a leadership capacity. We are specifically told that the chief

priests were in attendance as well as the "elderhood." This is more than a
little confusing, since ancient sources conflict with regard to the composition and makeup of the Sanhedrin. Some sources lead us to believe that it
was dominated by the priestly party, the Sadducees, while others suggest
that the Pharisees were the major component. The New Testament would
lead us to believe that it was split between the two parties, not unlike today's houses of Congress. The chief priests were balanced by the Pharisaic
sages of the day, the "elderhood." The chief priest seems to have been the
Father of the Court, the *Av Bet Din*, but who would have been his counterpart, as President and presiding officer?

As we read on in the narrative, we are introduced to another character from the "elderhood," code language for the Pharisees, whose voice
dominated in the assembly. He was the greatest Pharisaic sage of his day,
the illustrious Gamaliel I, "the Elder." His pedigree was impressive, being
the grandson of Hillel. In the great collection of Jewish law and lore, the
Talmud, he is given the title "Rabban," which is reserved for the head of
the Sanhedrin, the *Nasi*. And according to the other ancient compendium
of Jewish law, the Mishna, "Rabban Gamaliel used to say, 'Find yourself a
teacher, remove yourself from doubt, and do not overly guess in tithing'"
(author's translation). In other words, the scrupulous observance of religious precepts (such as tithing) follows directly in the wake of study, which
begins by enlisting a superb teacher. Here was a man who stood head and
shoulders above his contemporaries, whose word was revered and whose
authority was unquestioned.

To the High Priest Caiaphas, the same official who felt challenged
by Yeshua when he overturned the tables of the moneychangers in the
Temple, the *ma'aminim* represented a political threat to the Sadducean establishment.[4] The whole Sanhedrin, we are told by the narrative, stood
poised to condemn the movement. Even under the Romans the Jews had
maintained an independent judiciary, and the Sanhedrin was by no means a
toothless tiger. In the year 41 BCE, they had handed down a guilty verdict
against the current governor of the Galilee and future sovereign of all Israel,
the notorious King Herod the Great. Herod, who had ordered the murder
of the ringleader of the Zealot party, Hezekiah the Galilean, subsequently
found himself standing before the Jewish High Court. Having been tried
and sentenced to death, Herod had no recourse but to flee to Rome, where
he persuaded his friend Mark Antony and Octavian (later to become Caesar
Augustus) to crown him King of the Jews. Now it was the turn of the
ma'aminim to face the terrifying judgment of the Sanhedrin.

We should pause here and note that Rome had taken from its Jewish subjects the so-called "power of the sword," the ability to carry out an execution. It therefore appears that the book of Acts is engaging in a bit of literary exaggeration by declaring that the members of the High Court deliberately conspired to kill the *ma'aminim*. It is one more unfortunate detail in the account that helped spur centuries of Christian anti-Semitism. In any case, strong opposition from the Sadduccean priesthood needs to be considered in the historical context of those days. A negative judgment by the Sanhedrin may well have led to a direct appeal by the priesthood to the Roman authorities, to the effect that the new movement was stirring up insurrection.

But Gamaliel would have none of it. The Pharisees in fact had a long tradition of what they called "being moderate in judgment." They were bound to uphold the Torah on every point, including capital punishment, which the books of Moses had carefully prescribed as the punishment for an assortment of crimes, including Sabbath breaking. However, the Oral Law added so many preconditions to a sentence of death (including the requirement that an official "warning" be issued to a person about to commit a capital offense) that they made it virtually impossible to render a guilty verdict in a capital case. Without contradicting the word of the Torah, the Pharisees had virtually abolished capital punishment some two thousand years before western nations would adopt such moderation. Jewish law even stipulated that handing a Jew over to a foreign authority, such as Rome, was a sin that could never be forgiven.[5]

When the great sage Gamaliel now stood up in the assembly, all fell silent in his presence. In thunderous oratory he pointed out what everyone already knew, that messianism was by no means a new phenomenon in Israel. "For before these days," he declared, "Theudas rose up, boasting to be somebody" (Acts 5:36). This is code language for making a messianic claim. Indeed, no one could be defined as "Messiah" unless he had accomplished his task, namely to bring all the dispersed Jews back to the land of Israel and to bring about universal peace. A person was thought of only as "somebody" until he had succeeded. Gamaliel continued, relating the same events later described by Josephus: "A number of men, about four hundred, joined themselves to him who was slain. And all, as many as obeyed him, were scattered and brought to nothing."[6] Next he mentioned Yehuda (or Judas) the Galilean, who had fomented a violent resistance to a Roman tax imposed by the governor Quirinius in the year 6 CE. His father was Hezekiah, whom Herod had previously murdered. Now Yehuda, along with one Zadok (a Pharisee but with an unusually militant stripe), headed the Zealot party, which Josephus later called "the fourth philosophy" (the first three being Pharisees, Sadducees, and Essenes). Here was an example of a different messianic paradigm, that of a military deliverer rather than a Hasidic healer. Yet, he was also liquidated by the Roman response, which was characteristically ferocious. His followers, as expected, were dispersed, and the insurrection fizzled. He could only have claimed to be "somebody."

The typically Pharisaic wisdom of Gamaliel to the assembled Sanhedrin was therefore to leave these *ma'aminim* alone. After all, he claimed, if this new movement was the result of human connivance, it would collapse under its own weight and come to naught. But if, on the other hand, this movement was the result of divine initiative, then anything the council did to oppose it would itself come to naught. They might, he argued, even find themselves fighting against God. Gamaliel's authority was so imposing, his speech so reasoned, so articulate, so persuasive, that the narrative curtly reports: "They obeyed him" (Acts 5:40). Thereafter, the *ma'aminim* were beaten, but released. And where did they go? Back to the Temple Mount, which remained at the center of the movement.

Moderation had won the day, thanks to the leader of the Pharisee camp. The reality was a far cry from the common misconception that the early disciples, like Yeshua before them, had been overwhelmingly rejected by the Jewish people. On the contrary, this Hasidic oriented phenomenon was so well received that a tradition arose claiming that Gamaliel himself became one of the *ma'aminim*. The claim is probably an exaggeration, but Shaul (or Paul) would later insist that he had studied at the feet of Jerusalem's greatest Pharisee (Acts 22:3).[7] We can be sure that there was no incompatibility between the Way and Torah — true Judaism. Was Gamaliel's bold pronouncement something that a scrupulously observant Pharisee might have said regarding a sect that in any way abrogated the Torah, or disrespected the Temple sacrifice? Clearly, the early disciples were pious Jews, who made sure that they did everything in kosher fashion. And while Yaakov, the de-facto *Nasi* of the Way, remains in the shadows, the narrative tellingly records that the disciples continued to go "from house to house" (Acts 5:42). This is where the *Nasi* of the movement would have been found, orchestrating the mutual care of the flock and the communal meals of which they regularly partook, great repasts that would later be designated as "love feasts."

The Hidden Hand of Yaakov and the Seeds of Discord

While Yaakov's imprint was certainly present upon the developing "Jesus movement," he is almost completely ignored in the book of Acts narrative. Like a phantom, his presence is felt even as details about him are few. But the narrative does make it clear that the fledgling movement had a well-organized administrative structure, its own "Sanhedrin" of sorts, the "invisible" chief administrator of which was Yaakov. This *ad-hoc* "Sanhedrin" does come front and center, as the narrative pauses from its glorification of Shimon (Peter) and Yohanan (John) long enough to take up a dispute, the first major quarrel within the ranks of the movement. It had to do with the fact that the pietistic group of Galilean *ma'aminim* was, from the feast of Shavuot on, supplemented by a large contingent of Jews from abroad, from the Greek speaking world, who had come to the holy city on pilgrimage. They were representatives of what is called Hellenistic Judaism.

There were in fact enormous numbers of Jews, scattered across the Mediterranean world, in what was known as the Diaspora, the great "dispersion" of Jews away from the land of Israel. From the Greek root of this term comes our own English word "spore," a seed carried by the wind, which plants itself in distant fertile ground, to spawn a new and vital colony. From Alexandria to Athens to Rome and points beyond, these Greek and Latin speaking Jews created their own culture, uniquely Jewish, yet deeply syncretistic with the host culture of the Classical world. There was a natural tension between them and the Jews of the land of Israel, who were much less inclined to compromise with the surrounding Greco-Roman paganism. The native Israelite Jews were in a sense like the patriots in the young American colonies, who had developed their own unique American culture and who ultimately longed for independence from the mother country. The Hellenistic Jews were like the Tories, who were accustomed to being Englishmen and who opposed the hot-headed rebels. Needless to say, native Israelite Jews and Diaspora Jews didn't always get along.

The book of Acts narrative tells us that time has passed since the death and resurrection of Yeshua, though we don't know how much. What we do know is that the *ma'aminim* began living a seriously communal lifestyle, not unlike the ancient Essenes, the one Jewish group who strictly shared their possessions. The *ma'aminim* had apparently pooled their resources, and distribution was made (as Karl Marx would later put it) "to each according to his need." This is when a complaint was lodged from the ranks of the Hellenistic contingent that the widows among them were being neglected in the daily distribution of funds. At this point the twelve apostles are mentioned once again. Yaakov's name has again been edited out, though, as we have seen, the case can be made that he was one of the twelve and was in fact the leader of this "Sanhedrin." The narrative declares that the entire community of *ma'aminim* was summoned to what must have amounted to a legal hearing, the acting *Nasi* of which must have been Yaakov.

The nature of this dispute strongly reminds us of another New Testament tome that bears his name, the book of James, which echoes the concern of the first great argument in the history of the "Jesus movement," namely the treatment of widows. Notice how this Christian epistle defines "religion":

> Pure religion and undefiled before God and the Father is this, to visit orphans and *widows* in their afflictions, and to keep oneself unspotted from the world. (James 1:27)[8]

As we will later see, the likelihood is that the book of James came not from the hand of Yaakov himself but from one of the descendants of Yeshua's family, the so-called "Heirs." While the bulk of scholarship dates this book from a period long after the early days of the movement, re-counted by the book of Acts, it doubtless reflects very well the attitude of Yaakov and his compatriots toward religion and spirituality. Like all pious Hasidic Jews of the period, theirs was not a faith built on theology. As we have noted, they had no theology as modern westerners understand it. The complex and systematic theological grid of classical Christianity took centuries to develop and would have been completely incomprehensible to the heirs of Yeshua. For Yaakov and his fellow disciples, divine justice was meted out on the basis of Hillel's Golden Rule and was therefore pri-marily a function not of belief but of behavior.

We can imagine that, as *Nasi* of this new Sanhedrin, Yaakov might have felt shamed for having given preference to his fellow Israelite Jews over those from the Diaspora. It never dawned on the *ma'aminim* of those days that this movement was anything more than an elite corps of dedicated followers of the Way, intent on experiencing the abundant power of the Kingdom of Heaven in the present tense and in their daily lives. The idea of embracing large numbers of Diaspora Jews whose syncretistic notions of Hellenistic Judaism incorporated far too much of the pagan world must have seemed fairly traumatic to them. The idea that non-Jews might come into the movement as well was unthinkable.

We can only imagine how this grievance must have been presented, as a preference was alleged on behalf of native-born Israelites to the disadvantage of Diaspora Jews. Yaakov and his associates may indeed have maintained an air of superiority over Jews from other lands. After all, as Hasidim they were scrupulous in their level of piety, maintaining such a strict degree of kosher that they doubted whether the Diaspora Jews were, so to speak, up to snuff. In the end the solution adopted by the new "Sanhedrin" seemed elitist enough, though it was met with wide approval. The twelve disciples, who were too busy to bother themselves with such mundane affairs, established a "sub-committee" of seven individuals to handle the affairs of the Diaspora Jews. They all bear Greek names, including one non-Jew who, the text strains to tell us, had already converted to Judaism. Importantly, the "righteous proselyte" (or *ger zedek* in Hebrew) was by law considered Jewish in every way, though there was an implicit understanding that he or she might not be treated that way.

In any case, the needs of the Diaspora Jews were now officially taken care of, though we get the sense that as a group they were segregated from the native born Israelites. The applicable doctrine must have been "separate but equal."

Riot!

On a literary level, the book of Acts is known for its many speeches, for the thunderous oratory in the mouths of the disciples. But speeches alone don't move multitudes, and Jews in particular have traditionally been skeptical of words. There was something more vital that propelled this movement. It was not the eloquence of the apostles, but their *acts*. As with Yeshua before them, the Kingdom of Heaven was manifest in miraculous signs and inexplicable wonders performed by Yeshua's followers. It is estimated that in those days, roughly one quarter of the population suffered from some physical malady at any given time. There was not merely an interest in healing, there was a crying need. And when a man well known to be lame from birth, who sat begging alms at the "Beautiful Gate" of the Temple every day, suddenly stood on his feet and walked again, word spread like a violent late Spring torrent that the *Malchut Shamayim,* or the Kingdom of God, had been made manifest among them. A new generation of Hasidic healers had come, and their Torah caught on like a contagion.

Nevertheless (the movement's early success notwithstanding) it is clearly evident as the narrative of Acts progresses that the new movement was driven by conflict. One of the seven individuals put in charge of the Hellenistic contingent was a man named Stephanos, or Stephen. In one succinct line we are told that this Diaspora Jew performed miracles and wonders among the people, one more piece of evidence that the reign of God had come. But a man with such a public presence also became a magnet for nay-sayers, members of the so-called synagogue of the Freedmen (or Libertines). Jews of the ancient and classical world abhorred slavery and would go to great lengths to purchase the freedom of fellow Jews who ended up in this unfortunate condition. These "Freedmen," fellow Diaspora Jews, began arguing with Stephanos. We should notice, however, that this synagogue consisted of Jews from Cyrene and Alexandria and that they were joined in the dispute by other Jews from Cilicia and Asia, all parts of the Diaspora.

Scholars have observed that Diaspora Jews were the ones who were insecure about their religion and their very identity.[9] They had worked hard to cultivate their own expression of Hellenistic Judaism, as a peculiarly monotheistic philosophy, competing with a multitude of sects, cults and philosophic systems "duking it out" with each other across the Mediterranean world. They already had enough sects to cope with, and one more competing Jewish sect was irritating to the point of being egregious. It shouldn't surprise us that when Shaul (or Paul) traveled westward carrying the message of the *ma'aminim* in the decades to come, he ran into a good deal of trouble, not only from Gentiles but from his fellow Diaspora Jews. But the native Israelite Jews, among whom Yaakov and company resided, were surprisingly receptive to this new breed of Hasidim.

The situation with Stephanos, who replied to his Hellenistic opponents with Hellenistic-style oratory, was, however, another matter. The narrative tells us that certain individuals were bribed to declare that they heard Stephanos speaking against Moses and God. To this was added the charge that he claimed Yeshua would one day bring down the Temple itself. It sounds like an issue that would have been raised, not by Gamaliel or any of his Pharisee friends, but indeed by the Sadducees. We are told that Stephanos was brought before the council to answer the charges. But this could not have been the full Sanhedrin on which their ally Gamaliel sat. It was likely some sub-committee of the only group in the land of Israel that had ever felt threatened by Yeshua or his Heirs, the Sadducees. Scholars have argued that a "Temple Committee," consisting of the chief priests, priestly elders and scribes, minus the Pharisees, had previously condemned Yeshua and incriminated him before Pilatus. As scholars pore over the events leading up to Yeshua's execution, it appears that his single act of overturning the tables of the moneychangers in the Temple was what got him into trouble with the Sadducee-dominated priesthood. It was they, not the Pharisees and certainly not rank-and-file Israelites who pressured Pilatus for his execution. Now that Yeshua was out of the picture, they were at it again.

What followed has no precedent in Pharisaic/ "Rabbinic" law. It flies in the face of all the jurisprudence and civil procedure that the liberal-minded Jews of the land of Israel had established. Basically, it amounted to a lynching. The narrative depicts a group of crazed council members descending on Stephanos, dragging him out of Jerusalem, since it was illegal to execute someone within the city walls, and stoning him to death. Overseeing all this was a young man whom we now meet for the first time and who was destined to change everything, indeed to change the world. This man was Shaul, or Paul who appears to have been in the employ of the Sadducees, who were particularly ruthless in meting out punishments. As Josephus observed:

> The sect of the Sadducees … are very rigid in judging offenders, above all the rest of the Jews. (*Antiquities*, 20, 9)[10]

Shaul's collaboration with the Sadducees is curious in light of the fact that he later declared: "I am a Pharisee, the son of a Pharisee" (Acts 23:6). Certainly, his blood-thirst early on reminds us of nothing the Pharisees would have counseled. In a larger sense we need to question what is going on in the book of Acts' narrative, in that it downplays the role of Yeshua's Heirs in leading and guiding the movement. And while all the members of the Way were still Jews in these early days, there is a deliberate shift to highlight Diaspora Jews, as if to foreshadow the movement's inexorable progression (some would say "hijacking") to the west. We have to look to other ancient sources to fill in the blanks behind these events, which must have amounted to nothing short of a major riot in the city of Jerusalem.

The Phantom of the Apostles

One such source to which our inquiry leads us is a text called Pseudo-Clementines, a "religious romance" describing how the Church Father known as Clement became the traveling companion of the apostle Shimon (Peter). The story is told by Clement himself, and is addressed to none other than "James the Just" (our Yaakov), who is called "Bishop of Jerusalem." The specific language is: "Bishop of bishops, who rules Jerusalem, the holy Church of the Hebrews, and the Churches everywhere." We are told

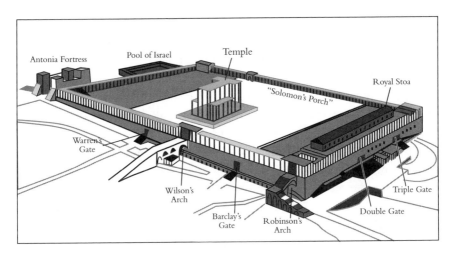

in this narrative how Shimon (Peter) asked Clement to travel with him from town to town, as they made their way to Rome. Shimon had been instructed by Yaakov to relate to him everything he was teaching, and for this reason Clement sent his account back to Jerusalem. While the book of Acts is fixated, first on Shimon and next on Stephanos, Pseudo-Clementines tells us that Yaakov was clearly in charge. In a note at the end we are told that when Yaakov received Clement's letter, he read it to the Jerusalem elders. However, it was in the future to be disseminated only one part at a time, and only to those who were circumcised, who were teachers, and who were "pious," a word which referred (at least in Jewish sources) to the ancient Hasidim.

The text recounts a heated confrontation between the disciples and the High Priest Caiaphas during which Shimon (Peter) prophesied the coming destruction of the Temple itself. Naturally, the Sadducean priest-hood was outraged, just as they had been at Yeshua. The account dove-tails with the book of Acts, stating that it was Gamaliel the Pharisee who came to the aid of the beleaguered *ma'aminim*, making a public speech on their behalf the next day. But while Acts has written Yaakov out of the story, Psuedo-Clementines tells us that at this point he boldly addressed the people in the great court of the Temple Mount for a full week. His oratory was so persuasive that large numbers were ready to go through the *mikveh* (ritual immersion, which Christian sources call "baptism") as initiates into the sect. This was the moment when an unidentified "en-emy," linked by modern scholarship with Shaul (Paul), stirred up a crowd against Yaakov. In wild rage they pummeled him and threw his limp body down the steps of the Temple, where he was left for dead.[11]

There was indeed a massive and monumental staircase at the southern end of the Temple Mount. It led up to two enormous arches through which subterranean ramps served as an exit onto the vast platform called the Court of the Gentiles. This was where the public would gather for all manner of religious and civil purposes. Within an immense open colonnade called the portico of Solomon, anyone with a loud voice could address an assembled multitude.

There was also a melancholy historical precedent vis-à-vis disturbances on the Temple Mount. In the second century BCE, the Jewish king Alexander Yannai was officiating at the Feast of Tabernacles. In his dual role as king and High Priest he was pouring out a liquid libation at the altar when it became apparent to a crowd of Pharisees that he was not performing the ritual according to the rigid precepts they had established. In a sudden rage they began pelting him with citrons, the fruit associated with the Festival of *Succot*, as it was called in Hebrew. An enraged Yannai unleashed his troops against them, perpetrating a bloody massacre in the sacred precincts. In Yaakov's case, the battered leader was left alive though badly injured, having broken his leg, or perhaps both legs. But as fate would have it, he was rescued by a multitude of his own adherents, some five thousand strong (an inflated number by anyone's estimation), who carried him to a safe refuge, somewhere near Jericho.

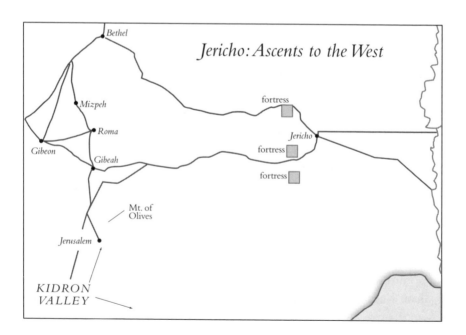

Jericho: Ascents to the West

We should point out that Pseudo-Clementines says nothing at all about a riot involving Stephanos, but Yaakov (James) remains front and center in the story. We might even go as far as to question whether Stephanos, in the Acts account, is not in some sense a surrogate for Yaakov, whom the writer would rather not mention. If so, it would have amounted to nothing less than a cover-up of the true leadership of the *ma'aminim*, a deliberate attempt to supplant the native Israelite Heirs of Yeshua with westerners of a very different cultural heritage.

Bear in mind, not a few scholarly voices dismiss Pseudo-Clementines as a fictional work rather than an historical account. Yet, it is reasonable that if there had been an altercation in Jerusalem involving the *ma'aminim*, then Yaakov must have been involved. It also makes sense that, had he been injured by his Saducean-backed adversaries, his escape route would have led in the direction of Jericho. After all, the region around Jericho had from time immemorial served as a safe haven for refugees of various sorts, from common brigands to the like of a Bethlehemite shepherd and member of the court of Saul, David. Recall that David fled for his life to the Wilderness of En Gedi, a lush desert oasis which gave him shelter from his own deranged king, Saul, who sought to murder him.

Exodus!

The flight of Yaakov and company also prefigures a much larger exodus, some three decades later, when the entire Jerusalem community of *ma'aminim*, now known as Nazarenes, perceived the coming apocalypse and uprooted themselves from holy Jerusalem to find a new domicile eastward across the River Jordan. It would prove to be the salvation and the continuation of the dynasty of the Master. But for now, the wounded leader of the Jerusalem community was in serious need of rest and recuperation, and this temporary relocation was the sensible thing to do.

By now a serpentine though well-maintained Roman road stretched due east from the city, marked with periodic milestones to gauge one's progress. It snaked its way from the hill country of Jerusalem through a series of natural ravines, desert wadis that had been eroded by the elements. Passing chalky and desiccated hills, the terrain slowly flattened into an unforgiving desert known as the Judean Wilderness. Off in the distance a faint band of blue could be discerned on the horizon – a brackish, sulfurous lake known as the Dead Sea. The traces of greenery that tenaciously clung to the hillsides in the environs of Jerusalem soon gave way to barren wasteland. In the horrific heat of the relentless desert, it felt

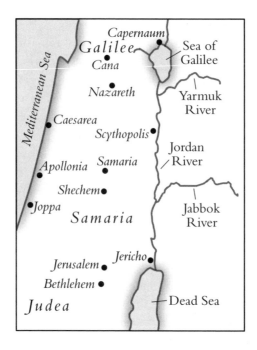

like a descent into hell itself. Roughly halfway along the modern road that sits astride its ancient counterpart, today's travelers encounter a landmark known as the Samaritan's Inn, where, in Christian tradition, the parable of the "Good Samaritan" played out.

We can hardly imagine a troupe of five thousand of Yaakov's supporters marching like an army down the road to Jericho, but ancient traditions, exaggerated though they may be, often rest on unambiguous reality. The idea that the bulk of Yaakov's community strategically retreated from the city of Jerusalem until the situation calmed down is entirely plausible. At the end of the road was an ancient settlement conquered more than a thousand years before by Joshua, whose command brought its famous walls crashing down. It was situated at the mouth of an underground spring that turned the blistering desert into a verdant oasis adorned by graceful date palms. While the Bible decreed that it be perpetually uninhabited, its lush environment made it too alluring to be kept in a state of desolation. In the days of King Herod the Great it was turned into the equivalent of a winter resort, with a sumptuous palace and even a swimming pool, for the personal use of the mighty potentate.

To the immediate east was the Jordan River, which cascaded down from the Galilee, emptying into the Dead Sea. Jericho lay astride lively

trade routes, catering largely to the spice traffic and linking the land of
Israel with the King's Highway in Transjordan. It wended its way south
and west down to Egypt, and in the other direction it meandered across
Arabia to points east. Between engaging in trade and fishing the Jordan
River, there was ample opportunity to earn a livelihood. Moreover, the
warmth, the sunshine and the therapeutic waters were amply suited for
Yaakov's healing and restoration.

We don't know how long Yaakov and company remained in the environs of Jericho, but it is quite possible that years passed in this self-imposed
exile. Sometime during this period, it seems that other "satellite" branches
of the Way sprang up. We can only conclude that emissaries (sh'likhim in
Hebrew), known in the New Testament as "apostles," took to the roads
to establish communities in other cities in greater Judea. There was well-
established precedent for this tactic, inasmuch as the sect who wrote the
Dead Sea Scrolls (identified by most researchers as the Essenes) had employed their own emissaries to set up satellite communities in various
Jewish cities. To be sure, there was one city, Damascus, that now boasted
a sect of ma'aminim in addition to a much older community of Essenes
(judging by its prominent mention in the Scrolls). Damascus was one of
ten Greco-Roman cities in the territory that was otherwise rooted in
Semitic culture, namely Jewish, Aramean and Nabatean. These were not
Diaspora cities, in spite of large number of pagans who were living there,
for in the days of the great King David, this was all Jewish land. Moreover,
the Jewish population of the Decapolis remained sizable, though in the
minority. Years earlier Yeshua had admonished his disciples not to go
into the "way of the Gentiles" at all, since his teaching (his "Torah") was
for Israelites only.[12] Yaakov, in dispatching his own emissaries, remained
faithful to this precept. And, in targeting the Decapolis, he was, as we
shall see, prefiguring the ultimate relocation of all the heirs in the decades
to come.

But for now we can at least be sure that Yaakov, while residing in
Jericho, did recover from his injuries. We are told that he continued to lead
the movement and even to give orders to the other disciples. According
to Pseudo-Clementines, he dispatched Shimon (Peter) to Caesarea on the
Mediterranean coast, for the purpose of confronting a sorcerer of famously ill repute, known as Simon Magus. At this point Pseudo-Clementines
conflicts directly with the canonical story recounted by the book of Acts,
which sets the confrontation between the two Shimons (Simon Peter and
Simon Magus) in the region sandwiched geographically between Judea

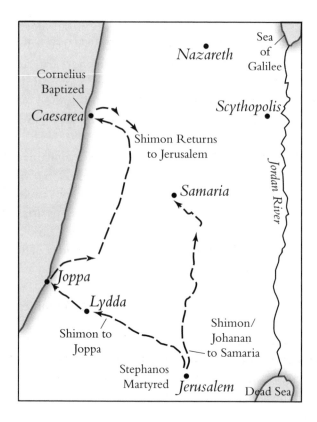

and the Galilee, Samaria. It appears that Acts has erred in its historical record, since Josephus speaks of one Simon, who lived in Caesarea around the year 40 CE.[13] The writer of Acts may simply have confused Simon Magus' original domicile, Samaria, with the location of his conflict with Shimon (Peter).

In any case, it was apparently the belief of an early sect of Gnostics (people who sought a private and personal knowledge of the divine) called Simonians that the infamous master of the dark arts (Simon Magus) was not merely a messiah ("anointed one"), but a god incarnate. The Church Father Ireneus wrote: "He was worshiped by many as a god, and seemed to himself to be one."[14] Such a doctrine was particularly distasteful to Jews, who considered it idolatry. But it is quite possible that in the cosmo-politan city of Caesarea many Jews felt a certain sympathy for him, per-haps in opposition to new messianic claims being made by the *ma'aminim* on behalf of Yeshua m'Natzeret.

With this background in mind, we are told that this Simon offered money to the other Simon (Shimon Peter) and to Yohanan (John) in return for receiving the power to impart the Divine Spirit (the *Shechinah* in Hebrew, a particularly "Hasidic" gift) through the laying on of hands. But Shimon (Peter) only retorted with a harsh rebuke, barking, "Your money perish with you!" (Acts 8:20). Again the narrative of Acts leaves Yaakov out of the picture, an odd editorial choice, given that the writings of the Church Fathers depict him as orchestrating all these events, both dispatching emissaries ("apostles") and receiving reports back from them.

We hear nothing more of Yaakov for some time to come. The canonical New Testament would remain silent about him, choosing to reference him only through the prism of the self-styled apostle to the west, whom it calls Paul (Shaul). As we shall see, this Shaul will end up in a bitter dispute with Yaakov, during which he will attempt to peel away support from Yeshua's brother and effectively take control of the entire movement.

Enter the "Interloper"

How did all of this come about? According to Christian tradition, it was all the hand of God, and was directly related to the most compelling conversion story in history. To be sure, the man called Shaul (Paul) was a complex character by anyone's estimation. He was indisputably a man of contradiction. He was both a Jew and a Roman citizen. As a Diaspora Jew, he nonetheless claimed to have studied at the feet of the Jerusalemite sage Gamaliel. He accordingly boasted of his Pharisee credentials, though he persecuted the *ma'aminim* in the name of the Sadducees. He boasted of being "an Israelite of the tribe of Benjamin, circumcised on the eighth day" (Phil. 3:5), though he spent the bulk of his life bringing the piety of a sect of Jewish Hasidim to the uncircumcised. He claimed to speak with complete apostolic authority, transmitted from Yeshua himself, yet he had never known nor even met Yeshua personally. He preached freedom from the restrictions of religious law, yet he practiced the most restrictive lifestyle the ancient world had to offer, celibacy. He was cantankerous and argumentative, and given the style of his epistles, now ensconced in the New Testament canon, prone to outbursts of emotion.

Modern commentators have called him homophobic, sexist and even anti-Semitic. To him the greatest oxymoron of all might be said to apply: an anti-Semitic Jew. His home town was Tarsus in Cilicia, located in modern-day Turkey. He was no stranger to Jerusalem, though if his claim is true that he had been a disciple of the liberal-minded Gamaliel, then it is beyond bizarre that he would have been in attendance at the brutal stoning of Stephanos. One therefore suspects that Shaul's association with the Pharisaic sages and their teachings is more than a little exaggerated. It was the Sadducees, not the Pharisees, who were ruthless in their suppression of rival religious groups, and it was the Sadducees alone who possessed the temporal power, as "lackeys" of the Romans, to engage in any form of persecution. Given the "cold war" between Sadducees and Pharisees, the Acts narrative is odd in relating that the High Priest gave Shaul "letters of introduction" to the synagogues of Damascus, "… so that if he found any of the Way, whether they were men or women, he might bring them bound to Jerusalem" (Acts 9:2). One element of the story that rings true is that the devotees of Yeshua continued to gather for worship where Hasidim, Pharisees and rank and file Israelites had always congregated, the synagogue. The *ma'aminim* had not been cast out of synagogues, and their worship resembled that of their fellow Jews in every way.

Nonetheless, the story recounts that Shaul, with letters in hand, was traveling the trade route that led to Damascus when he was knocked from his horse and sent sprawling to the ground, blinded by a brilliant, divine

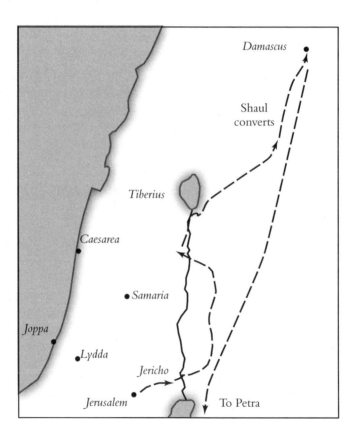

light. A voice from the heavens thundered, "Shaul, why are you persecuting me?" (Acts 9:4; 22:7). In a Hebrew context it reminds the reader of
an incident from long ago, when young David was being pursued by an
earlier Shaul, King Saul. David encountered the king, fast asleep in a desert cave, and shouted to him from a distance, "Saul, why are you chasing
me?" (1 Sam. 26:18).[15] It happens that the Hebrew verb *radaf* has a double
meaning, "chase/pursue" and "persecute." And perhaps the narrative of
Acts is trying to tell us that Shaul of Tarsus, in persecuting the *ma'aminim*,
was, ironically and subconsciously, "chasing" or "seeking" Yeshua himself. It all sets the stage for the amazing narrative to come.

Unable to see, Shaul's traveling companions led him on to Damascus,
at which time a member of the Way was supernaturally directed to find
Shaul and impart healing, the recovery of his sight, through the laying
on of hands. It is one more gift of healing that we might expect from a
"Hasidic" sect such as the Way. Amazingly, Shaul himself immediately
became a member of the Way, undergoing ritual immersion in a *mikveh*
as a manifestation of his new identity. We are told that he went to the
synagogues of the city, where he now made messianic claims of his own
on behalf of Yeshua. We are also told of his daring nocturnal escape from
those who now sought his life through an opening in the city wall, by
being lowered in a basket.

The Acts narrative next tells us that he returned to the city of Jerusalem,
but this directly contradicts what he wrote in his own later epistle:

> Nor did I go up to Jerusalem to those apostles before me, but I
> went into Arabia and returned again to Damascus. Then after
> three years I went up to Jerusalem to see Peter (Shimon), and
> stayed with him fifteen days. But I saw no other of the apostles,
> except James the Lord's brother. (Galatians 1:17-19)[16]

Shaul, a quintessential city dweller, can hardly be pictured living the life
of a hermit, alone in the desert of Arabia. But there was in those days a
vast and impressive city, which had risen in the Transjordanian desert to
the east of the Dead Sea. It was called Petra, a city carved into the rocky
cliffs and controlled by Nabatean Arabs, though cosmopolitan enough. It
is likely that Shaul spent his next three years back and forth between Petra
and Damascus, developing a complex and systematic theology, representing a syncretistic blend of ideas from across the Near East, sprinkled with
a heavy dose of Essene dualism, influenced directly or indirectly by the
Dead Sea Scrolls.

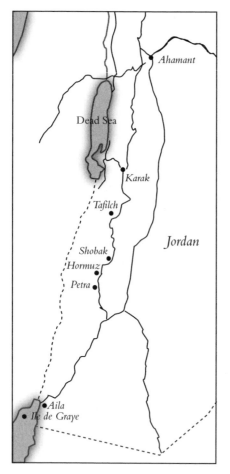

A single verse in Acts (9:31) tells us that this was a time of peace for the movement called the Way. The native Jewish population of the region was, as we have seen, largely receptive to this fundamentally Hasidic group. It was strong, it was vital, and with the help of the *Shekhinah* (the Divine Presence, which Acts calls the "Holy Spirit"), it grew significantly in numbers. What the book of Acts conveniently omits is the individual directly responsible for its growth and success, whose very presence must have been seen as a threat to those who would later "hijack" the Way and take it far to the west, ultimately severing it from its Jewish roots. This unnamed leader was of course Yaakov, the unheralded "phantom" of the apostles.

Notes

1   See R. Eisenman *James the Just in the Habakkuk Pesher* (Leiden: E.J. Brill, 1986), 3. See also Epiphanius, *Haeres* 29.3; 78.13 and Jerome, *Vir. ill.* 2. For a discussion of the character attributes and ascetic lifestyle that gave rise to the early designation "James the Just," see C.C. Torrey, "James the Just, and His Name 'Oblias'," *JBL* 63.2 (1944): 93-98.

2   See H.J. Schoeps, *Paul: The Theology of the Apostle in the Light of Jewish Religious History* (Philadelphia: Fortress Press, 1961), 67. See also R. Eisenman, *Maccabees, Zadokites, Christians and Qumran: A New Hypothesis of Qumran Origins* (Leiden: E.J. Brill, 1983), 12-16. Eisenman has gone as far as to posit a Zadokite/ Zealot/ Saducean movement. However, many scholars cast doubt on his conclusions. See J. Vanderkam, Review of Eisenman (1983), *JAOS* 105.4 (1985): 798-9.

3   For an examination of the role of *Nasi* and *Av Bet Din*, see S. Zeitlin, "The Titles High Priest and the Nasi of the Sanhedrin," *JQR* 48.1 (1957): 1-5.

4   While the "official" High Priest was Annas, the Romans had replaced him with Caiaphas, who served in an "acting" capacity. For more on the Sanhedrin vis-à-vis capital punishment, see T.A. Burkill, "The Competence of the Sanhedrin," *VC* 10.2 (1956): 80-96. Burkill argues that certain religious offenses were indeed punishable with death.

5   See the rabbinic tractate *Seder Olam Rabbah*, end, chapter 3.

6   There is an inconsistency here, in that Theudas is said to have risen prior to Judah the Galilean, whose activities are dated to the period of taxation in 6-7 CE. By contrast, Josephus dates Theudas to 45-46 CE, long after Judah the Galilean and post-dating Gamaliel the elder. Solutions to this contradiction are multiple. Luke (who wrote the book of Acts) may have been mistaken in his reading of Josephus. This would of course assume that Luke wrote after Josephus (post 70 CE). Alternately, both Luke and Josephus may have used a separate, inaccurate source regarding Theudas. A third option is that Josephus was simply mistaken in his chronology. One final possibility is that there were several individuals named Theudas and/ or Judah of Galilee. See C. Clemen, "Josephus and Christianity," *BW* 25.5 (1905): 361-75.

7   See M.S. Enslin, "Paul and Gamaliel," *JR* 7.4 (1927): 360-75.

8   This verse is sometimes linked with Michah 6:8: "He has shown you, O man, what is good. And what does the Lord require of you but to do justice and to love mercy and to walk humbly with your God?" James' definition of religion is in keeping with the pietistic view that the essence of life is service to others – to something outside of one's self. The concept has been defined in traditional Christian terms as "loving ministration," or as being "in the world but not of it." See H.M. Haydin, "Three Conceptions of the Christian Life, A Study in the Epistles of James, 1 Peter, and 1 John," *BW* 23.1 (1904): 18 ,20.

9   For a detailed discussion of the origins of the "schism" between Jewish Christians and their fellow Jews, see Flusser, *Judaism*, 617-44.

10   For more on the distinction between the Sadducees in their harshness and the Pharisees in their moderation, see L. Finkelstein, "The Pharisees: Their Origin and Their Philosophy," *HTR* 22.3 (1929): 185-261.

11   See Eisenman, *James the Just*, 4.

12   See Matthew 10:5: "Jesus sent out these twelve, commanding them, saying, "Do not go into the way of the nations, and do not enter into *any* city of *the* Samaritans."

13   See Josephus, *Antiquities* xx.7.2. According to Pseudo-Clementines (which has been preserved in two forms, the *Homilies* and the *Recognitions*), Shimon (Peter) was welcomed to Caesarea by Zacchaeus, who related to him the actions

of Simon Magus. The account is not present in the *Homilies*, perhaps because it is not consistent with canonical Acts.

14   *Adv. Hæreses* i.23.1

15   Lit. "Why does my lord pursue after his servant this way?"

16   Some scholars view Shaul's sojourn in Arabia as purely allegorical, or figurative of Damascus itself. See C.W. Briggs, "The Apostle Paul in Arabia," *BW* 41.4 (1913): 255-9. However, in light of what we know about Petra, it is now possible to take Shaul (Paul) at his word.

3

The Great Debate

"Little Boots" – Big Problem

BACK IN ROME A MOST UNUSUAL EMPEROR HAD MADE HIS MARK on history. His name was Gaius, though everyone knew him by the nickname he had acquired in childhood when he tagged along on military campaigns with his parents, Caligula or "Little Boots." Dressed in a soldier's uniform, the young lad looked adorable. But when he came of age, and upon taking the reigns of empire at the death of Tiberius in 37 CE, the rambunctious child became a bloodthirsty tyrant of the first order. For the Jewish inhabitants of Judea the consequences would be nearly catastrophic.

"Little Boots" perpetrated bloody executions, staged spectacular orgies, and made love to his own sister. But the most infamous of Caligula's misdeeds, in the eyes of his own people, concerned his inflated self-conception. While a swollen ego was hardly foreign to Roman emperors, Caligula's went beyond the pale. His great-grandfather, Augustus, had been officially promoted to divinity by the senate, though only after his decease. Caligula, however, was disinclined to wait. He took the outlandish step of deifying himself. It was said of him:

> On nights when the full moon brightly shined, he regularly entreated the moon goddess to his bed for sex. In the daylight hours he whispered in conversation with Jupiter, as if the god were speaking into his ear. Sometimes he even shouted with rage. On one occasion he uttered this threat to Jupiter: "Unless you

exalt me to the heavens, I will throw you into hell!" (Suetonius, *The Twelve Caesars*, author's paraphrase)

With Caligula there was for the first time an emperor who not only considered his deity a fact but played the role with gusto. He wanted the world to know of his divine status and to pay him due obeisance, but for his imperial subjects and for his Jewish subjects in particular, this arrogance was the ultimate provocation.

Drunk with godhood, Caligula surveyed his empire and realized that of all the temples in all the cities honoring such a variety of deities, one alone stood out, which lacked any image of a god or goddess and was surprisingly empty. It was the temple of the God of Israel in Jerusalem. Here was a building of stunning beauty, yet, as far as Caligula was concerned, devoid of any god at all. He determined that something must be done about this. The province of Judea was in those days under the military jurisdiction of Syria, and he therefore dispatched a new governor to the region, a legate named Publius Petronius, with orders to bring an army into Jerusalem and erect an enormous statue of the emperor within the Temple's great hall.

As the sculptors began work on Caligula's monumental visage, delegations of thousands of Jews pleaded with Petronius that he not follow through with the hideous order, which would make a mockery of the First Commandment: "You shall have no other gods before Me." What is not commonly known is that Petronius may in fact have been one of the so-called "God-fearers," a term which referred to an entire class of non-Jews, who nonetheless allied themselves with the one God of Israel.[1] They voluntarily kept the Sabbath and many of the feast days of Judaism, without being circumcised or formally converting to Judaism. Having grown weary of the multiple deities of the pagan world, they saw Judaism as a lively alternative, the only truly monotheistic alternative ever to arise in human society. In their tens of thousands, they were becoming a significant presence within the empire, and they were soon to become targets for proselytism into the new movement called the Way.

As one who was well-acquainted with Jewish sensibilities, the governor Petronius knew that the installation of Caligula's statue within the holy Temple would be considered an unforgivable abomination, which the Jews of Israel would go to any lengths to prevent. The Israelites as a people would lay down their lives in unison rather than to allow a human being, even the emperor, to be worshipped as a god in the Temple. It was a brewing crisis, poised to rock Rome on its foundations. Petronius tried to stall for time and he wrote back to Caligula, "Unless you are prepared to obliterate this land and all its people, you should consider revoking this order!"[2]

The impulsive Caligula became furious and dispatched another letter across the Mediterranean, commanding Petronius to fall on his own sword. But the letter was delayed by a storm at sea. After some time a second letter was dispatched to Petronius, bearing much better tidings. It related that Caligula had been ambushed and assassinated by his own Praetorian Guard. The ship bearing this missive was not delayed, and it reached Petronius first. The governor of Syria breathed a huge sigh of relief, and when the original letter arrived, commanding his suicide, we can imagine him chuckling as he cast it into the flame. The year was 41 CE and a massive Jewish insurrection had narrowly been avoided.

Why were these events not recorded in the New Testament? Perhaps the book of Acts was too absorbed with the exploits of Shimon and Yohanan (Peter and John) to concern itself with a Jewish national emergency. But Jewish law on the subject of "holy war" was clear. There are some things not worthy of making oneself a martyr to defend. For example, if someone were to hold a sword over you commanding you to break the Sabbath, then submit and break the Sabbath, so you will be alive to keep it next week. But on the question of idolatry there is no compromise. It is better to lay down one's life than to allow the unity of God to be profaned. On this point there was complete unanimity among all Jewish sects, and all were prepared to go to war to uphold it.

What would have been the position of Yaakov and the Heirs during these unsavory events? One thing is certain. Contrary to popular stereotype about the first "Christians," the *ma'aminim* had not abandoned the Temple, and they would have been in complete solidarity with their fellow Jews in standing up to the edict of "Little Boots." For a people living under the not-so-little boot of Rome, who had for decades been on the verge of revolt, these days amounted to a serious exercise in "brinkmanship."

King of the Jews

The great irony about Caligula is the fact that from his very accession to power, his reign brought new hope for the inhabitants of Israel. One of his friends happens to have been Agrippa, the grandson of the notorious King Herod and his beloved Jewish wife, Miriamne. Agrippa had fared surprisingly well while growing up in faraway Rome where he was sent to be educated. (It was said that the only people in Herod's entire household

who turned out halfway "normal" were his grandchildren.) Agrippa was a thoroughly Jewish leader who had descended from an Israelite princess, and his people knew it. Of course being well placed among the Roman aristocracy didn't hurt. Caligula, who had regarded him well from his youth, made him governor of the northern territories of the land of Israel in the year 37 CE, on his rise to the imperial throne. Agrippa used his new position to good advantage and, as the years passed, actively lobbied for Jewish interests during the crisis over Caligula's statue, thus endearing himself to his people. He so positioned himself with the ruling elite that he eventually lobbied to have Judea's status as a mere Roman province annulled and to have himself declared king over the entire land of Israel.

Oddly, the book of Acts paints him as a villainous, even murderous megalomaniac, but for most of the Israelites it amounted to an "Era of Good Feeling."[3] Moreover, at some point Yaakov and the Heirs (presumably including Miriam and Clophas as well as his brothers and sisters) must have returned to Jerusalem to reestablish the movement in the Holy

City. The house of Yohanan the Priest may have continued to serve as their headquarters, though, with the members of the sect pooling their resources, we can imagine that a number of homes and villas in close proximity to each other must have been pressed into service.

During Agrippa's tenure Sadducean persecution of the Way continued sporadically. The book of Acts records that another Yaakov ("James the brother of John") was in those days put to death by the sword. Not surprisingly, Agrippa gets blamed. Additionally, Shimon was arrested, until, according to the narrative, an angel miraculously appeared and led him out. In a Jewish context it was one more miracle experienced by a Hasidic sect that thrived on miracles. In any case, scattered pockets of disciples must have cropped up in various locales, including the Galilee (where Agrippa served as governor), and one town in particular where Yeshua had spent much of his career as a sage, Capernaum. Nestled along the shore of the lake called Kinneret (the Sea of Galilee), it must have become, very early on, the Galilean headquarters of the movement.

Archaeology has shown that one house in particular was revered by the *ma'aminim* as a sort of shrine and that it was most likely the home of Shimon (Peter). The fact that it was situated just a short distance from the synagogue of the town indicates what some have called a symbiotic relationship between the Way and the other streams of ancient Judaism. One might in fact have gone to any synagogue in the land and found the *ma'aminim* praying alongside observant Jews of other persuasions. In such an environment of tolerance, the claims made by the Believers on behalf of Yeshua may have become increasingly bold, even to the point of calling him the "anointed one" – the *Mashiakh/* Messiah. Their belief in his resurrection had only strengthened, being confirmed by the experience of the *Shekhinah* (the Divine Presence/ "Holy Spirit") in their lives.

But messianism has never been the central element of Judaism and all Jews are "messianic" in the sense of adhering to the concept of an anointed deliverer to come who will sit on the throne of David. It has long been an adage that wherever two Jews are gathered, there are at least three opinions. So it is today and so it was then. Some believed in a militant messiah, some in a purely spiritual messiah.[4] Some, like the Essenes (who wrote the Dead Sea Scrolls) believed there would be two messiahs, a Davidic messiah and a priestly messiah. But no one could be judged a "good Jew" or a "bad Jew" on the basis of what he or she thought about the deliverer to come. The goal was to make the world a better place today, so that the Messiah (whatever his identity) would want to come. And what better way to improve the world than to express and experience the "Kingdom of Heaven," including miracles, signs and wonders, in the here and now? This was the essential "Torah" of the Heirs of Yeshua.

Suspicious Arrival

We are told that during this same period (approximately 37 CE) Yaakov was visited by an individual whose background was suspicious at best and menacing at worst. It was the very man who had orchestrated the riot in which Stephanos was murdered and Yaakov seriously injured, Shaul of Tarsus. He had withdrawn to the desert for three years following his miraculous conversion, and now he was back in Jerusalem seeking entrance into the very sect he had assailed, the Way. Naturally, they all had good reason to fear him. The book of Acts again makes no mention of Yaakov, as though the leader of the movement and spokesman for the Heirs didn't even exist. It is only in the later Pauline epistle of Galatians that we are told of his meeting with Yaakov, specifically referenced as "the Lord's brother":

> Then after three years I went up to Jerusalem to see Peter (Shimon), and stayed with him fifteen days. But I saw no other of the apostles, except James (Yaakov) the Lord's brother. (Gal. 1:18-19)

Clearly it was Yaakov who evaluated Shaul and who "did not believe that he was a disciple" (Acts 9:11). It took a Diaspora Jew of priestly pedigree named Yosef (Joseph), renamed Barnabas by his Hellenistic friends, to come to Shaul's defense and persuade the *ma'aminim* that his conversion was genuine.

Perhaps Yaakov felt some shame over the fact that the Diaspora Jews had been mistreated earlier and for this reason he was inclined to accept Shaul and even allow him to reside with the community. The narrative relates that he went about the city arguing and debating with Greek-speaking Jews. Why not native Israelites? Perhaps because the movement under Yaakov's leadership was gaining ground among the native population, who were disinclined to debate with a Diaspora Jew whose knowledge of the Torah was less than their own. Shaul certainly had more in common with Greek-speaking Jews, who were ever-present in cosmopolitan Jerusalem. But the Diaspora Jews were more insecure about their identity and more inclined to be offended by a lunatic who had come in from the desert, having propounded a distasteful new theology. Did they really try to kill him, as the

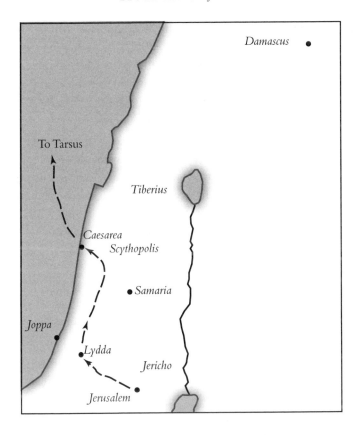

book of Acts maintains? It is curious that neither Yaakov nor any of the Heirs were threatened, only Shaul. The best solution was to get him out of town, indeed out of the country. Shaul was spirited away to Caesarea on the Mediterranean coast and then off to his home town, Tarsus. His focus and his theology would now turn to the west, transforming the character of what was still a "Hasidic" Jewish sect beyond recognition. Years would pass before he would see Jerusalem – and Yaakov – again.

Shaul was not, however, to be dissuaded. He was clearly a man of ambition who wanted to "be somebody," to make an impact. As a Diaspora Jew, however, it was obvious that he could never make a great impression on native-born Israelites, and among the movement of *ma'aminim* he would always be considered an outsider at best. Having failed to convince Jerusalem's Diaspora community of the rectitude of the Way, he turned his attention to Jews who had natively made their homes in the Diaspora, starting in his own city of Tarsus, where these realities must have crystallized in his mind. While he could never match the learned erudition of Israelite sages like Gamaliel or Yeshua's brother Yaakov, he must have realized that the Diaspora was a very different arena, where even among Jews an exhaustive knowledge of the Torah was a rare commodity. One wonders whether Shaul might have been familiar with some ancient variant of the adage, "In the land of the blind, the man with one eye is king."

One-Eyed King

But even in the Diaspora Shaul's efforts were destined for failure, probably for the same reason that Jerusalem's Diaspora Jews shunned him. They were an inherently insecure lot. Unable to define themselves by their status as inhabitants of Israel, they could only cling to their culture and their religion, which was often imperfectly grasped, their Jewish education generally being substandard. In the land of Israel, new and disparate ideologies were debated, considered and entertained, but in the Diaspora those same ideas represented an identity crisis. "Who is a Jew?" has been a pressing question throughout the generations of Israelites. Moreover, they must have asked, "Are we Torah-true Jews, or are we sectarians?" In such an environment, Shaul made an easy target for attack, and he was lambasted. It has alternately been quipped that in the land of the blind, the man with one eye is stoned to death. Moreover, Shaul was precisely the sort who took things personally. In his character he was high-strung, emotional, even given to occasional outbursts. Rather than understanding the essential predicament of Diaspora Jews, he branded them as rejectionists of the true Way, a stiff-necked people in the tradition of their ancestors who had come out of the land of Egypt.

In the verbal equivalent of shaking the dust from his sandals, Shaul petulantly uttered a single remark that would inexorably alter the course of world civilization:

> It was necessary for the word of God to be spoken to you first. But since indeed you put it far from you and judge yourselves unworthy of everlasting life, lo, we turn to the nations. (Acts 13:46)

It was a declaration that would give rise to the scurrilous charge hurled against Jews across the centuries, that they had *en-masse* rejected Jesus the Christ. Shaul's statement completely ignores the reality of a strong and vibrant community of *ma'aminim* in Jerusalem and in cities and towns across the land, which were piously Jewish and intent on infusing the most

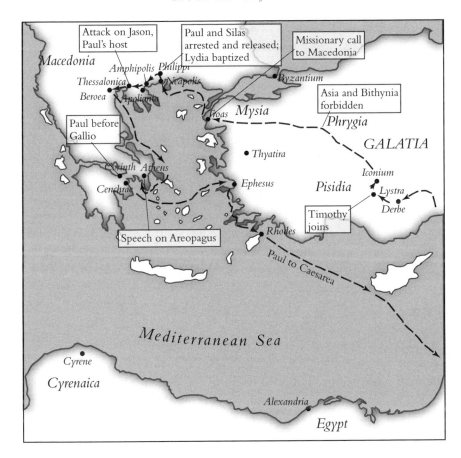

minor commandments of the Torah with divine, regenerative power. But of them the book of Acts maintains its silence.

Instead, we follow Shaul in his journeys across Asia Minor and throughout Greece. In that era the cities of the Greco-Roman Diaspora were a cauldron of contending cults, where debate over religion was the order of the day. Israel's God had to compete for adherents among a polyglot assortment of deities, from Athena, to Mithras, to Zoroaster, to Jupiter. Jews, who have been known throughout history as a people who do not proselytize others into their faith, were surprisingly active in seeking converts to Judaism in the classical world. The Torah had centuries before been translated from Hebrew into Greek for consumption in the west, and the great Jewish philosopher of Alexandria in Egypt, Philo Judeaus, made it his mission to explain Judaism in terms palatable to the philosophically oriented Greeks.

By contrast, the Stoic philosopher Seneca wrote of the Jews with derision, yet recognized their prominence within the empire:

The practices of this villainous nation have so prevailed that they are adopted by people everywhere. The vanquished have made laws for the conqueror![5]

In Shaul's mind, what was the Way but a specialized sect within Judaism, which likewise might gain adherents in the west? As an advocate of a growing sect of "Hasidic" Judaism, Shaul might even become "somebody," albeit a one-eyed king, within the greater Jewish outreach to the non-Jewish world.

But even his speeches to the *goyim* fell on largely deaf ears. The most poignant example of this is when he later journeyed to the city of Athens, ascending a rocky outcropping known as Mars Hill, sandwiched between the Acropolis and the Agora. Here, Athenians would regularly gather to debate the issues and the philosophies of the day. Shaul's remarks to those assembled were eloquent enough, calling attention to a nearby altar bearing an inscription "To an unknown god."[6] Israel's single Deity was both known and knowable, and, according to Shaul, had revealed the divine will through his servant Yeshua, whom God had miraculously resurrected from the dead. But Shaul's remarks had little impact on the crowd. A few listened intently and "joined themselves" to Shaul, but others remarked that they would "hear you again concerning this."[7] Still others scoffed in derision, hardly the stuff from which dynamic new movements are launched.

Shaul had learned the hard way that to sell a monotheistic sect, it is best to start with people who are already sympathizers with monotheism. They were the "God-fearers," known in Greek as the *sebomenoi*, from the Greek root *seb*, meaning "to fall down," as in homage before the Almighty. In virtually every city in the Greco-Roman world where there were communities of Diaspora Jews, God-fearers were also to be found. They accepted Israel's "jealous" Deity, turning aside from all forms of paganism. They observed many Jewish customs, including the Sabbath and various dietary restrictions. They honored Jewish festivals, such as Passover and the High Holy Days: the New Year, the Day of Atonement and the Feast of Tabernacles. Some decided to become full proselytes to Judaism, which involved circumcision and ritual immersion in water. But others decided to remain as they were, non-Jews who had discovered "ethical monotheism." Jewish communities accepted them as such, emphasizing that they were under no compulsion to be circumcised or abide by any of the Torah's laws directed to Israel.

Nevertheless, to be a God-fearer was not to be counted as a Jew, and they therefore had the dubious distinction of being considered not proselytes, but "semi-proselytes." This is the point at which Shaul performed a degree of mental gymnastics, taking the unprecedented and even revolutionary step of allowing these semi-proselytes full membership in the piously observant sect of *ma'aminim*. Such a leap would involve a redefinition of the sect itself, which was already being called by other names. In the land of Israel they were known as the Nazarenes (in Hebrew *Notzrim*), referring to the home town not only of Yeshua, but of all his family members, the Heirs. Further up the Mediterranean coast, however, in the Diaspora city of Antioch, a Greek term was coined to describe the movement,*Christianoi*, a derivative of Christos ("anointed"), the Hellenistic equivalent of the Hebrew *Mashiakh*.[8] This was the genesis of the word Christian, though it was hardly the beginning of Christianity, since everyone understood that the movement was entirely Jewish. This was in no sense a new religion, only a single sect of a very old faith.

The "Defection" of Shimon

For the first time, however, as a result of Shaul's missionary work, there were individual non-Jewish members of the sect from among the "semi-proselyte" God-fearers. This development was not without precedent, for the book of Acts famously records an incident in which a man named Cornelius, a God-fearer, became a "believer." Cornelius, who was a Roman military commander, reminds us of the centurion who came to Yeshua. Certainly, the two had much in common, being God-fearers. Moreover, the visceral response of Shimon was not unlike that of his teacher, Yeshua, to avoid the company of such men. Both ultimately did have dealings with the non-Jewish God-fearer who had sought them out. But here the similarity ends. For Shimon, we are told, offered water for ritual immersion, a *mikveh*, not only to Cornelius but to an entire group of Gentiles who were with him. This Yeshua would never have done.

Bear in mind that in Judaism the *mikveh* was employed for two distinct purposes. It was a sign of ritual purity, utilized by Jewish men on a regular basis, especially prior to the weekly Sabbath, and periodically by women following the menstrual cycle. Secondly, it was employed as an initiation rite into the Jewish faith. In a real sense it symbolized rebirth, and attaining a new Jewish identity. But it was only one step in the process of conversion, for it had to be accompanied by a gift to the Temple and by circumcision, as well as the studied observance of Jewish law. The idea that a non-Jew might enter a Jewish sect by immersion in a *mikveh* alone sounded absurd to the pietists of the Way back in Jerusalem.

It would also have been unthinkable for Shimon, were it not for the fact that he had received a vision in which he saw all manner of un-kosher food being lowered in a net, accompanied by a voice which told him to rise, kill and eat. Significantly, there is nowhere any indication that Shimon actually violated the laws of *kashrut* (kosher food).

The meaning of the vision was simply that non-Jewish God-fearers should not be coerced to observe Jewish dietary restrictions in order to be accepted by the *ma'aminim*. This step alone was revolutionary and shocking, suggesting to some researchers that Shimon was being "co-opted" by the new theology of Shaul. It was certainly enough to provoke the ire of Yaakov and the Heirs back in Jerusalem, whom the Acts narrative casts in negative light: "Those of the circumcision contended with him, saying, 'You went in to uncircumcised men and ate with them'" (Acts 11:2-3).

Who were "those of the circumcision"? They could only have been the leaders of the community of *ma'aminim* in Jerusalem, now broad-brushed with a pejorative term, kept in the shadows and not even referenced by name. It is a clear indication of a deepening rift within the movement. No sympathy is extended to their position or to the fact that in ancient Judea, eating meals was an important aspect of societal identification, and a meal had to be consumed in a scrupulous state of ritual purity. This was especially true of the Essenes who required a rigorous three-year probation before an initiate could partake of the "pure meal of the congregation."[9]

Yeshua himself, while not an Essene, appears to have subscribed to this level of purity. According to two separate Gospel accounts, he was approached by a Roman centurion, who asked that his paralyzed son[10] be healed. From the context it is apparent that Yeshua did not want to speak to this man at all, since he was a non-Jew. Only after the disciples pointed out that he was a benefactor of the Jews and had even built them a synagogue did Yeshua hear his request. In other words, he was a God-fearer. But the centurion distinctively understood that Yeshua would not ritually defile himself by entering his home, where he might be expected to partake of un-kosher food. He therefore shouted from a distance, "I am not worthy that You should come under my roof; but only speak the word, and my boy will be healed" (Matthew 8:8). Yeshua healed the boy, but only from afar, making sure to keep his distance. Such details come as a shock to modern readers, who routinely imagine that the message of "the Christ" was to all humankind, specifically embracing the Gentile world.

But the great sage of Nazareth would never compromise his Jewishness. This was the same Yeshua who declared, "I am not sent except to the lost sheep of the house of Israel" (Matthew 15:24) and who instructed his flock, "Do not go into the way of the Gentiles" (Matthew 10:5).

If this were the attitude of Yeshua, why should we be surprised to find that it was also the attitude of his family members, Yaakov and the Heirs? The real surprise is that one of Yeshua's personal disciples, Shimon, a fellow Galiean well acquainted with Jewish piety, would be prepared, not merely to speak with non-Jews, but to invite them to become full members of the very exclusive sect known as the Way. It was as though he had "defected" from the movement, or at least been strongly affected by a new and disparate ideology deriving from circles associated with Shaul.

Paradigm Shift

Shimon's change in attitude amounted to a fundamental paradigm shift, perhaps best explained by a modern-day analogy. Consider the largest, most dynamic branch of Hasidic Judaism in the world today, the Habad-Lubavitch movement. They are viewed as not only orthodox, but ultra-orthodox, stringently observant of Jewish law. In terms of dietary laws, ordinary kosher food is not sufficient for them. They require an even higher level, known as Glatt-kosher, which mandates that meat consumed must come from animals with defect-free, "smooth" lungs. Their members wear black coats and black hats, and are usually fully bearded, with long side curls. They actively reach out to fellow Jews, many of whom become members of the movement. They are, consequently, the fastest growing sect within all of orthodox Judaism. They also have a message for non-Jews, encouraging them to keep a series of seven laws for all humankind. Known as the seven laws of the sons of Noah, they are not connected with Judaism per se and their focus is not to proselytize anyone into Judaism. They are basic ethical commandments by which all people should live and which will make the world a better place, someday ushering in the messianic age. There is even a Habad-Lubavitch reggae-rap singer, who performs concerts before huge crowds – mostly non-Jewish – and who conveys a message of ethical monotheism, as embodied in the Noachide laws.

Are non-Jews welcome in Habad-Lubavitch synagogues? Absolutely. They are welcome to observe, even to join in the prayers. They are not counted as members of the congregation, nor can they come up to the *bema* (the elevated platform on which the Torah is read). But their presence is always welcome. Would a member of Habad eat in the home of a non-Jew? Certainly not. However, non-Jews are not to be disparaged or shunned, since they are not expected to keep Jewish law.

Now imagine, hypothetically, a non-Jew becoming interested in the Habad-Lubavitch movement through the influence of the reggae-rap artist. What if this person not only visited one of their synagogues, but donned a black coat and hat and expressed a sincere interest in becoming a member? This would not be allowed. Habad is a movement for Jewish renewal and is not for the non-Jewish "nations." A formal conversion to Judaism is the only way that such a person could ever be welcomed as a full member of the congregation. Such a conversion, however, is deliberately made difficult. In fact, the person must first be discouraged as much as possible, to the point of being rebuffed and turned away. (Recall that once Yeshua refused even to speak with a non-Jewish, Syro-Phoenician woman, until she quipped that even the "dogs," a pseudonym for "Gentiles," get the scraps from the table[11]) Conversion to Judaism is a serious step, which requires time, reflection and dedicated study, coupled with the difficult and painful requirement of ritual circumcision. The very idea of a *trefe-* (un-kosher food) eating non-Jew becoming a full-fledged member of Habad-Lubavitch is ludicrous. The movement may have its own reggae-rap singing sensation who performs for spellbound audiences of Gentiles, but its character and composition has always been and ever will be Jewish. Nor would anyone call them xenophobic or "legalistic" for preserving their essential character.

The book of Acts, however, paints the "party of the circumcision" in almost villainous tones, as though they were trying to block the path of salvation for a multitude of Gentiles who had already been divinely gifted with the Holy Spirit. It amounts to such a fundamental misunderstanding of what ancient Hasidic Judaism (and the Jesus movement as one expression of it) was all about that we have to ask what must have possessed Shimon in those days. When the narrative records his vision of the net descending, it must be straining to tell us that he had a drastic change of heart, which drew him away from the traditions and customs that had shaped his life. Perhaps Shimon had some personal dealings with Shaul of which we are not told in the Acts narrative. Perhaps Shaul, during his three years in the desert, had been hard at work formulating the kernel of a radical new theological system, which he now transposed back upon Yeshua, and into which he successfully corralled Shimon.

In any case, as Shaul embarked upon his missionary journeys across Asia Minor and into Greece, the details of his theology took shape and

were expressed in a series of letters he wrote to the communities he founded in these areas. These letters, known as the "Pauline epistles," would
become a lens through which two millennia of Christians would ultimately view Yeshua himself. While dealing with sundry issues of concern
to those fledgling communities/ "churches," their overarching theme was
a response to the "party of the circumcision," whom later ecclesiastics
would brand as the "Judaizers."

In sweeping tones Shaul now preached "freedom from the Torah,"
the Law, while castigating those who preached righteousness through observance of legal precepts and ritual practices. Oddly enough, Shaul utilized some of the language and vocabulary of Jewish mysticism in making
his argument. For example, the mystics taught that when the Messiah
comes, at the end of days, the Torah itself will slowly fade away, being
no longer required in a perfected world. Since Shaul was now making
bold messianic claims on behalf of Yeshua, he was now able to assert that
for the God-fearers the Torah had indeed faded away, that they should
be accepted as full proselytes into the Nazarene sect without becoming
proselytes at all into Judaism. As Shaul journeyed westward, this radical
idea was greeted with both intense skepticism by insecure Diaspora Jews
and increasing acclaim by God-fearers, who did not have an identity crisis
and were intrigued by the idea that while they could never be accepted as
bona-fide members of the Jewish community, they could at least be accepted as members of the Jewish sect of the Nazarenes. Shaul would have
to work hard to justify this new and unorthodox approach, and the complex theology he built, summarized by the term "justification by faith,"
was the result.

What is usually forgotten, two millennia removed from Shaul, is that
he would never have dreamed of nullifying or even relaxing either the
ethical or ritual aspects of Jewish law for the Jewish members of the sect.
He had no authority in Jerusalem, where Yaakov and the Heirs reigned
supreme, and it was implicitly understood that the Jewish *ma'aminim*
would forever abide by the Torah, from the keeping of Sabbaths to the
consumption of strictly kosher foodstuffs. On one of Shaul's missionary
journeys he encountered a young man of mixed parentage by the name of
Timothy whose father was Greek but whose mother was Jewish. Timothy
sought membership in the Nazarene sect, but when Shaul recognized
that his mother was Jewish, he took him aside and personally performed
what was for an adult an excruciating procedure, the rite of circumcision.
Shaul himself, on his final trip to Jerusalem, underwent a most rigorous

and elaborate ritual purification procedure, even going to the extreme of shaving his head. In his epistles he wrote that he had become "all things to all men."

And so he continued on his journeys, rebuffed by Jews who were strug-gling to live observant lives in a pagan world and who must have thought that Shaul had lost his mind, but striking an ever deeper chord with God-fearers, who now gathered regularly in private homes to hear the mys-teries of this monotheistic sect propounded on a weekly basis. As Shaul wandered through the hellenistic towns of Asia Minor, he was clearly "on a roll," establishing "churches" far and wide. (The term "church," *ecclesia* in the Greek, stems from the root *kaleo* meaning "to call," suggesting a group "called out" from the surrounding pagan population.) But while the great majority of these new "believers" were non-Jews, the churches of those days were hardly an expression of a new religion, but were in fact patterned after Diaspora synagogues (from the Greek *synagoga*, which in turn was a translation of the Hebrew *bet knesset*, "house of gathering"). The church, like the synagogue, was essentially a communal center, where the Torah was studied.

As Shaul's movement grew, however, it could no longer be relegated to the fringes of Jewish society. Was Shaul creating a Judaism without the Torah? Even more menacing as it grew in size, might it even overwhelm Judaism itself? The Diaspora Jews who voiced these concerns are of course cast as villains. Worse still, they are simply identified as "the Jews," who are depicted as inciting crowds against Shaul and even stoning him and leaving him for dead (Acts 14:19). Such characterizations directly stimulated centu-ries of Jew-baiting and anti-Semitism across Christian Europe and continue to feed Christian stereotypes of Jews to the present day. Shaul is painted as the victim of attack by Diaspora Jews on the one hand and by the party of the circumcision, the "Judaizers," on the other. The Acts narrative tells us that he took up residence for an extended period in the city of Antioch.

During this period, we are told that a famine struck Judea with such severity that it necessitated relief measures from *ma'aminim* in other Diaspora communities, specifically Antioch. Shaul, who orchestrated this aid, must certainly have risen in prestige and authority during the "crisis," and Yaakov must have felt diminished and weakened:

> And in these days prophets from Jerusalem came to Antioch.
> And one of them named Agabus stood up and signified by the
> Spirit that there should be great famine over the world (which

also happened in the days of Claudius Caesar). And the disciples, as any were prospered, determined each of them to send for ministry to those brothers who lived in Judea, which they also did, sending to the elders by the hand of Barnabas and Saul. (Acts 11:27-30)

It was also during Shaul's Antioch residency that a number of *ma'aminim* came up from Judea and began insisting that the Nazarenes were a Jewish sect, composed only of Jews, and that its members must fully convert to Judaism. While they too are cast as villains by the New Testament, we ought to recognize with hindsight that they had a point, namely, that without the requirement of conversion/ circumcision, the time would probably come when non-Jews in the movement outnumbered Jews, and the entire Jewish character of the Way would be lost. In this, of course, they were correct, and this is precisely what happened. It happened so thoroughly that in the twenty-first century, most of Christendom is surprised, even shocked, at the very idea that the "Christianity" of "Paul" was in no sense a new and separate faith, but rather an expression of pietistic, semi-mystical Hasidic Judaism.

Enter, the Ebionites

The active assumption is that these "Judaizers" were emissaries from Yaakov and the Heirs, back in Jerusalem, who had reluctantly accepted Cornelius and his compatriots as non-Jewish members of the sect, due to the efforts of Shimon, but were by no means ready to embrace a whole flock of Shaul's God-fearers into the movement without insisting on full conversion. There exists, however, another possibility, that these emissaries were not from Yaakov, but rather from another mysterious sect of *ma'aminim*, all but forgotten by history, know as the *Evionim*, or Ebionites.

The story of the Ebionites is one of the enduring puzzles of New Testament scholarship that continues to perplex as much as it intrigues. There was at one time an actual text produced by this Jewish-Christian sect, known as the Gospel of the Ebionites, which unfortunately has been lost in time. However, selections from this text survive through the fourth century hunter of heresies named Epiphanius who quoted portions of the Ebionite gospel as part of his full-scale broadside against Jewish Christians. From this and other ancient sources we know that the Ebionites consisted of Jewish followers of Yeshua, scattered across the Mediterranean world between the first and fourth centuries, who authentically maintained their

Jewish lifestyle, even while making messianic claims on behalf of *Yeshua m'Natzeret*. No one should have been surprised that their approach remained strictly monotheistic, until the Pauline communities "morphed" themselves, over a few centuries, into a distinctly separate religion, severing all connections with Yeshua's own Judaism.

By the time Epiphanius came along, the ecclesiastical structure of orthodox Christianity had already made the bold claim that Yeshua was in fact divine, that is, of the very substance of God, an eternal Deity. The formulation of the Holy Trinity, Father, Son and Holy Spirit, as three distinct "persons," representing a single unity, had become ensconced as inviolate theology at the Council of Nicea in the year 325 CE.[12] *Iesus*, as he was now called in Greek, was God incarnate, "begotten," not "made," from the Eternal Father. Any deviation from this sacred dogma was completely suppressed, and of deviants there were many.

The Ebionites in particular emphasized their belief that Yeshua, whom they accepted as Israel's *Mashiakh*, was in any case not a divine being, and he was certainly not God. Judaism, while it has no formal theology, does insist on one theological point, that there is only one God and that no human being is to be confused with this God. The worship of any created being, such as the *Iesus* now worshipped by Christians, was considered nothing short of idolatry by traditional Jews and by the Ebionite "believers"/ *ma'aminim* as well. This abiding respect for true monotheism left them much in common with traditional Jews, and it also resulted in their condemnation as heretics by the likes of Epiphanius.

The very existence of the Ebionites should alert us to the fact that the Jewish side of the Jesus movement continued for centuries into the common era. But the Ebionites also took the radical position that Yeshua's execution amounted to such an efficacious and universal sacrifice that the entire sacrificial system at the Jerusalem Temple had been rendered null and void. This goes well beyond the attitude of the Jerusalem *ma'aminim*, including Yaakov and the Heirs, who never abandoned the Temple and who must have seen ongoing meaning in the sacrifice of animals. But the Ebionites went even farther, taking the additional step of adopting a strictly vegetarian diet, due to the fact that meat in the classical Greco-Roman world was generally obtained through the sacrifice of animals. This is reflected in a particular passage of the Ebionite gospel, which declares that the diet of John the Baptist was wild honey, fashioned like pancakes, with no reference to the traditional Gospel account that he ate locusts, technically considered "meat."

The Ebionite gospel also lacks the traditional nativity story of Yeshua's birth, including the miraculous account of the virgin birth, later cited as proof of his divine nature. The lack of such significant details in the Ebionite gospel was enough to get it, as well as the entire sect, excommunicated completely from Christian orthodoxy. The term Ebionites derives from the term *Evionim*, which means "poor ones," a term used repeatedly in the Dead Sea Scrolls to describe the sect that produced them, generally identified as the "Essenes." They could be considered "poor" because they held all their possessions in common, and none individually owned anything. As a group, however, they were well to do, lacking no cultural or material amenities.[13]

There is some confusion among ancient sources, some of which link them with the Nazarene sect. They were, however, most likely a distinct movement with their own agenda. Other ancient sources tell us that they held Yaakov, Yeshua's brother, in great esteem, while villainizing Shaul, whose radically lax approach vis-à-vis the God-fearers undercut their most hallowed principles.

The picture that emerges, then, is of multiple "Christianities" and even multiple "Jewish Christianities," the Ebionites representing a Jewish group allied with Yaakov and the Heirs while remaining separate and distinct.[14] To what extent Shaul was arguing with the Ebionites as opposed to arguing with Yaakov's Nazarenes is impossible to say. But Shaul clearly spent most of his apostolic career in an extended rant against them and in making a theological justification for a faith not dependent upon the Torah. Shaul of course would never have countenanced lifting the requirements of Jewish law from Jews themselves, including the *ma'aminim*. It took subsequent generations of Christian clerics to do that.

Yaakov's "Summons" and the Council of Jerusalem

In the meantime Shaul found himself making a return trip to Jerusalem to make his case before the Sanhedrin of Yaakov. As we have noted, Yaakov appears to have been systematically excised from the Acts narrative, as if the author wants us to know nothing about either him or the Heirs. But all of Shaul's missionary endeavors notwithstanding, and for all of the "churches" he established in Diaspora lands, it is clear that the administrative center of the sect remained in Jerusalem. It is also clear that Yaakov, as head of the Jerusalem community, exercised legal authority over all other communities. For all the talk of a miraculous lifestyle, accompanied by a "hasidic" goodness and even "signs and wonders," the Jewish *ma'aminim* remained Torah-true.

Yaakov and the Heirs engaged themselves in the same practice that universally occupied the minds of Israelites of that age, namely, the formulation and hammering out of *halakhah*, as it was called – Jewish law – a word that literally means "walking," because it delineates the step-by-step behavior of its adherents on a daily basis. Every possible behavior had to be categorized on the basis of whether it was "kosher" (that is, "proper") or not, from what to eat to what to avoid eating, to what actions were permissible on the Sabbath. All had to be evaluated, all had to be debated, and all had to be adjudicated. Whatever decision was made in Jerusalem was binding upon all. Yaakov may have been all but ignored by the ongoing narrative of Acts, but no writer could ignore him at this point. Nor could he be conveniently edited out.

For Shaul the appearance before the Sanhedrin of Yaakov, alternately known as the Council of Jerusalem, was the most critical juncture of his life and career. For Shaul's new interpretation of the Torah, it was "make or break" time. He alludes to his journey in one of his later epistles, saying, "Fourteen years later I went up again to Jerusalem, this time with Barnabas" (Galatians 2:1).

The consequences of Shaul losing the ensuing debate would have been staggering, in fact world-changing. Yaakov might well have decided that the admission of Cornelius and company into the ranks of the *ma'aminim* was enough but that the admission of a host of non-Jewish God-fearers threatened to swamp the entire movement. Yaakov and his Sanhedrin might simply have decided to bar them from full participation in the sect and to forbid Shaul from establishing any more such communities. Had this been the council's decision, then the entire non-Jewish religion called Christianity, which became the bulwark of western civilization and the dominant religion on the planet today, would in fact have been stillborn.

For Shaul this would have been a disaster, but for the Jewish *ma'aminim* it might have been a much preferable outcome. Later clerics like Epiphanius would surely never have risen to choke out the Jewish roots of the Jesus movement. There simply would have been no Christianity as a separate religion. The entire Roman empire would not have tilted toward Christianity as it did under the emperor Constantine, and the world as we know it would be a very different place. The Acts narrative tells us that upon Shaul's arrival in Jerusalem there was intense debate and that Shaul himself was hotly opposed by *ma'aminim* from among the Pharisee party. We have already noted that Gamaliel the Pharisee was moderate toward the sect and that opposition to Yeshua's movement had never come from these quarters.

From this single verse in the narrative it is clear that the Pharisees, to whom the Hasidim had historically been aligned, remained a significant segment in the sect's composition. The Pharisees, contrary to popular stereotype, were moderate and liberal in their interpretation of the Torah, all the while stressing that it be honored and kept. They now declared to the assembled Sanhedrin that all non-Jewish *ma'aminim* must go through a formal conversion process.

Shaul never debated whether Jewish *ma'aminim* should continue to abide by the Torah; that was understood. He was entirely consumed with arguing that non-Jews be allowed to remain non-Jews and still be counted as Nazarenes. The Acts narrative dutifully reports the speech of Shimon on behalf of Shaul, further evidence that Shaul may have influenced this disciple of Yeshua and "peeled him away" from the rest of the Jerusalem community. Shaul and his sidekick Barnabas went on to report a series of miracles they had witnessed during their journeys, something which clearly impressed the Hasidic-oriented sect, which relished above all the miraculous manifestation of the Kingdom of Heaven in people's everyday lives.

At the end of lengthy deliberations it came time for Yaakov to render the verdict. After referencing the speech of Shimon (whom he deliberately did not call "Peter"), he pointed out that it was the vision of the prophets of old that the Gentile nations should partake of the knowledge and blessings of Israel's single God. He therefore decreed that Shaul's God-fearers should legally be obligated to keep not all of the Torah's precepts, but only four:

1) to refrain from food such as sacrificial animals that had been offered to pagan gods

2) to avoid sexual immorality

3) to not consume the meat of any animal that had been strangled and

4) to refrain from consuming blood

These laws were in essence a concise restatement of the "seven laws of the sons of Noah," which traditional Judaism had already decided were the only laws incumbent on the whole host of God-fearers in the Gentile west. They specifically require the abstention from:

1) idolatry

2) blasphemy

3) bloodshed

4) sexual sins

5) theft

6) eating the flesh of a living animal (part of the general Jewish sensitivity toward all living things)

They also mandated:

7) the establishment of a legal system to fairly adjudicate disputes.

Some scholars today maintain that there were originally only three of these "Noachide laws," prohibiting idolatry, bloodshed and sexual misconduct, expanded by subsequent generations of rabbis. In any case it is clear that Yaakov was making reference to these principles, asking how they, as a Jewish sect, could require more of the Gentiles than God had required. The result amounted to a great compromise, which appeared to solve the problem to everyone's satisfaction.

But did it really? Yaakov's Sanhedrin never addressed the fundamental question of whether there was now one great community of *ma'aminim* or two. Would Jewish and non-Jewish *ma'aminim* be able to dine together? Certainly not, if the laws of kosher were still to be upheld. Would they be allowed to intermarry? Certainly not, if the Jewish *ma'aminim* were to continue to abide by the *halakhah*. Could the sect remain Jewish at all, if, as time would show, the majority of its members were to be non-Jews living in the Gentile west? All of these issues remained unresolved as, in the course of time, what had been a Jewish sect evolved into something else entirely.

Notes

1   While some scholars question the role of the "God-fearers" in the Roman empire, there is evidence from archaeology, published as late as 1987, that supports the historical reality of this class. One city in Asia Minor, Aphrodisias, has provided important inscriptions bearing on this issue. One, dating from the third century CE, lists contributors to a charitable endeavor, possibly a soup kitchen. A list consisting mainly of Jews is found on one side of the inscription, while fifty-two "*theosebis*" ("God-fearers"), among them nine town councilors, are listed on the opposite side. These *theosebis* clearly comprise a distinct group, representing almost half of the donors. In Sardis, also in Asia Minor, the largest Diaspora synagogue ever excavated has yielded a plaque in the central hall, reading: "Aurelios Hermogenes, citizen of Sardis, God-fearer, from his gifts of Providence, I made (donated?) the seven-branched candlestick." While this individual was not a Jew by birth or conversion, he was sufficiently motivated to make a donation to the synagogue, which was receptive enough to memorialize it. See M.P. Bonz, "The Jewish Donor Inscriptions from Aphrodisias: Are They Both Third-Century, and Who Are the *Theosebeis?*", *HSCP* 96 (1994): 281-99.

2   See Josephus, *Antiquities*, XVIII, 257; *War* II, 184. Josephus records that Petronius "marveled at the providence of God," additional evidence that he may have been a "God-fearer."

3   See Acts 12:21-23: "And on a certain day, Herod sat on his throne, dressed in royal clothing, and made a speech to them. And the people gave a shout, saying, It is the voice of a god and not of a man! And immediately the angel of the Lord struck him, because he did not give God the glory. And he was eaten by worms and gave up the spirit."

4   H. Stegemann, who favors the Essene identification of the sect, does not find militancy in the approach of the Habakkuk Commentary, which he concludes was written soon after the plundering of the Temple by the Romans in 54 BCE.

On the contrary, the enemies of Israel (Rome) are depicted with "unconcealed admiration," paying tribute to their might. They are viewed as God's instrument for punishing the unrighteous of Israel. This of course amounts to purification via the crucible. See H. Stegemann, *The Library of Qumran* (New York: Brill, 1993), 131.

5   See John M. Cooper and J.F. Procope, *Seneca: Moral and Political Essays* (Cambridge: Cambridge University Press, 1995).

6   Acts 17:23.

7   Acts 17:32, 34.

8   Acts 11:26.

9   See James VanderKam, *The Dead Sea Scrolls Today* (Grand Rapids: Eerdmans, 1994), 88-89. Trever (1985: 89-102) made the assertion that the author of the book of Daniel was none other than the leader of a non-militant/ 'pacifist' branch of the ancient Hasidim. According to Trever, it was they who refused to join Mattathias and the Maccabees in their revolt against Antiochus IV, fleeing into the Wilderness of Judea as a place of refuge. He further suggests that the author of Daniel became the Qumranic 'Teacher of Righteousness'.

10   The Greek word can refer to either a child or a servant/ slave.

11   Matthew 15:27.

12   On Athanasius, see S. Hornblower and A. Spawforth, eds., *Oxford Classical Dictionary*, 3rd ed. (Oxford; New York: Oxford University Press, 1996).

13   Flusser found a link between 1QM 11:10 ("You will ignite the humble of spirit like a fiery torch of fire in a sheaf, consuming the wicked"), and Mt. 5:3 ("Blessed are the poor in spirit"). In each case the reference is to the sect itself or to the future "Israel of God." See Flusser, *Judaism*, 106. Stegeman (*Library*, 262) points out that the War Rule elucidates the meaning of "poor in spirit" as those who are permeated by the divine essence/ 'Holy Spirit' and are thus capable of genuine humility.

14   The Church Fathers occasionally drew a distinction between the Ebionites and the Nazarenes, the latter being a distinct group of Jesus' disciples. They may be understood as a branch of the original "Church" of Jerusalem, roughly between the years 30 CE and 135 CE. The earliest sources also speak of a Judeo-Christian "synagogue" of sorts on Mount Zion, between 70 and 132 CE. Jerome, however, apparently thought of the Ebionites and Nazarenes as a single sect. However, given the lack of primary source material, it is difficult to determine the rationale behind this differentiation. Indeed, one Church Father seems to rely on another. See Epiphanius, Panarion 30.22.4.

4

Who Killed Yaakov?

THE FLEDGLING NAZARENE SECT HAD PROVED CAPABLE OF governing itself, of making difficult decisions and navigating through the art of compromise. It would, however, remain a movement torn between its two halves, dominated by Yaakov and the Heirs in the east and by Shaul in the west. East would meet west in the Council of Jerusalem, but that encounter only bandaged the fact that the movement's two leaders were inexorably leading their respective flocks in opposite directions. Caught between them was the disciple to whom Yeshua had entrusted the "keys to the kingdom of heaven," Shimon.

When it comes to the community of *ma'aminim* in Jerusalem, we continue to get a picture of a movement divided. We are even told that Shimon, a Torah-true Jew, refused to dine with non-Jewish *ma'aminim*, notwithstanding his earlier vision of the net descending and the voice commanding him to "rise, kill and eat." The narrative hints that when he later came to the city of Antioch, near the southern coast of Asia Minor, Shaul upbraided him for "reverting" to the practice of refusing to eat with Gentiles, even though he had previously been sharing meals with non-Jewish *ma'aminim* (Galatians 2:11-14). According to tradition Shimon ultimately made his way to Rome, where he, like Shaul, was destined to meet his end.

However, when it comes to the real issues facing the organization and direction of the movement, we are exposed only to Shaul's perspective, and the position of Yaakov is never mentioned. We are left to wonder: How could so many generations of Bible-readers have missed the obvious slant? To discover the real story of what happened, we have to don our detective caps and press our investigation forward.

Shaul *versus* Jerusalem

The last time we hear in the book of Acts narrative of Yaakov and the Sanhedrin he established in Jerusalem, he was meeting once again with Shaul, the new leader of the Nazarene movement in the west. The great "emissary" (more popularly known by the term "apostle") was on his final trip to the holy city, feeling strangely compelled to make the journey, as part of his spiritual destiny. Of course the narrative skews everything in favor of Shaul, who is depicted as warmly received by the Jerusalem *ma'aminim*. Nonetheless, as though visiting a great dignitary, he was not immediately entitled to see the movement's leader. He had to wait until the next day.

How odd it must have seemed for Yaakov to be hosting this man, who years before had come in off the desert and was looked upon askance by nearly everyone, but who now approached Yaakov as de-facto champion of the Nazarene communities of God-fearers to the west. There was still no question, however, that Yaakov was ultimately the boss. Other ancient sources equally attest to this fact. One such text, the First Apocalypse of James, was never accepted into the New Testament, and while it is rightly considered "pseudepigrapha" (an anonymous work falsely attributed to a well known person), it does authentically recount early traditions. Specifically, it tells us that Yaakov (James) wielded unassailed authority over all eleven other disciples. There can be no doubt that Shaul had entered the presence of a man of considerable stature in the city of Jerusalem.[1]

What followed amounted to a bit of Middle Eastern theatrics. Yaakov said nothing at first. It was Shaul who felt obliged to give a report of how the movement was spreading among the God-fearers. In accordance with the rules of decorum, as practiced across the Levant (the eastern Mediterranean), the *ma'aminim* first praised Shaul, noting his great spiritual labors among the Gentiles. The New Testament uses the word "Gentiles" to refer to Shaul's converts, though the term is technically inaccurate. "Gentiles," in Hebrew *goyim*, refers to the pagan "nations" around Israel. To call someone a Gentile was to call that person an idolater. Shaul's converts, as we have already seen, were overwhelmingly from the class of "God-fearers," people who had already abandoned paganism in favor of Israelite monotheism. In any case, Shaul was given high marks for his efforts.

But the polite praise only masked another sentiment. For immediately afterwards, Yaakov's *ma'aminim* proceeded to put Shaul in his place. "Look at the size of our community in Jerusalem," they remarked. "See how many thousands have joined the ranks of the Nazarenes." It was a way of saying, "Don't brag about what you have done in the west; the headquarters of the Way is still here in Jerusalem and you must pay obeisance to us, not the other way around." They were clearly suspicious of why Shaul had come to Jerusalem, as if they needed any help. Shaul, of course, had never fared particularly well in Jerusalem. Years before he had quarreled with the city's Diaspora Jews, whom he had tried to win into the sect. Now all the *ma'aminim* themselves were giving him a hard time, masked by initial politeness.

At this point they added an additional phrase, calculated to be biting: "And all are zealous for the Torah" (Acts 21:17). This single verse speaks volumes about Yaakov's community of Jerusalemite *ma'aminim*, for even as Shaul was off in the west, raving about how the Messiah, the Christ, had "set us free from the Law," the entire eastern half of the movement remained piously observant in Hasidic fashion. They clearly saw things differently. For them the martyrdom of Yeshua, while perceived as a sacrificial death with atoning power, was by no means a substitute for the Temple sacrifice and certainly not for the Torah, which in their mind must continue to be observed eternally.

Shaul was not only allowing non-Jews, even though they were God-fearers, into the sect in large numbers, he was actively teaching and preaching that there was no longer a distinction between Jew and Greek. He was turning traditional Jewish ideas about the value and sanctity of the Torah upside down.

Whatever Was Shaul Thinking?

One example of Shaul's inversion of the Torah comes from a letter he had written to the community he had founded in Asia Minor in the

region of Galatia, in which he took hallowed Jewish images and inverted them:

> Abraham had two sons, the one out of [Hagar] the slave-woman (Ishamael), and one out of [Sarah] the free woman (Isaac). But, indeed, he out of the slave-woman has been born according to flesh, and he out of the free woman through the promise; which things are being allegorized... (Galatians 4:22-24)

In Jewish tradition Isaac was the child of promise. Hagar, a bondwoman, brought forth Ishmael, whose descendants were destined to be a thorn in the flesh of the Israelites. But for Shaul and his non-Jewish disciples, everything became reversed. He continued:

> For these are the two covenants, one indeed from Mount Sinai bringing forth to slavery, which is Hagar. For Hagar is Mount Sinai in Arabia, and answers to Jerusalem, which now is in slavery with her children. (Galatians 4:24-25)

Sinai, in the Jewish mind, was where the Almighty came down and touched the earth, delivering the Torah into the hands of Moses. It should be equated with Sarah and with Isaac but is here linked with Hagar and Ishamael. Sinai was an enduring symbol of freedom from the bondage in Egypt. But Shaul wrote of it, along with Jerusalem, as an emblem of slavery, symbolic of Hagar and a different kind of bondage, along with the Torah itself.

Moreover, he painted the Jewish people uniformly as rejectionists of the Nazarene movement, who should be "cast out" like Hagar:

> But what does the Scripture say? "Cast out the slave-woman and her son; for in no way shall the son of the slave-woman inherit with the son of the free woman." (Galatians 4:30)

Never mind the myriads of *ma'aminim* under Yaakov and the Heirs. The whole Jewish people were equated with Hagar, bringing forth children under slavery, that is, the Torah. It was Shaul's non-Jewish followers who were depicted as the new children of promise.

This was the dawn of what would come to be called "replacement theology," the idea that the non-Jewish "Church" had literally replaced the Jews, becoming the new, spiritual Israel.[2] What, then, of traditional Jews, who, regardless of their level of devotion and piety, could not be counted among the Nazarene movement? They were doomed, cut off, to be eternally damned, world without end. Shaul had spelled it out even more vehemently in another of his letters, addressed to the members of the Nazarene community of Thessalonica:

> For you also have suffered these things by your own countrymen, even as they also by the Jews; who both killed the Lord Jesus and their own prophets, also driving us out and they do not please God and being contrary to all men, forbidding us to speak to the nations that they might be saved, to fill up their sins always; but the wrath has come upon them to the uttermost.
> (1 Thessalonians 2:14-16)

Such passages appear to us today not only as mean-spirited, but as the very genesis of anti-Semitism. Yet, it was Yaakov's Jewish *ma'aminim*, the elders of the Nazarene community, who are depicted as mean-spirited by the book of Acts narrative. *They* were mean-spirited when they declared:

> … You teach all the Jews who are among the nations to forsake Moses, saying that they ought not to circumcise their children, nor to walk after the customs. (Acts 21:21)

Of course Shaul was not really telling Jews not to be Torah-observant. He was after all rigorously observant himself, and he had personally circumcised Timothy, since he was born of a Jewish mother. But his rhetoric had indeed become so strident, as he railed against the likes of the Ebionites, that it must have sounded to many as though he were counseling the complete abrogation of Jewish law and custom.

Little wonder that Yaakov's elders would make a specific demand of Shaul, as if to ask, "Are you, a Jew, willing to observe Jewish law and custom yourself? You are in the holy city; join those among us who have vowed to perform the purification rite." This elaborate ritual involved not only complete immersion in water (the *mikveh*), but also the complete shaving of one's head and body to make sure that the water made contact with every pore of the skin. It is startling proof that Yaakov's Nazarenes continued to abide by the most rigorous details of Jewish law. Identification as a "believer" in Yeshua, including "baptism" into the movement, did not eliminate the requirement for ongoing purification, as a part of normal Jewish ritual.[3]

Would Shaul, who preached a radical "freedom from the Law," now submit personally to this most stringent requirement? His answer was an unqualified yes. Was Shaul being duplicitous, even while systematically try-ing to "hijack" the entire Jesus movement to the west? Some would say yes, though Shaul himself would have stressed that his message of "free-dom from the Law" was never intended for Jewish *ma'aminim*, only for his unique flock of God-fearers.

As head of the Sanhedrin, Yaakov himself remained silent, letting the elders speak for him. They pointed out again the compromise reached at the Council of Jerusalem, noting that a letter had been sent to the new non-Jewish members of the sect, requiring nothing more than observance of the "Noachide laws": abstention from idolatry (including food sacri-ficed to idols), sexual immorality, and things strangled (i.e. cruelty to ani-mals). Yaakov's compromise was thereby reaffirmed. There would be two communities of *ma'aminim*, functioning by entirely different sets of laws. Shaul could do as he pleased with his communities abroad, but this was Yaakov's turf, on which Shaul was a guest. His welcome was conditioned on his observance of the strictest rules of purification, which he proceeded to perform without question.

The book of Acts narrative proceeds to follow Shaul, as he encoun-tered a group of Diaspora Jews from Asia Minor (notably, not native Israelites), who stirred up a crowd and got him arrested. From the outset, Shaul's very presence in Jerusalem is a point of intrigue, since Yaakov's community was at the time thriving without his assistance He must have known that his presence in the holy city would be provocative. It was as

though he wanted to stir up controversy, even to get himself arrested, perhaps to steal the thunder, as it were, from Yaakov.

When given a chance to speak openly and defend himself (an important provision of Jewish law), he made sure to address the crowd in Hebrew ("the Hebrew dialect") and he made sure to appeal to the one group that was naturally aligned with the *ma'aminim*, the Pharisees. In spite of his earlier affiliation with the Sadducean priesthood, he declared, "I am a Pharisee, and the son of Pharisees" (Acts 23:6), "and I am on trial here for preaching the resurrection," a particularly Pharisaic doctrine. As we have noted, he even claimed that he had studied at the feet of Gamaliel (Acts 22:3). Nonetheless, readers of the text have, down through the ages, received the impression that he was being accused by "the Jews" as a people. After all, the crowd is quoted as shouting:

> For we have found this man a pestilent fellow, and a mover of sedition among all the Jews throughout the world, and a ringleader of the sect of the Nazarenes. (Acts 24:5)

The narrative goes on to relate a plot against his life, followed by a trial before the Roman governor Felix, followed by a hearing before King Agrippa himself. Notably, his opponents included a mixture of Sadducean elements (who had always opposed the Jesus movement, beginning with Yeshua himself) and Diaspora Jews (whose inherent insecurity caused them to fear new forms of messianism that they didn't understand). The king, being a man of moderation, found no harm in Shaul or in his message and declared that he would have released him had he not appealed directly to Rome, as a Roman citizen.

The remainder of the book of Acts follows Shaul's journey to the heart of the empire, where martyrdom would be his ultimate fate. This is precisely where readers of the New Testament lose track of the entire Israelite branch of the Nazarene movement. For the text is so preoccupied with the apostle to the west that its entire focus shifts inexorably to Rome. It has been seen historically as "preparing the way" for an inevitable break with the Jewish faith and the formal birth of a new religion, headquartered in a new holy city, founded by the Caesars, which would become the seat of the Church Universal, formally "Catholic" and thoroughly Roman.

Whatever Happened to Yaakov?

After Shaul's arrest on the Temple Mount, the Acts narrative never again mentions Yaakov or the elders of his Sanhedrin. The entire

Nazarene movement in Israel, also known as the Way, simply disappears from the pages of the New Testament. People of faith don't seem to be bothered with such details, but the objective reader cannot help but ask: What became of this enormous movement? Where did they go? Did they disappear from the face of the earth? Did they simply vanish into thin air? It is one of history's greatest mysteries, perhaps the greatest mystery in the whole pageant of world religion. The Christian canon will henceforth maintain a stony silence about the multitudes of Jewish *ma'aminim* and about the fate of their communities, which now peppered the landscape of Israel, including the region known as Yeshua's birthplace, the Galilee. And what of Yeshua's brother, Yaakov? To discover the fate that awaited him, we have to play detective once more and turn to sources beyond the New Testament. It has in fact been said that we know more about the historical Yaakov from non-Biblical sources than we know about any other New Testament character. Aside from Church historians there was the greatest of all ancient Jewish historians, Josephus, whose account must be the next stop in our sleuthing.

According to Josephus, an "impostor" from Egypt had arrived in the days of the procurator Felix (52-60 CE) and ascended the Mount of Olives, which must have been a locale of great significance for prophets, promising to make Jerusalem's imposing walls, hewn from enormous limestone ashlars, collapse into rubble at his command. Josephus' choice of words, "impostor," indicates that this Jewish Egyptian had actually made a messianic claim, which was by no means unusual in such tumultuous and chaotic times. The Roman governor, we are told, launched a massive assault on the "impostor's" swelling ranks, even as they were assembled on the rocky ridge overlooking the city, putting four hundred to the sword and capturing another two hundred. The Egyptian "messiah" was lucky enough to escape, though his fraudulent identity was unmasked.

How would Yaakov have felt, recognizing that so many wanted and expected a militant messiah who would deliver the land from the Roman yoke and foment a glorious revolution, such as had transpired two centuries before in the days of the Maccabees? He had to have sympathized with the overall desire of the freedom fighters to rid themselves of Roman oppression. But he also represented a sizable segment of the population whose messianism was of a different sort – mild and moderate, humble and peace-loving. A generation before Yeshua, the great Judean sage Hillel had said, "Be among the disciples of Aaron: Love peace and pursue peace; love your fellow creatures and bring them near to Torah."[4] The only question was, whose version of messianism would win out? The answer would not be to Yaakov's liking, as trouble broke out in Caesarea, the great Herodian port city on the Mediterranean, between Jews, who claimed the city should be considered Jewish and that they should therefore have precedence, and Syrians, who heartily disagreed. The governor Felix intervened, unleashing his troops, who in the end perpetrated a massacre entirely of Jews.

Looking out at the world politically from the movement's headquarters in Jerusalem, Yaakov must have been deeply torn and seriously distressed. The atmosphere in those days was probably not unlike the mood in colonial America in the years leading up to the Revolutionary War. There was growing opposition to a foreign tyranny that was becoming ever more oppressive. The American colonists were increasingly aware that the British sovereign, King George, was going mad. In first century Judea, it was equally clear that the Roman emperor, Nero Caesar, was at least behaving like a madman.

Nero's pedigree was impressive, since his mother Agrippina was the great-granddaughter of Caesar Augustus. For several years after his accession, his best advisors, including the philosopher Seneca, ran the ship of state. But in the year 59 he began to assert his own power, which he demonstrated by having Agrippina murdered. This was only the beginning of a spate of killings, including his wife Octavia, daughter of the previous emperor, Claudius. Even members of the Roman Senate, the ancient seat of democracy and relic of the glorious days of the republic, found themselves under the blade of the executioner for questioning Nero's policies.

Much like the American patriots centuries later, the Judeans were a chaotic rabble that called itself an army, up against the world's greatest empire. Anyone living in Jerusalem in those days had to have been aware of the downward spiral into violence. But Yaakov also had to have been aware of Yeshua's admonition nearly three decades earlier that if someone (such as a Roman soldier) should ask you to carry a heavy burden a distance of a mile, you should carry it for two (Matthew 5:41). Do not make trouble with temporal authorities, Yeshua proclaimed, for it will only lead to the destruction of the nation.

This was of course no easy admonition. While King Herod Agrippa had fought hard for the interests of his people, his death had brought about a re-imposition of direct Roman rule and a slow descent for the land of Israel into a chaotic abyss. The Zealots became increasingly active in their agitation and civil unrest, and while Felix the procurator was at first conciliatory, his main objective became the suppression of the "freedom fighters."

His successor, Festus, had an even more difficult time, his rule being marked by violent clashes, especially in Caesarea, where the ultimate question continued to be whether this was a Jewish or a Greek city. While the Jews possessed greater wealth and power, their Greek foes relied on the military, garrisoned in nearby Sebaste.

Somewhere along the line, according to Josephus, certain signs and portents of doom began to manifest themselves within the holy city. The Jewish historian mentions a crazed prophet, a rude peasant by the name of Jesus, Yeshua, who, during this time, began to march back and forth through the city streets, with a single, bold, bone-chilling prophecy:

> A voice from the east,
> a voice from the west,
> a voice from the four winds,
> a voice against Jerusalem and the Holy House,
> a voice against the bridegrooms and the brides,
> and a voice against this whole people! (*War*, 6.5.3)

Who was this mysterious Jesus, who, like the earlier prophet of Nazareth, pronounced "woe" upon the city of Jerusalem? And are the striking similarities between this man and that other peasant, the prophet from the Galilee, pure coincidence? Perhaps Josephus, in writing about this particular Jesus, son of Ananias, was actually borrowing certain traditions regarding *Yeshua m'Natzeret* and transposing them upon this Jerusalemite for dramatic effect. It is one more mystery befitting an age replete with mysteries. In any case, it starkly illustrates the fact that during the early reign of Nero, when Jerusalem was still enjoying relative prosperity, when work on the massive Temple complex was nearing completion, there were those who clearly saw the writing on the equally massive city walls, who correctly understood that the Zealot phenomenon was not going away, and that if it continued, the result for all of Israel would be calamitous.

Yaakov, at the head of the Way, must have been aware of this Yeshua, and he had to have been aware of the similarity between him and his own brother, who, according to the Gospels, faced Jerusalem and prophetically pronounced its imminent doom. Some modern scholars have dismissed the Gospel account of Yeshua's prophecy, which he uttered while perched on the Mount of Olives:

> Do you not see all these things? Truly I say to you, There shall not be left here one stone on another that shall not be thrown down. (Matthew 24:2)

"It is obviously a subsequent addition to the text, added decades later by religiously motivated editors!" So say the scholars. But given that Josephus independently recorded the prophecy of that "other Jesus," at a time when Jerusalem was still at peace and years before the outbreak of war, we have to wonder whether the prophecy of Yeshua m'Natzeret was that unusual. Perhaps there really was a sense of foreboding in the air that those gifted with insight merely reflected.

Hindsight being twenty-twenty, this would have been an auspicious time for Yaakov to have left the troubled capital of the Jewish nation, just as he had done years before, when he reportedly retreated to Jericho with a host of his followers. But for some unknown reason he did not. Perhaps he sensed the time was not right. Perhaps, as leader of the "Sanhedrin" of the Way, he felt obligated to remain. After all, the movement was by now so well established as a permanent fixture of the city, that any such exodus would be perceived as a frightened rout. And so he stayed on in Jerusalem, even as a series of events, some religious and some purely political, were coagulating, both at home and abroad, that would bring about his most untimely demise.

"Judicial Murder"

After the death of Festus in 62 CE, Nero sent a replacement by the name of Albinus to the troubled region. With no intermediary to plead their cause with the emperor, the Jews felt increasingly helpless in the face of forces they could not control. The second King Herod Agrippa (the last king of the Herodian dynasty) used this occasion to appoint a new High Priest by the name of Ananus. His father, Annas, had served in this capacity along with the notorious Caiaphas, who had tried Yeshua m'Natzeret for blasphemy. The younger Ananus, Josephus tells us, was even more harsh after the manner of the Sadducees. Again, the devil is in the details. Twenty centuries of anti-Semitic propaganda have declared that the Jewish people en-masse rejected Jesus and persecuted his followers, including the early "Church" in Jerusalem. But all of our ancient sources agree that it was specifically the Sadducee party that acted in a stern and punitive manner, being "very rigid in judging offenders, above all the rest of the Jews" (Josephus, *Antiquities*, 20:9.1).

Moreover, since Festus was deceased and Albinus had not yet arrived, Ananus felt emboldened to unleash any fury he wished. Specifically, he took aim at the Way, known by this time as the Nazarenes, a growing faction that had been a thorn in the flesh of the Sadducees for three decades and

whose revered founder had caused a ruckus and deliberately insulted the
entire Temple hierarchy by overturning the tables of the moneychangers.
He called together an *ad-hoc* assemblage of the Sanhedrin and hauled before
it, in Josephus' words (composed in Greek), "...the brother of Jesus, who
was called Christ, whose name was James, and some others, [or, some of his
companions]" (Josephus, *ibid.*). Who were these "others," who were brought
before the Jewish high court along with Yaakov? Doubtless, they were elders
of the Nazarene movement in Jerusalem, perhaps serving on its "Sanhedrin,"
or perhaps even fellow family members; we can only speculate.

The Great Sanhedrin was, even in its most corrupt incarnation, a legal body, bound by jurisprudence, and by no means could it hand down
punishments without following judicial procedures. What, then, were
the formal charges against a Jewish sectarian movement, beloved of the
people, who had so much in common with the Hasidic sages of previous generations? "They have transgressed the Torah!" The charge was
ridiculous, which is why this kangaroo court had to be convened between
one procurator (Festus) and the next (Albinus). For even the bloodthirsty
Romans would not have allowed such trumped-up charges to stand.

We do have to ask, however, why a charge of transgressing the Law
would have been entertained to begin with, even by a corrupt Sanhedrin,
rather than some other charge, like sedition. Weren't Yaakov and his
Jewish *ma'aminim* strictly observant, living strictly "kosher" lifestyles?
True enough, but the compromise reached at the Council of Jerusalem,
allowing for sizable numbers of Shaul's non-Jewish disciples to be admitted into the sect, may have given the appearance that Yaakov and the
Heirs were abrogating Jewish law and counseling others to do the same
when nothing could have been further from the truth. It was Shaul whose
obsession with building a theological argument for "freedom from the
Law" led to statements that appeared to trivialize if not nullify the Torah,
and with it, the whole fabric of Jewish life. The Sanhedrin of Ananus may
have fallen into the trap of "guilt by association," assuming that Shaul's
anti-Torah stance applied equally to Yaakov and company.

Unfortunately, we know none of the details of the proceedings. We
are only told that the High Priest Ananus "... delivered them to be stoned"
(Josephus, *ibid.*). This is the last we hear of Yaakov. Through these brief
words, we understand that the life of this remarkable man who, along
with his extraordinary older brother, changed the course of human civilization, was snuffed out. We don't know how many of Yaakov's company
were executed along with him, nor do we know their names.

As for the method of execution, stoning was, according to the Bible itself, the preferred means of eliminating those convicted of murder, blaspheming God, or leading the people into religious apostasy. In some instances adulterers could also be stoned to death. Stoning allowed for a sense of anonymity with respect to the execution itself, since it was impossible to know whose stone delivered the final death blow to the victim. The progressive-minded Pharisees, however, were loathe to execute anyone, and the Talmud later records that only those who received an official warning in the presence of at least two witnesses and who yet committed a capital offense before those witnesses, could be put to death. In light of such scruples, rabbinic records boast that only eight individuals were executed under their watch in the course of four centuries. Clearly, the Pharisees, classic villains to this day in the minds of Christendom, had nothing to do with the stoning of Yaakov.

Complicating the record is the fact that the book of Acts, which records in detail the tribulations and trials of Shaul, including his own ordeal in Jerusalem and subsequent journey to Rome, maintains a stony silence about the execution of the brother of the Christ himself and the leader of the entire Nazarene movement in the land of Israel. This is especially odd, given that it takes care to point out the martyrdom of the other Yaakov, James, son of Zebedee:

> And [Herod Agrippa] killed James the brother of John with the sword. (Acts 12:2)

But it is clear that Ananus the High Priest had chosen to decapitate the Nazarene movement by eliminating Yaakov as its titular head. What does this say about the size and strength of the movement in those days? Were they a tiny, beleaguered sect, who had been overwhelmingly rejected by the Jewish people? That is certainly the stereotype that has been carefully crafted for long centuries in the Christian west. It is, moreover, an anti-Semitic stereotype. But we need to rethink things, remembering that rulers don't persecute a small inconsequential movement that has few followers and no influence. They persecute a movement that is growing and is large enough to threaten the established order, in this case the Sadducean priesthood, who had always viewed Pharisee-oriented groups as arch foes precisely because of their popularity with the common people. Indeed, the Nazarene sect had grown to be a substantial presence in the holy city. Far from threatening Judaism, of which it was very much a part, far from spreading anti-Roman sedition, which it had never done, it threatened the very hegemony of the Sadducees, whose support among the masses had been waning for some time and who could ill afford to allow this "Hasidic" sect to steal away any more hearts and minds.

What Did Eusebius Know?

In any case, Josephus was not alone in recording the execution of Yaakov. Eusebius, in writing his history of the Church, referred to the earlier work of the church historian known as Hegesippus, from whom he borrowed a disparate account of the demise of Yaakov. The account has long been suspected to be no more than legend, but with so few sources to draw on and the conspicuous silence of the Acts narrative, we are forced to consider it. Eusebius relates that when Yaakov refused to deny his belief that his older brother Yeshua was in fact the Anointed One, he was dragged to the southeast corner of the Temple Mount, the great retaining wall of which stands to this day, also known as the "pinnacle" of the Temple. It was the same place where Yeshua, according to hallowed tradition, was tempted by the Adversary and offered all the kingdoms of the earth if only he would bow down and worship him. From this spot Yaakov's accusers threw him down into the Kidron Valley, over a hundred feet below. Somehow, Yaakov managed to survive the fall, whereupon he was promptly stoned. The account is especially suspect, since Eusebius identifies the evildoers as Pharisees (whom we have already seen were sympathetic to the movement), while Josephus correctly paints the Sadducean priesthood with blood on their collective hands.

Eusebius' account goes on to record that Yaakov, as though he were imbued with some supernatural power, survived even the stoning. In the end, we are told, he was bludgeoned to death with a fuller's club. Some have argued that Eusebius likely combined three separate accounts of Yaakov's death: being thrown from a high place, being stoned, and being clubbed. However, on the side of the account's general authenticity, there is a chilling passage in rabbinic literature, describing a "place of stoning" in the vicinity of the Temple. It was required to be at least double the height of a person, from which the hapless victim was hurled by one of the witnesses to the offense. If the condemned person failed to die from the fall itself, a second witness dropped a heavy stone on his heart. If that failed to produce death, the entire multitude joined in the stoning, until it was certain that the person was no longer alive.[5] Consequently, while hurling Yaakov from the pinnacle of the Temple sounds at first blush like a wild exaggeration (since

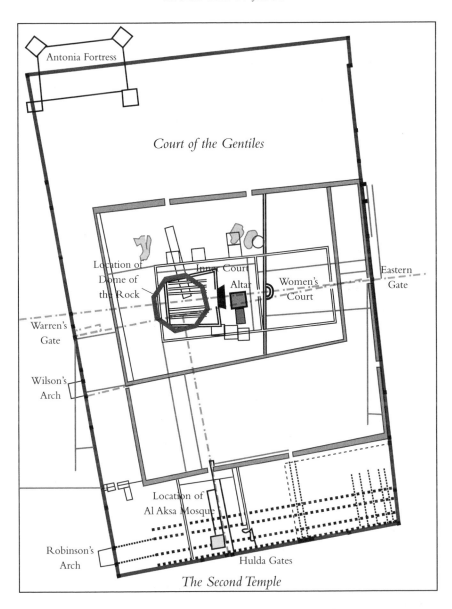

The Second Temple

it amounted to far more than "twice a man's height," as stipulated by Jewish law), it does accord well with the concept of incapacitating if not killing the victim through a fall, prior to the actual stoning. In short, Eusebius' account may contain more than a kernel of truth, when we consider the rabbinic ordinance regarding the execution of a person, as it were, "in stages."

After this savage deed was done, there is no question as to where the people's sympathies lay – not with the Sadducees, not with Ananus the

High Priest, but with the condemned individuals, Yaakov and his un-named comrades, who were perhaps also among the Heirs. While pre-tending to follow the outward form of Jewish criminal law, the executions themselves were viewed as nothing short of "judicial murder," in gross violation of the heart and soul of the Torah. A good part of the city, most likely those of Pharisee orientation, were appalled. Josephus records:

> But as for those who seemed the most equitable of the citizens, and such as were the most uneasy at the breach of the laws, they disliked what was done. (Josephus, *ibid.*)

When the new procurator, Albinus, was on his way from Alexandria (where he had been stationed) to the province of Judea, a delegation of disgruntled Jerusalemites intercepted him en-route, to protest against the outrages that had been perpetrated by their own High Priest. They charged that Ananus had no authority to convene the Great Sanhedrin without the expressed consent of the Roman procurator.

The last thing Albinus wanted at the beginning of his procuratorial rule was to alienate the rank and file Judeans. He therefore complied with the request of the delegation and promptly wrote an angry letter to Ananus, threatening to exact upon him a harsh punishment. This moment brought the direct intervention of King Herod Agrippa II, who, just three months after appointing Ananus High Priest, ignominiously sacked him. It is remarkable that the Jewish people as a whole would rally round the Nazarene movement and that a Jewish king would honor their request to punish the one responsible for executing the Nazarene leader. Of course, those who are aware of the sect's deep devotion to Judaism should not be surprised at all. Josephus relates that after Ananus was deposed, the king appointed a new High Priest named, ironically enough, Jesus (Yeshua), son of Damneus.

From this point the trail of evidence regarding the "real" Yaakov, the physical brother of Yeshua and the definitive face of the Nazarene move-ment, grows cold. The New Testament text extolls Shaul, whose epistles make only brief reference to the man who led the sect from Jerusalem, and the non-Jewish Church fathers and historians make only passing refer-ence to him while tracing the westward spread of the movement's Roman incarnation as it eventually separated itself entirely from Judaism and be-came the dominant religion on the planet. We have no sources to indicate what became of Yaakov's body or where he was interred after his execution, but he must have been deeply mourned and highly revered among the Nazarenes, and even among the Jewish people at large.

Does Limestone Speak?

But all that was to change in October of 2002, when a rather diminutive stone box carved of chalk was unveiled before a thunderstruck assemblage of reporters. It was a simple ossuary, the ancient equivalent of a "casket," into which the bones of the deceased were deposited. During the period of the Second Jewish Commonwealth, there was in fact a unique practice in Jewish burial that was never used before and has never been employed since. Within twenty-four hours of a person's death, the body would be laid out on a perpendicular "shelf" in a rock-hewn tomb, wrapped in perfumed burial garments with no other embalming and left to decay within the hastily sealed sepulcher for a period of a year.

After twelve full months (the normal grieving period in Judaism to this day) had elapsed, the bereaved family would return to the tomb. Finding that all the flesh had rotted away, "Ashes to ashes, dust to dust," the bones would then be carefully collected and interred in a stone box, or ossuary. This would in turn be deposited in a perpendicular niche in the wall called a *cokh*. There it would reside for eternity, alongside other relatives, in what amounted to a family tomb. The inscriptions on those ossuaries tell us a much about the society of ancient Judea and about quite a few ancient Judeans in particular.

In 1990 there was a good deal of commotion when the ossuary of none other than the High Priest Caiaphas was discovered in his family tomb, some two miles south of modern Jerusalem. The elaborate carvings on the limestone box, along with the inscription itself, made it evident that this could be the ossuary of none other than the infamous High Priest who turned Yeshua over to the Romans for execution. It was a major find of historic importance. But even this discovery paled in comparison to this much simpler, relatively unadorned chalky ossuary. When it was revealed to the world at a press conference, it bore an inscription that would transfix the world. In easily discernible Aramaic letters, which looked like they had been carved yesterday, it read: *"Yaakov, bar Yosef, akhui d'Yeshua,"* "James, son of Joseph, brother of Jesus."

There were of course many Yaakovs living in ancient Jerusalem, and just as many Yeshuas, quite popular names in antiquity. The latter only later fell into disuse because of its association with the founder of Christianity. Most ossuaries listed the name of the deceased, followed by an identifica-

tion of the person's father, and that was all. But this inscription contained
something more. This Yaakov was deliberately identified as the "brother
of Yeshua." Doubtless, this must have been a very famous Yeshua, so important that his name had to be added to that of this Yaakov's father. How
many Yaakov's in ancient Jerusalem, who lived during the single century
when ossuaries were commonly in use, had a very famous brother named
Yeshua? There could be only one, the titular head of the sect called the
Way, brother of the most famous Yeshua in history, Jesus of Nazareth.

It should come as no surprise, however, that when spectacular claims
are made, one encounters equally bold counter claims and detractors galore.
The trouble is, declared the Israel Antiquities Authority, the words "*akhui
d'Yeshua*" ("brother of Jesus") do in fact look as though they were carved
yesterday. Indeed, as paleographer Rochelle Altman pointed out, the second part of the inscription appeared to have been carved by a distinctly
different hand than the words "*Yaakov bar Yosef*" ("James, son of Joseph").
According to some authorities, the whole thing smelled like a carefully
contrived forgery, designed to make a good number of headlines and an
even greater amount of money. If the inscription turned out to be authentic,
it would represent the only archaeological record of the historical existence
of Yaakov and Yeshua m'Natzeret. What was initially hailed as one of the
greatest archaeological finds in history was soon enmeshed in controversy.

In which exact family tomb had this ossuary been discovered? No one
knew. It had been pilfered anonymously, the typical *modus operandi* of grave

*The James ossuary was on display at the Royal Ontario Museum from November
15, 2002 to January 5, 2003.*

robbers, and put up for sale on Jerusalem's antiquities market. Thereafter, in the mid-1970s, it was bought by an Israeli engineer and antiquities collector named Oded Golan, who claimed that the unique nature of the inscription had gone unnoticed by the dealers themselves and even by him. He had believed that he was buying just one more ossuary to add to his collection, only later to be struck by the words "*akhui d'Yeshua*" ("brother of Jesus"). Then and only then did he go public with his find.

Little did he imagine that in time he would be charged with having personally forged what had quickly become the world's most famous inscription. Of course the hand that wrote "*akhui d'Yeshua*" was different, or so it was alleged. It was suspected that it was Oded Golan's hand. In due course the Israeli collector found himself handcuffed and under arrest, to face trial for forging antiquities. The question of the ossuary's authenticity would remain unresolved, with experts weighing in on both sides. Renowned Semitic scholar and scriptologist Frank Cross of Harvard University first rendered his opinion that the inscription was genuine, only to reconsider and declare the stone box genuine but the inscription a forgery. Others would decry the authenticity of the artifact, noting that every inscription collects a certain chemical residue in the small crevices created in the stone by an inscriber's chisel, called patina, and its presence indicates the antiquity of an inscription. In this case, doubters maintained, patina found on the James Ossuary had been faked. In fact, clever forgers have even been able to replicate this residue by covering a fake inscription with a solution of chalk powder dissolved in hot water, an instant patina.

As the controversy regarding the "James Ossuary" continued to swirl, fresh scientific tests were made on the patina in an attempt to determine whether this residue was ancient or modern. If ancient, how does one account for the second part of the inscription being in a different hand than the words "*Yaakov bar Yosef*" ("James, son of Joseph")? Supporters of the ossuary suggest that someone else came along after Yaakov's decease, perhaps a family member, one of the Heirs, and subsequently chiseled the words "*akhui d'Yeshua,*" so that posterity would know without question which Yaakov this was. As of this writing, the final verdict remains "conclusively inconclusive."

Jude the Obscure

If anything is true of mysterious ancient accounts, such as those relating to the demise of Yaakov, it is that they raise more questions than they answer. For example, how many of his kinsmen were caught up in the judicial madness of the Sadducean High Priest? How many of the Heirs survived these most gruesome and bloody executions? What of Miriam, the mother of the whole clan, about whom traditions are legion but facts are in short supply? Aside from wild rumors that she made her way to France, there are later Christian traditions that record her death in Jerusalem and her burial on Mount Zion, where an imposing church called the Dormitian today marks the spot, not only of her decease, but her presumed ascension into the heavens.

When we look to other New Testament documents, we also have an epistle ascribed to "James," our Yaakov, purportedly issuing from the very hand of Yeshua's brother. Strangely, however, direct reference to Yeshua is so scant in the letter that it makes the author appear to have not known him personally, hardly what we would expect from a physical brother. The scholarly consensus is that the epistle must have been written some time later. But how much later? As with so much else, it remains an unresolved issue.

Nor can we ignore another diminutive New Testament epistle, sadly overlooked by most readers who are too busy digesting the ins and outs of Pauline logic to pay it much attention. Known to English readers as the letter of Jude, the writer identifies himself as "Yuddas" (in Hebrew "Yehuda"), the "servant" of Yeshua, the *mashiakh*/ "Anointed One," and brother of James, again our Yaakov. Once again we have a text that presents us with a classic riddle wrapped inside an enigma. Was this Yehuda one of Yeshua's four physical brothers? Was this James/ Yaakov one of Yeshua's brothers, or merely some other Yaakov in the Nazarene movement? Was this Yehuda a descendent, perhaps even the son or grandson, of Yeshua's brother? Was the text written early, when Yaakov was still alive, or later? And if so, how much later? Was the initial greeting and superscription simply added to a later document to lend it weight and authority?

For whatever reason, modern researchers tend to be "minimalists," taking an almost perverse delight in impeaching ancient sources, especially religious ones. "This is unquestionably a later writing!" most will say, while trying to camouflage their inward smirks. But the fact is, we have virtually no concrete evidence to go on. And as one seasoned scholar quipped, "The absence of evidence is not evidence of absence." However popular it is to post-date ancient texts, when it comes to this epistle, it is difficult to imagine that the James/ Yaakov referred to could be anyone but the brother of Yeshua, which, if the superscription is authentic, would make Yehuda not only a "servant" of Yeshua but his brother as well. That would make this brief letter one of the only surviving documents composed by the so-called *Desposyni* or Heirs.

And what of the message of this Yehuda, as related in the short epistle? When it comes to Yehuda himself, there is no question regarding his religious and cultural orientation, which had to have been authentically developed in Israel and molded by generations of Jewish folklore. The concerns he addresses have to do with false teachers, who had adopted a "libertine" approach to their faith. The identity of these false teachers is one more facet of the overall mystery, but we can make some educated guesses based on Yehuda's rhetoric. He tells us that these people had distorted the concept of "grace" in order to disguise their own immoral behavior.

While the word "grace" today means many things to many people, in first century Israel it was defined by the Hebrew word *hesed*. The word is deliciously suggestive of divine, unrequited favor, bestowed without condition upon a people who had defined their existence in terms of the eternal covenant of the Torah. The ancient Jews who, more than any others, embraced this "loving-kindness" (the preferred translation of the term in today's English) and who expressed it through the working of wonders, from bringing rain in times of drought to healing those stricken with illness, were known as the Hasidim.[6] They were the Pious Ones, to whom, as we have suggested, the Nazarenes were most closely related.[7]

Who, by contrast, were these "ungodly" false teachers, intent on nullifying the Torah, worthy of judgment and intent on converting divine mercy into licentious behavior, intent on canceling its ethical commandments and adopting an "anything goes" attitude? On justifying virtually any behavior on the basis of being "free from the Law"? They were the kind of people who might well have been devotees of the apostle to the west, the one named Shaul, whose antinomian approach unintentionally spurred what even he would call "immoral" conduct. It was Shaul who wrote: "You were called to liberty; only do not use the liberty for an opening to the flesh" (Galatians 5:13). It is likely that there were those who, for better or for worse, understood Shaul's teaching as abolishing the commandments (Hebrew *mitzvot*), at least for the non-Jewish God-fearers, if not for Jews themselves, and who took this to mean that any kind of conduct could now be counted as "kosher."

In spite of Yaakov's attempt at compromise during the Council of Jerusalem, Yehuda and others must have felt that Shaul's radical doctrines embodied a "death wish" of sorts for the whole movement that threat-

ened to shipwreck them all. Yehuda's brief letter is therefore a poignant
reminder of Judaism's ancient precept, that *hesed* is intricately balanced
in the invisible spiritual realm by the equal and opposite divine attribute
of judgment. For in Jewish thought the paramount value has never been
placed on what a person believes or the theoretical correctness of "doctrine" but on one's concrete actions by which all humanity will one day be
weighed in the balance. Consequently, Yehuda mentions those Israelites
who came forth from Egypt in the days of Moses only to be destroyed in
the desert for their disobedience.

He also mentions a bit of ancient Jewish folklore regarding a class of
disobedient angels known as the Watchers who left their heavenly estate
in order to cohabit with earth women, thereby spawning a race of giants.
It was their licentious behavior that brought upon them divine judgment.
Yehuda's reference is to an ancient Jewish book banned from the Bible
by later rabbinic sages known as the first book of Enoch.[8] It was hugely
popular in the days of Yehuda and considered divinely inspired by at least
this "Heir" of Yeshua. Yehuda, now paraphrasing Enoch (14:5), declares
that those disobedient Watchers have been confined in the Underworld
until the great Day of Judgment.

He goes on to cite yet another example of long-forgotten Jewish
folklore, ultimately deleted from the authorized list of books considered
holy writ, the Assumption of Moses. In mysterious tones, it relates an account of how the Archangel Michael argued with the Evil One (known in
Hebrew as Satan, the Adversary) about the body of Israel's great lawgiver,
Moses, for the Bible itself records that no one knows the place of his burial
to this day. The ambiguity of the biblical text opened up the possibility
that some kind of cosmic confrontation must have transpired immediately
after Moses' death.

Yet, as the Assumption of Moses, now cited by Yehuda, relates, even
the mightiest of angels, Michael, did not rebuke the Evil One directly,
but merely quoted one of the prophets (Zechariah 3:2), saying, "The Lord
rebuke you!" It is a form of classic Jewish reasoning called "light and
heavy" (*kal v'khomer*), if one thing is true, how much more another. If
the Archangel Michael "respected" Satan, how much more should these
rebellious ones, the subject of Yehuda's epistle, respect spiritual authority.

From such examples we get a sense of the high place such otherwise
forgotten Jewish literature occupied in the hearts and minds of the early
Nazarene community. Though subsequent ecclesiastical authorities far to
the west would expunge such literature from the developing Christian

canon that came to be called the New Testament, there is no doubt about the fact that these "questionable" Jewish writings (later called pseude-pigrapha, or "false writings") were very much a part of the Bible known to Yeshua's earliest followers.

In that spirit Yehuda incorporates an almost direct quotation from the book of Enoch, noting that this ancient patriarch, the seventh descendant of Adam, once declared:

> Behold, the Lord came with myriads of his saints, to do judgment against all, and to rebuke all the ungodly of them concerning all their ungodly works, which they ungodly did, and concerning all the hard things ungodly sinners spoke against him. (Jude, 14-15; cf. 1 Enoch 1:9)

It is all by way of warning, in the expectation that history is indeed going somewhere on an inexorable march toward a cataclysmic end. Yet its blows are not random, but calculated to bring about proven character and sobriety in the face of the awesome judgment to come.

This was not time for "greasy grace," to which Shaul had perhaps un-wittingly opened the door. To be sure, the whole nation seemed perched on the abyss, ripe for some sort of catastrophic calamity. We cannot prove with certainly that this little epistle was written at an early date. Nor can we know with any confidence that its author was Yeshua's physical broth-er. But its overriding theme, warning of judgment, cautioning sobriety while holding out the hope of deliverance, seems almost perfectly suited to the tumultuous years during which Yaakov was executed, the years leading up to the most harrowing ordeal the Jewish people would ever face during their long history. For the land of Israel was about to descend into hell itself, which, in the year 66 of the Common Era, would open its jaws like a ravenous beast and swallow the nation alive.

Notes

1   William J. Scarborough adroitly summarized the relevant sources concerning James the Just. Much material regarding the later Nazarenes has been anachronistically read back into James. The pseudo-Clementine literature conversely depicts James as a proponent of a kind of primitive Ebionism. What can be said conclusively is that

James led the Jerusalem church from 42 - 62 CE. He appears to have represented a "conservative Jewish Christianity," characterized by an "ascetic piety," whereby he managed to reconcile Jewish and non-Jewish branches of the Jesus movement. See W.J. Scarborough, "James the Just," *JOBR* 9.4 (1941): 234–8.

2   This narrow theology of the "true Israel" reminds many of the Essenes, whose narrow soteriology doomed all others. David Flusser wrote convincingly that a "second wave" of early Christianity, patterned on Essene ideas, gradually divorced itself from Yeshua m'Natzeret, who in fact had little stomach for Essene teaching. See Flusser, *Judaism*, xviii.

3   Lawrence Schiffman dispels the notion that Jewish purification laws lack religious and ethical dimension. He points to Qumranic law as evidence that by the first century BCE the spiritual significance of ritual was being emphasized. According to the sect ritual purity is to be coupled with an "inner turning" and sincere repentance. See L. Schiffman, *Reclaiming the Dead Sea Scrolls: Their True Meaning for Judaism and Christianity* (New York, Doubleday, 1995), 299.

4   David Flusser suggested that Hillel's proverbial meekness was in fact a sign of his strength and self-awareness, an attribute similar to that attributed to the pietistic Jesus. See D. Flusser, *Judaism*, 512. The assertion of Liebermann that Hillel is speaking about God rather than himself is unwarranted in light of Hillel's other sayings. See S. Libermann, *Tosefta ki-fshutah, Order Zera'im*, Part I (New York: Jewish Theological Seminary, 1955), 124.

5   "The place of stoning was twice the height of a man. One of the witnesses knocked him down on his loins; if he turned over on his heart the witness turned him over again on his loins. If he straightaway died that sufficed; but if not, the second took the stone and dropped it on his heart. If he straightaway died, that sufficed; but if not, he was stoned by all Israel, for it is written, The hand of the witnesses shall be first upon him to put him to death and afterward all the hand of all the people." (Mishnah Sanhedrin 6:4)

6   The personal piety of the Hasidim was often coupled with an emphasis on the virtue of poverty, and some were involved with healing the sick or performing deeds of Tzedakah. See Safrai and Stern 1987: 319. Also known as Assidaeans, the Hasidim initially supported the Hasmonean dynasty, while frowning on the regime's increasingly Hellenistic tendencies. See M. Grant, *The Jews in the Roman World* (New York: Macmillan, 1973), 40.

7   For an insightful discussion of Jesus' relation to the Hasidim, see Flusser, *Jewish Sources*, 35.

8   1 Enoch 12:2

5

Blood and Fire

IRE. THE GIFT OF THE GODS TO PRIMITIVE HUMANITY, SENT down from Mount Olympus for warmth, for light and cooking. But fire was also the great destroyer. Unharnessed and untamed, the emblem of hell itself. Fire was the friend of the citizenry, but the ultimate foe of the cities they inhabited. Even the greatest city on earth, sprawled across seven hills along the River Tiber, was no match for the fury of flame that erupted into a sudden conflagration on the night of July 18 in the year 64 CE. Starting at the southeastern end of the Circus Maximus, which hosted the city's great chariot races, it was uncontainable, soon engulfing four of the city's fourteen districts. In the five long days of the fire's reign, it severely damaged seven more districts of the imperial city.

As the smoke and ashes subsided and the extent of the devastation was assessed, the central question was, "Who started this?" According to some, it was the increasingly mad emperor, Nero himself, who devised the fire as a means of clearing the city for new construction. The historian Tacitus, however, placed Nero elsewhere at the time of the fire, in the city of Antium. But was Tacitus merely covering up the popular story that the emperor found cheerful distraction during the conflagration by singing and playing his lyre? Did Nero really, as Tacitus records, rush back to Rome and organize a relief effort, personally subsidized from his own resources? Perhaps such reports were merely imperial PR. But whatever the emperor's complicity or lack thereof, he was in dire need of a scapegoat, someone to blame for the fire.

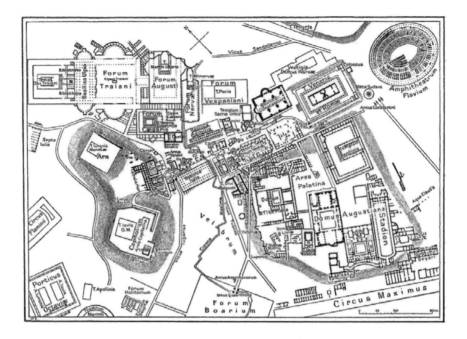

He might have accused an odd set of subjects in his empire, who had conspicuously avoided assimilation, thereby imperiling, at least in Nero's mind, the famed "Pax Romana." They were the Jews. Nero's consort, Poppea, had other opinions with respect to this ancient people and their hallowed religion. She, it seems, was a God-fearer, and was able to exert her considerable influence on the emperor to assure that no harm came to the seed of Abraham.

There was, nonetheless, one sect among the God-fearers whom Poppea had no interest in protecting. Known in Greek as the *Christianoi*, the Christians, they possessed none of the special immunity from emperor-worship granted to Jews and were, consequently, easy targets for Nero's wrath. While the emperor hesitated to strike the Jews themselves, he could at least strike this odd sect that hovered between Jewish and non-Jewish status. Thus began the first great imperial persecution of Roman "Christians," who were now officially rounded up.

Human Torches and the Great Apocalypse

Some Christians were thrown to the dogs, some were crucified, and still others were burned at the stake. Some were even used as human torches to light Nero's imperial gardens. It is at this point that one of the most studied, yet misunderstood books of the New Testament, called in

Greek the *Apocalypsis*, the "Revelation" of Yohanan (John), weighs in
with its cryptic commentary. As if describing the torment of those who
were first incarcerated, then incinerated, we find the following:

> They will not hunger any more, nor thirst any more, nor will
> the sun light on them, nor any heat. (Revelation 7:16)

Religious minded folk have always read and continue to read the great
Apocalypse as a "blueprint" of sorts for the end of the world, with no
reference to concrete historical events, and certainly with no understanding of the geopolitical realities of first century Israel. Nonetheless, while
the Heirs (*Desposyni*) and the Jewish "Jesus movement" they piloted are
systematically ignored by the book of Acts, they are in fact at the center of
the book of Revelation. Unfortunately, virtually no one knows it.

To be sure, the Apocalypse of Yohanan is enigmatic on multiple lev-
els. When was it written? Was it really the apostle Yohanan (John) who
authored it, or someone else? Was it attempting to forecast the future,
or was it, *post-facto*, describing events that had already transpired? Most
modern scholarship rejects the notion that its putative author, Yohanan
the apostle, actually wrote the book. Is this the sort of document that
might have been produced by the son of Zebedee, a fisherman from the
Galilee? Or is it more likely to have been composed by someone who had
a deep familiarity with the rituals performed at the Jerusalem Temple, the
details of which pepper this apocalyptic document?[1] Someone who cast
the fearful events he was describing in terms of the liturgical elements
of the High Holy Days, particularly *Yom Kippur*, the Day of Atonement?
Someone who had a priest's knowledge of the Temple itself and the liturgy connected with it? Might the author of the Apocalypse have been
himself a priest? Not Yohanan (John), the son of Zebedee, but that "other
Yohanan," the "beloved disciple," Yohanan the Priest?

Tradition has it that after Yohanan (John) completed his banishment
on the Island of Patmos, mentioned prominently in the book, he subsequently settled in Ephesus in Asia Minor, where he may have dictated
the document to yet another John, the elder of the Greek-speaking community of *Christianoi* in that city. This might account for Eusebius' claim
that this official in the Ephesian church was actually responsible for the
Apocalypse.[2]

Some argue that the Greek of the text is rather awkward and that
it must be a translation from an earlier Semitic document, composed in

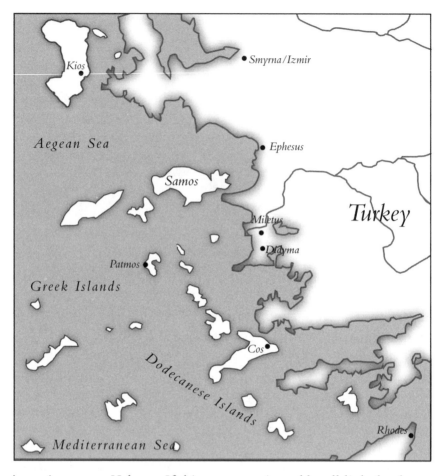

Aramaic or even Hebrew. If this were true it could well link the document with someone who had been part of the community of *ma'aminim*
in Jerusalem, someone like Yohanan the Priest. Most modern scholars, for
whatever reason, dismiss such intriguing possibilities, it being ever popular in academic circles to disprove most everything and leave us certain of
virtually nothing. They insist that the author was not one of the original
disciples of Yeshua at all, but merely an anonymous writer who made no
claim to apostolic authority. They go on to suggest that the book was
written in the mid-nineties of the Common Era, during the reign of the
emperor Domitian. Hard evidence is lacking, and with only hunches to
go on, almost any scenario is feasible. But one thing we can say with some
confidence is that the book's subject matter, far from relating to some
distant time at the "last days" of history, primarily concerns events that
are very much within our grasp, which took place long ago in the first

century of the Common Era, for the book in fact relates intimate details regarding the great Jewish revolt against Rome.

As the Apostle Yohanan (whichever Yohanan/ John it is) relates his spectacular vision, he describes a creature which defies artistic depiction on any concrete level, with seven heads bearing ten torn horns. There can be little doubt that what we have in this description is a mystical depiction of the Roman empire, sprawled across seven hills on the River Tiber. The horns may be taken to represent the first ten Julian emperors: Julius Caesar, Augustus, Tiberius, Caligula, Claudius, Nero, Galba, Otho, Vitellius and Vespasian.[3] It is as though the whole book is written in a mysterious code language that makes sense only to those "in the know," whose lives were most affected by the fearful happenings of those days, the members of the Nazarene sect. It is not unlike the Dead Sea Scrolls, which also make reference to geopolitical events in code language. They always refer to the Romans, who threatened their very existence, by the mysterious term *Kittim*.

The Apostle goes on to say that the beast looked like a leopard, stately and elegant, but that its feet were like bear claws, well suited to shredding its victims, and that its mouth was like a lion, devouring many. The beast's authority, power and dominion was bestowed by the dragon, who represents the Evil One, a malevolent force in the universe, an evil "dark side" of the Divine. Such dualism may seem out of place in strictly monotheistic Israel, but given the evidence of the Dead Sea Scrolls, which routinely characterize this evil power as a sort of "anti-God," it achieved a surprising popularity. Good and evil are painted in starkly contrasting tones by the Apocalypse, and Rome is cast as the very emblem of malevolence.

When Nero launched his campaign of annihilation against Rome's *Christianoi*, it appears that a good number quickly opted for full conversion to Judaism and the immunity it granted. How ironic that circumcision, which Shaul had so passionately argued against, became for many an attractive option. But for the writer of the book of Revelation, this was the wrong reason to enter the covenant of the Torah. It was fashionable, following Pauline logic, to denounce circumcision when there was nothing to gain by it, but when a simple surgical snip would grant legal immunity from imperial persecution, some in the Nazarene movement were more than troubled by the sudden change of heart. Another passage from the Revelation of Yohanan, normally read in a vacuum, suddenly comes into focus:

> I know the blasphemy of those saying themselves to be Jews, and
> are not, but are the synagogue of Satan. (Revelation 2:9)

Often taken to be a New Testament "anti-Semitic" passage, the historical context places it in a different light entirely. There must, in any case, have been considerable sympathy among the Nazarenes of Israel for their non-Jewish counterparts in the west, who suffered so grievously as "culprits" in a crime they did not commit. Nevertheless, the headquarters of the sect in Jerusalem had other things to worry about in the period after the death of their leader, Yaakov, and a number of his comrades. Who took the helm during this difficult period? How many of Yeshua's immediate family survived the cruel blow of the Sadducean priesthood, designed to sever the movement's head? Did the Israelite Nazarenes have clear leadership at all, or had this become a rudderless ship?

Were they, as some scholars suggest, social revolutionaries, as some also believe Yeshua to have been? Were they political revolutionaries, who, as others maintain, helped stoke the flames of revolt against Rome? Or did they adopt, as a few "renegade" researchers stubbornly insist, a deeply spiritual anti-war stance, consistent with the Hasidim of that troubled age, as well as certain Pharisee leaders, such as the famed sage Yohanan ben Zakkai, who would not support the rebel cause and who watched in horror as "rebel mania" consumed the landscape?

According to the biblical book of Ecclesiastes, there is a time for "every purpose under heaven" (Ecclesiastes 3:1-9), a time for love and a time for hate, a time for peace and a time for war. In the minds of an increasing number of Israelites, the time for war had come, but according to a significant number of others, it most certainly had not. True, Roman authority had become increasingly oppressive, denying to its subjects any sense of self-determination. Roman taxation became an ever-heavier burden, and for all the hyperbole about a cosmopolitan "Roman peace," the Jews in particular felt enslaved.

Every Spring during Passover they would celebrate their liberation from bondage in Egypt in the days of Moses, yet bitterly lament their current bondage under the imperial eagle. On the other hand, however, Rome never compelled its Jewish subjects to abrogate Mosaic law. They continued to enjoy immunity from emperor worship, and their "peculiar" customs, from kosher food to Sabbath-keeping, though sometimes ridiculed in Roman society, were by no means outlawed. If Rome ever demanded idolatrous practices from its Jewish subjects, as in the days of

Caligula and the graven image he planned to erect in the Temple, there would have been immediate revolt, not only in the land of Israel, but among Jews living across the empire.

Indeed, those who were wise recognized that support from the Jewish Diaspora was essential for any revolt to be successful. Conversely, without such support, any revolt would be doomed from the start. The surviving members of the family of Yeshua must surely have been on this side of the growing debate. But being "rudderless" and without a clear leader, a certain inertia must have taken hold, promoting a "wait and see" attitude. After all, the Zealots had by now been active for decades, yet the land had escaped the scourge of war. "Promote the Kingdom of Heaven" was the Hasidic message, and fret not about politics.

The Mark of the Beast

It was nonetheless impossible to ignore the looming reality that Rome's grip on Judea was becoming increasingly tight. Even financial transactions became expressions of imperial tyranny, as no one was allowed to buy or sell without the official seal of the emperor. The imperial stamp, made by a signet ring pressed into wax, was required on every document dealing with monetary matters. Worse still, the stamp bore the image of the emperor, and was therefore conceived of by Jews as another emblem of Rome's rampant idolatry. Another image from the book of Revelation immediately becomes clear:

> And he causes all, both small and great, rich and poor, free and bond, to receive a mark on their right hand, or in their foreheads, even that not any might buy or sell except those having the mark, or the name of the beast, or the number of its name. (Revelation 13:16-17, RSV)

Why was the mark to be placed on the right hand or on the forehead? The imperial seals were in actuality placed on transactions recorded on parchment and papyrus, but this highly symbolic language relates them to something else entirely. Jewish liturgical practice involved the wearing of small, intricately carved boxes, in which tiny scraps of parchment were wound up and inserted. Known as "Phylacteries," they were delicately inscribed with the most important declaration in Judaism, taken from the book of Deuteronomy, the *Sh'ma*:

> Hear, O Israel, the Lord our God is One. (Deuteronomy 6:4)
> Scripture commands the following:

> You shall ... bind them for a sign upon your hand, so that they
> may be as frontlets between your eyes ... And you shall write
> them upon the door posts of your house, and upon your gates.
> (Deuteronomy 11:18, 20)

Jewish faith and practice took these commands literally, and its adherents, including the *ma'aminim*, who never relinquished pietistic Jewish observance, literally bound these phylacteries to their foreheads and left forearms and hands with long black cords, in such a fashion that the cords themselves spell out the Hebrew letters of the word *Shaddai*, or "the Almighty." The left forearm, where the cord is knotted to form these letters, is designated because it is closest to the heart. Thus, the observant Jew symbolically binds the heart, the actions of the hands, the mind, and even the process of thought to divine service. On the contrary, however, those who accepted the idolatrous imperial stamp were symbolically receiving the "mark of the Beast," negating, as it were, true worship. The book of Revelation is even more poignant in the detail about the "mark of the Beast" being applied to the *right* hand, the hand opposite the one designated by Jewish tradition. In the minds of the ancient Hasidim and kindred sects (including the Nazarenes) imperial edicts amounted to a mockery of Jewish piety.

Additionally, we find in the Apocalypse a symbolic representation of a mysterious personage who has riveted the attention of readers for the last two millennia:

> Here is wisdom. Let him having reason count the number of
> the beast, for it is the number of a man. And its number is 666.
> (Revelation 13:18)

Which man could this be? Traditional Christianity has branded him the Antichrist, with many candidates for this role having been considered through the ages. We can, however, do better than resorting to mere guesswork, considering the fact that in the ancient Hebrew alphabet, every letter carries with it a numerical value. Numbers are commonly expressed as letters and every word written down can also be expressed as a number. An entire "science" called *gematria* developed to examine the Scriptures for numerical values. Complex numeric schemes have been seen imbedded in the biblical text.

Bearing the numerical value of Hebrew letters in mind, when we consider the name of the reigning Roman emperor, Nero Caesar, an interesting phenomenon takes place. Once we convert his name from Latin into Hebrew, we find that the Semitic equivalent is *Neron Keisar*, consisting of precisely seven letters, each carrying a specific numerical value:

Nun, or "N": 50
Resh, or "R": 200
Vav, or "O": 6
Nun, another "N": 50

Kuf, or "K": 100
Samekh, or "S": 60
Resh, another "R": 200

Added together, the sum of these numbers is exactly 666. Put simply, it is likely that everyone who read the book of Revelation understood that the nefarious "Beast" envisioned by Yohanan "the Revelator" was none other than the murderous tyrant, Nero. Again we should ask, was Revelation composed in the late first century, looking backwards to Nero, or does at least some of its contents date to the reign of Nero himself, from 54 to 68 CE, referring to him cryptically so as not to endanger those who circulated and read the text?

As noted, there have been other nominees for the "Antichrist" title down through history. Napoleon Bonaparte tried to resurrect the old Roman empire and led a vast army, "conquering and to conquer" (like the rider of the white horse in Revelation 6:2). And the twentieth century became witness to the Italian dictator, Benito Moussolini, who ruled from Rome. But every attempt to match an individual's name with the number 666 has failed. In truth we need look no further than the infamous tyrant on the Tiber, who made the streets of Rome flow with the blood of martyrs. But how did the Neronic "spirit of 666" lead, inexorably, toward a climactic confrontation between the despotic emperor and the province of Judea? And how did the Nazarene sect, struggling amidst the pangs of those days, weather the storm? How did they survive at all? These are issues we can only appreciate by returning to the crisis of politics that developed between the empire and her Jewish subjects.

Rumbles, Revolt or Revolution?

Little did anyone perceive that events in the Mediterranean port city of Caesarea (that had already proved a flash-point of conflict between Jews and Greeks) were soon to result in bloody carnage throughout Israel. The Jews of that city had built an impressive synagogue there, which was not surprising given that everything in the city was impressive. Adjoining land, however, belonged to a Greek citizen who decided to build some workshops nearby, leaving only a narrow approach to the Jewish place of worship. It was a typical property dispute that soon got out of hand as the Jews first tried to buy the Greek's property, offering an exorbitant price to no avail. Next, they tried to bribe the new Roman procurator, Florus, who accepted the eight talents of silver they offered only to leave the city for nearby Sebaste.

Adding considerable insult to their already injured pride, a local Greek arranged a mock sacrifice in front of the synagogue on the following Sabbath, slaughtering birds on an upside down pot. A major scuffle broke out, after which a delegation of Jews carrying a scroll of the Torah immediately set off for Sebaste to beg Florus' assistance, while reminding him of their earlier contribution to his coffers. But he ignominiously threw them into prison for, of all things, having disgraced the Torah by moving it from its home.

In Jerusalem the news was met with universal outrage. Florus, as if determined to provoke a full-scale revolt, personally marched to the holy city and pilfered an additional seventeen talents from the massive Temple treasury. An impromptu mob hastily assembled on the Temple Mount, shouting contempt for the procurator. Some even passed around a basket, begging alms in mocking derision for "the poor beggar Florus." The people's reaction was understandable. In revolutionary America such sentiments were equated with patriotism. But as in colonial America there were those who realized, the Heirs among them, that revolution, for all its "glory," would exact a terrible butcher's bill at the end of the day and that the ranks of those same patriots would feel the full brunt of imperial wrath.

Florus took this occasion to bring an army into Jerusalem, only to be met with mock salutes and defiant gestures. The procurator next issued a summons to the chief priests, Sadducees all, who begged pardon on behalf of the offenders. They wished as always to preserve the status quo, which is why they had persecuted the Way and any other sectarian movements whose messianism might, at least in the minds of some, have led to insurrection. Florus, however, was not so easily assuaged. He promptly unleashed his troops to wreck havoc in the city. They plundered the open market, indiscriminately killing all they met, and then began breaking into homes, slaughtering the occupants. The streets of Jerusalem turned blood red, as between three and four thousand men, women and children were hacked to pieces by Roman swords. How many Nazarenes were among those murdered we cannot know, but within twenty-four hours the city's upper market was packed with those mourning their dead.

When additional troops arrived from Caesarea, more brutality ensued. Many helpless Jerusalemites fell before the Roman stampede, being beaten with clubs, trampled or crushed to death. By now the enraged citizenry were assaulting the Romans from their roofs, while a mob seized control of the massive Antonia fortress, which overlooked the Temple complex, destroying the porticoes that linked it to the the great plateau beneath. It was the equivalent of storming the Bastille. One is reminded of the words of King Louis XVI, who, on hearing the news that the Bastille had fallen, asked incredulously, "Is it a revolt?" To which his attendant replied, "No, Sire; it is a revolution."

King Herod Agrippa II, who had been away in Egypt during these events, hastily returned to Jerusalem, attempting to avert total war. His efforts, however, were of no avail, since the population seemed utterly determined to take on the "evil empire." Josephus Flavius, while pretending to write objective history, cannot help asking a rhetorical question at this point in his narration. How could the Jews hope to succeed in fomenting revolution when the world was ruled by Rome?[4] In this detail ancient history dovetails again with the book of Revelation:

> And they worshiped the beast, saying, Who is like the beast?
> Who is able to make war with it? (Revelation 13:4)

God, Swords and Guts

The "Beast" himself, Nero reacted with rage to reports that were soon coming in from the province of Judea. A contingent of the most radical of rebel groups, the Sicarii, now assaulted Masada, the immense stronghold in the Judean desert overlooking the Dead Sea. Masada, which in Hebrew means "fortress," was built up in the days of the so-called Hasmonean dynasty, the last kings of a truly independent Judea. Under King Herod the Great, Masada experienced its heyday, boasting an enormous three-tiered palace, an elaborate bathhouse, impregnable walls completely surrounding the plateau, vast cisterns and even a swimming pool. Herod had taken delight in confounding nature, with fresh water pools in the midst of the unforgiving desert of Judea. It was considered so inviolate that the Romans had left only a token force to secure it.

The Sicarii, the infamous "dagger men," were known not only for

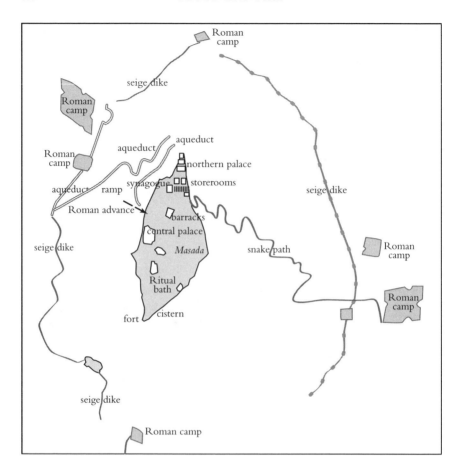

attacking the Romans, but for murdering those suspected of "collaborating" with the Romans. That was one way to radicalize the whole population and fan the flames of revolt. But this new act of storming to the top of Masada's great plateau and slaughtering the Roman guards there meant that there was no turning back.

Back in Jerusalem, those who favored revolt had an ally in Eliezer, son of the High Priest Ananias, who made sure that no sacrifice or offering be accepted from a "foreigner," which in effect halted the customary prayers and sacrifices offered on behalf of the emperor. An extraordinary moment of solidarity followed, as a number of leading Pharisees joined the chief priests in pleading that these offerings not be discontinued, since their ancestors had always received the gifts of non-Israelites. We are even told that some of the people began hastily rebuilding the porticoes connecting the Temple Mount with the Antonia Fortress in a last-ditch attempt to avoid the inevitable conflict with Nero's legions.

What we know from these events is that a significant faction of Jewish Jerusalem had no interest in launching an anti-Roman revolt. We also know that a sizable segment of the Pharisee party was moderate to the point of being "pacifist," opposing armed insurrection at any cost. And since we have seen that the Pharisees were closely aligned ideologically with the Nazarene movement, agreeing on most points of religion and behavior, it stands to reason that the Heirs – as a branch of the Hasidic movement – shared this "anti-war" stance. However mad "satanic" Nero was, they understood as Yeshua had before them the devastation that war would bring. The book of Revelation may be seen as a series of dire warnings about what was to come, not in some distant epoch, but in the "Revelator's" own day and age.

History repeats itself. The modern Hasidic group discussed earlier, Habad-Lubavitch, headquartered in Crown Heights, Brooklyn, also lost their revered leader, the venerable Rebbe Menachem Mendel Schneerson, who died in 1994. Like the ancient Nazarenes after the death of Yaakov, they have continued as a prominent Jewish sect, though leaderless. They are staunchly Zionist in orientation, proudly supportive of the State of Israel, yet they do not take up arms or fight in its wars. They pray, they remain steadfast in observance of the Torah, and they let God do the rest. There is in modern Israel no small degree of controversy regarding all such ultra-Orthodox Hasidic groups, who receive all the benefits of Israeli citizenship, yet do not serve in the military and are not prepared to put their lives on the line to uphold the state. There is in fact a great deal of enmity vented by fellow Israelis against them. Some describe it as virtual civil war. So it is today and so it was in antiquity.

An odd coalition of the chief priests and "all who favored peace" (presumably including moderate Pharisees as well as members of the Way) temporarily took control of the so-called Upper City, where the city's most sumptuous villas were located. While there was no love lost between the *ma'aminim* and the Jerusalemite priesthood, this was in fact the likely location of the home of the mysterious "thirteenth disciple," Yohanan the Priest, the same individual who, some speculate, may have been the real author of the book of Revelation. While tradition has it that he was exiled to the Roman penile colony of Patmos, it is possible that his family villa in Jerusalem continued to serve as the hub of the Nazarene movement. This would place them in exactly the part of the city that chose to oppose the rebels.

Meanwhile, the Temple Mount and the so-called Lower City, lower

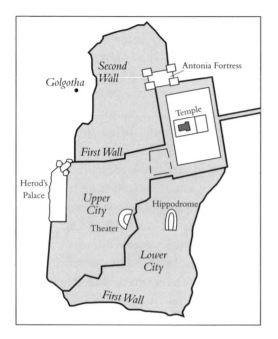

in altitude and in affluence, fell to the rebels, who next slaughtered the Roman garrison quartered in the Antonia fortress. At this point Jerusalem witnessed the arrival of a man of illustrious character and equally illustrious fame. His name was Menakhem, the son of the Zealot faction's greatest leader, Yehuda the Galilean. He had come from Masada, where he and his followers had robbed King Herod's armory of its weaponry. Josephus relates that when he came into the holy city he was greeted like a veritable king. This language suggests to some scholars that this was no ordinary revolt, but had messianic overtones from the outset. It was the ancient equivalent of *jihad*, a "holy war" that would succeed by supernatural agency to reestablish the throne of King David. Perhaps this Menakhem was himself the Messiah, at least in the eyes of the Zealots.

But we should again bear in mind that ideas about the Messiah were sharply divided and that more than a few Israelites, most likely including the Nazarenes, viewed the anointed deliverer not in military but in spiritual terms. Notwithstanding a few modern researchers who make the case that the Nazarenes were themselves of the Zealot persuasion, their true position must have been closer to the moderate Pharisee camp, which viewed the arrival of Menakhem with horror.

The rebels for their part saw things in starkly dualistic terms of right and wrong, good and evil. Theirs was the just cause, and we can only imagine that if Patrick Henry had been alive in their day, he would have taken up arms with them, shouting, "Give me liberty or give me death!" They did not seek to perpetrate massacre but were merely trying to free themselves from the Roman yoke. When the rebels therefore laid siege to Herod's great palace in Jerusalem, now used as the headquarters of imperial jurisdiction, the outnumbered Romans within were allowed safe passage to the sea. "Why obey the Romans," asked the imperious Menakhem, "when God alone is our Master?"

But any unity of purpose among the rebels was to be short-lived. After the murder of the High Priest Ananias and his brother, Ananias' son Eliezer accused Menakhem of a tyranny on par with the Romans'. Discovering the rebel leader in the Temple, dressed in royal raiment as befitting a "messianic" king, Eliezer had him and his cohorts publicly tortured to death. One of Menakhem's relatives, another Eliezer known as the "son of Yair," managed to escape, fleeing to Masada, where he would lead the most intransigent of rebel forces, the Sicarii. In time Eliezer ben Yair would transform the plateau into a universal emblem of defiant freedom that would live forever in legend and myth.

Meanwhile, the conglomeration of moderates in Jerusalem – priests, Pharisees and, we must presume, Nazarenes – hoped that the violent death of Menakhem would bring an end to the budding rebellion. But fanaticism, like the fire that burned Nero's capital, is difficult to quench. Eliezer son of Ananias so pressed his siege of the remaining Roman forces that they consented to lay down their arms, turning over their weapons and property in return for their lives. Such protocols, however, mean little to fanatics, who in this case proceeded to shed the blood of their Roman victims, even as they shouted, "But what of the agreement; what of the oath?" In this act of carnage, perpetrated on the Sabbath, the rebels of Jerusalem transformed themselves from revolutionaries akin to the colonial Americans to the likes of the French revolutionaries, whose butchery would one day subject countless Parisians to the guillotine.

When news of the massacre reached the Mediterranean coast, the Greek citizens of Caesarea took matters into their own hands, mounting a genocidal attack on the Jews of that city. Within a single hour some twenty thousand had been slain, virtually emptying Caesarea of its Jewish inhabitants. According to Josephus, another thirteen thousand Jews were butchered at the inland city of Scythopolis. Massacres in other cities followed, including Alexandria in Egypt, where a strong Jewish community had thrived for centuries. Yet the rebels continued their advance, slaughtering a Roman garrison near Jericho and occupying another Bastille-like fortress called Makhaerus.

The entire land of Israel, being under the Roman military jurisdiction of Syria, was the immediate concern of Gaius Cestius Gallus, who served as legate of the province. The buck stopped, so to speak, with him, and he could not afford to let the situation get completely out of hand. The time

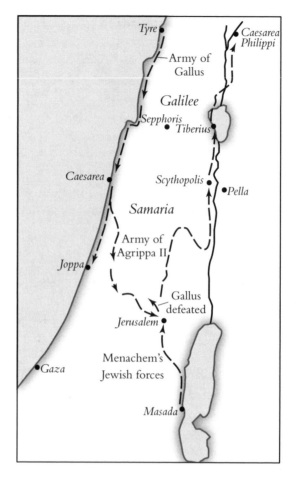

for negotiation had passed. The unruly Israelite rebels had to be crushed immediately. The legate led a massive army down the coast from Antioch, attacking the port city of Joppa and killing its citizens. But this was to be total war, and even the annihilation of whole communities would not suffice. Gallus gave orders that the countryside itself be set afire, in a fierce conflagration that would render the land unlivable.

What the Oracle Said

The communities of *ma'aminim* scattered across Israel and the Diaspora could not have been living in splendid isolation and could not have been unaware of the devastation going on around them. The question was, how does a pietistic Jewish sect respond in the face of events that must have seemed to be proof that the world was coming to an end? The book of Revelation once again makes relevant commentary on these days, as though its author is taking a page directly from the writings of Josephus Flavius:

> The first angel sounded, and there followed hail and fire mixed
> with blood, and they were cast on the earth. And the third
> part of trees was burned up, and all green grass was burned up.
> (Revelation 8:7)

Prophetic warnings of this nature were not unique to Israel. The Greeks
had always had their oracles, such as the famed Oracle at Delphi, which
had always been taken seriously by peasants and kings alike. Are we to
assume that the Nazarenes had no such oracles, simply because it isn't
fashionable to speak of "fortunetellers" in the world of modern scholarship? What if the book of Revelation was not written long after the fact,
in the days of the emperor Domitian? What if at least a good deal of its
content dates from the period of the revolt itself, having been transmitted
perhaps from "Yohanan the Priest" or someone like him, or from multiple
Nazarene "oracles," as cryptic yet dire warnings, preparing the entire
community of Jerusalemite *ma'aminim* to take flight?

Amazingly, there are similar images of conflagration among the
hymns of the Dead Sea Scrolls, ancient Hebrew documents that also date
to the first century:

> The torrents of Satan shall reach to all sides of the world. In all
> their channels a consuming fire shall destroy every tree, green
> and barren, on their banks; unto the end of their courses it shall
> scourge with flames of fire, and shall consume the foundations of
> the earth and the expanse of dry land. The bases of the mountains
> shall blaze and the roots of the rocks shall turn to torrents of pitch;
> it shall devour as far as the great Abyss. (Dead Sea Psalm 5)

In another Dead Sea hymn we find this:

> The flame of (their) javelins is like a consuming fire among trees.
> (Dead Sea Psalm 2)

Scholars continue to debate the identity of the Judean sect who wrote the
Dead Sea Scrolls, but the most widely accepted theory links them with an
apocalyptic group known as the Essenes, who, sometime during the second
century before the Common Era, abandoned the city of Jerusalem and took
up residence along the northwest shore of the sea of salt, at a place today

known as Qumran, under the direction of a mysterious leader known as the Teacher of Righteousness.[5] They persevered in the desert and ultimately established satellite communities across the length and breadth of ancient Israel. Jerusalem was home to one such community, and there was even an Essene Quarter of the city as well as an Essene Gate, which pointed in the direction of the Judean Desert, toward the Dead Sea and Qumran.

The Nazarenes had to have been aware of the Essenes, as did the rest of the population, though an open question remains: How much did the Essenes, with their apocalyptic mentality and expectation of an imminent "end of the world," impact the general population of those days? Did their mentality govern the fanatical mania of the rebels, as the revolt continued on its gruesome course? Did the Essenes sympathize with the rebel cause, even to the point of joining the revolt?

Some have speculated that the Nazarenes were deeply influenced by the Essenes, deciding to emulate their communal lifestyle and to share all things in common.[6] French historian Ernest Renan once made a bold proclamation that early Christianity was nothing short of "Essenism that succeeded."[7] Or was it? The Dead Sea Scrolls certainly share a number of concepts common to the writings of Shaul, including a militant apocalypticism, strong cosmic dualism of light and dark, good and evil pitched in battle on the world stage, and a radical predestination which sees human beings as helpless in the hands of predetermined fate. Such ideas, assuming that they went beyond the confines of the Essene community, may have served to energize the rebels and propel their cause. But a strong case can be made that they are absent from the teaching of Yeshua m'Natzeret and just as absent from the mindset of his lineal descendants. As we have already seen, one of Yeshua's disciples was known as Shimon (Simon) the Zealot, which may or may not identify him with the anti-Roman revolutionaries. But even if this Shimon were himself a revolutionary, Yeshua would by no means have been in the same camp. In fact, Yeshua seems to be loosely quoting the Dead Sea Scrolls in his famous saying:

> You have heard that it was said, "You shall love your neighbor and hate your enemy." (Matthew 5:43)

In the Scrolls the command was given to love all the Sons of Light and "hate all the Sons of Darkness" (Manual of Discipline 1:10). If the term "Sons of Darkness" applied to anyone in those days, it was the Romans. Yeshua sought to reverse this philosophy by adding, "But I say to you,

Love your enemies" (Matthew 5:44). In other words, he acknowledged the xenophobic attitude of the Essenes, but proceeded to shred it.[8]

Messianic Mania

Did the leaderless Heirs of those days live up to Yeshua's admonition, even when so many of their comrades had joined the ranks of the freedom fighters? Did they ignore other Essene prophecies, such as the famous Dead Sea War Scroll? This mysterious ancient text, found in 1947 among the cache of ancient documents at Qumran, is, like the book of Revelation, a cryptic text with messianic overtones that describes war at the end of the age between the so-called Sons of Light and Sons of Darkness. The hostilities would be foreordained from on high and divided into a series of seven battles. Three of these engagements would be won by the Sons of Light and three more by the Sons of Darkness, leaving the final, seventh battle to be won by a coalition of men and angels who would descend from heaven and defeat the forces of evil.

Assuming that this "messianic mania" of the Essenes did in fact influence the rebels of Jerusalem, who fought with a fanaticism that bordered on madness, some have argued that the Nazarene sect actually joined the rebel cause and that its messianism dovetailed with that of the Essenes and the Zealot freedom fighters. This, we have seen is unlikely, given the pietistic rather than militant approach of Yeshua himself. We must nonetheless ask: Is it coincidental that the rebels adopted a symbol that must also have been near and dear to the Nazarenes, the chalice? The chalice appeared as the central image on coins struck during the revolt.

Under Jewish law no person's image could be depicted, as they were on Roman coins, since this would be considered a "graven image" and therefore equivalent to idolatry. As a result, coins struck during the revolt bore only this inanimate object on one side and a simple leaf on the reverse. Round about the chalice the year was listed, starting from the year the revolt broke out (66 CE) as Year 1. As the principal image of the Lord's supper, later called the eucharist, the cup was an integral element of the communal meals of the Nazarenes and must have carried with it a messianic significance. Likewise, the Essenes, in a ceremony detailed in the Dead Sea Scrolls, turned the communal meal into a "messianic banquet." In a ritual bearing an uncanny resemblance to the protocol instituted by Yeshua, a priest first extended his hand over the wine chalice, then over bread. The use of the chalice image by the Judean rebels may thus be seen as one more example of the fanatical "fever" that drove the revolt, even against overwhelming odds and what looked from the outset like certain defeat.

Despite the evidence of this shared imagery, however, we cannot assume that the Nazarenes and the Essenes were united in the revolt against Rome. Each group had its own set of oracles, delivering opposite counsel at this most critical time. According to the Dead Sea Scrolls, all was predestined, including the final victory over the Roman Sons of Darkness. The Nazarene oracles, however, counseled the reverse. Assuming at least that the contents of the book of Revelation are early, we can imagine that the *ma'aminim* were disseminating stern advice to all their comrades: "This is not the 'just cause,' nor the 'righteous war' that the rebels imagined. We may be living at the end of the age, but what is foreordained is not rebel victory, but *our* survival. This is not the time to rise up, but to hunker down." And that is precisely what the Nazarenes did, even as the pro-Roman Jewish king Agrippa II and his sister Bernice fled Jerusalem for the Galilee where they surrendered to the Romans.

Gallus, in spite of sizable reinforcements, met ignominious defeat in central Israel in the battle of Bet-Horon on the border between the tribes of Benjamin and Ephraim. During their humiliating retreat, the illustrious Legio XII Fulminata (the legion organized by Julius Caesar), lost its standard, bearing its famed "thunderbolt" emblem, to the rebels. For Nero, this was the ultimate outrage. He dispatched his most capable general, Vespasian along with his son Titus, to replace Gallus and head to Judea province with all haste.

The rebels, for their part, chose their most capable commander, a man with military experience and a scholar in his own right, a prolific writer who would become the greatest Jewish historian of the age, Yosef ben Mattatiyahu, known to history as Josephus Flavius. He would be given command of the Jewish forces in the fiercely independent Galilee. But for all the pious intent of the Zealot horde he commanded, they were at the outset little more than a disorganized militia, up against the most efficient fighting force in history. His task was to introduce his troops to Roman military discipline.

Vespasian's strategy, however, allowed his adversaries no safe haven and little time for training. Vespasian planned to subdue the Galilee first, since this region had been the hotbed of resistance ever since the Romans first arrived in the land of Israel in 63 BCE. Only when the Galilee was firmly in his grasp would he turn his attention to Jerusalem. He therefore decided to wait with the fifth and tenth legions in the northern coastal city of Ptolemais for the arrival of Titus, who was coming up the coast from Alexandria with the fifteenth legion. Titus, as we shall see, would be no bit player in the drama about to unfold in Israel, but was destined to dominate the coming battle for Jerusalem.

Josephus recorded the legendary tactics, regimen and "look" of the Roman army in meticulous detail:

> When, after this, they are gone out of their camp, they all march without noise, and in a decent manner, and every one keeps his own rank, as if they were going to war. The footmen are armed with breastplates and head-pieces, and have swords on each side; but the sword which is upon their left side is much longer than the other ... Each horseman has a long sword on his right side, and a long pole in his hand; a shield also lies by him obliquely on one side of his horse, with three or more arrows that are borne in his quiver, having broad points, and not smaller than spears. They have also head-pieces and breastplates, as do all the footmen. (*War*, 3.5.5)

Liberty or Death?

The Jewish historian's description of the Roman army reminds us of another passage in the book of Revelation, which describes them in terms of an invasion of locusts:

> And the shapes of the locusts were like horses prepared for battle. And on their heads were as it were crowns like gold, and their faces were like the faces of men. And they had hairs like the hairs of women, and their teeth were like the teeth of lions. And they had breastplates like breastplates of iron. And the sound of their wings was like the sound of chariots of many horses running to battle. And they had tails like scorpions, and there were stings in their tails... And they had a king over them, the angel of the bottomless pit, whose name in the Hebrew tongue is Abaddon, but in Greek his name is Apollyon. (Revelation 9:7-11)

These latter two names both mean "destroyer," and aptly describe how Vespasian and Titus appeared to the freedom fighters. Once again, what modern readers imagine must have something to do with events relating to the "end of the world" is in reality a depiction of Israel's first century

Roman foes, couched in the language of apocalypse. Again we ask, was this written years or even decades after the revolt, and if so, what purpose would it have served? Is it possible that the Greek text of Revelation rests on early Semitic writings that may go back to the revolt itself – "oracles" for the Heirs and the *ma'aminim* of Judea and the Galilee – counseling them to avoid the rebels and to stay out of harm's way?

Josephus, however, found himself at the epicenter of the conflict, well aware that he was not only leading a lost cause, but an exercise in madness that would result only in carnage and suffering on an unimaginable scale. He wrote:

> Indeed I foresaw the final catastrophe toward which the Jews were heading… but I would not betray my command. (*War*, 3.6.3)

He gathered his forces and hastily retreated to a fortified Galilean settlement, perched on a hillside called Yodfat (Jotapata in Greek), where he attempted to make a last stand against the legions of Caesar. In due course Yodfat was surrounded by the combined forces of Vespasian and Titus. A lengthy siege ensued, in which colossal catapults and battering rams were pressed into service. In language evocative of one of the plagues from Pharoah's Egypt Josephus describes what befell the hapless defenders:

> And they threw stone by catapults and the lances launched by the bows hissed, and arrows dimmed the light … and the Jews dared not stand on the ramparts. (*War*, 3.6.19)

Yohanan the Revelator, while not specifically describing Yodfat, employs images that conjure the horrific siege in our minds:

> From the sky huge hailstones of about a hundred pounds each fell upon men. And they cursed God on account of the plague of hail, because the plague was so terrible. (Revelation 16:21)

The siege engines at Yodfat proceeded in their relentless assault. Merciless in their onslaught, the Romans broke into the settlement, butchering everyone save for twelve hundred women and children, who were taken as captives. The legionaries scoured every potential hiding place for more victims, even as many of the defenders preferred to die by their own hand. What was it that drove them to such desperation, even to such a fundamental violation of Jewish law as suicide? Could it be one more aspect of the "messianic" character of the revolt? In modern times we think of fanatical cults such as Jonestown, the Branch Davidians and Heaven's Gate whose misguided followers have gone so far as to take their own lives, invariably convinced that the "end of the world" was at hand. Those Jews at Yodfat were perhaps motivated by the same religious fervor.

Josephus, who was with a small band of holdouts hiding in a cave, describes what transpired in terms reminiscent of the warnings of Revelation:

> I called to mind the dreams which I had dreamed in the night time, whereby God had signified to me beforehand both the future calamities of the Jews, and the events that concerned the Roman emperors... I put up a secret prayer to God, and said,

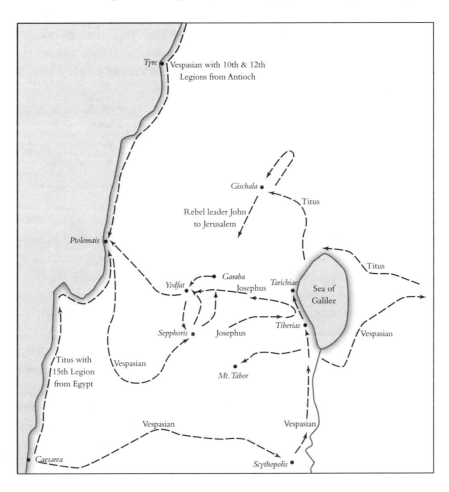

"Since You have chosen me to foretell what will come to pass hereafter, I am content to live. I declare openly that I do not go over to the Romans as a deserter of the Jews, but as Your servant." But those with me began to thrust their swords at me, and threatened they would kill me, if I thought of yielding myself to the Romans. (*War*, 3.8.3)

Josephus attempted to dissuade his comrades from killing themselves, but they would hear none of it:

Desperation had shut their ears, as having long ago devoted themselves to die, and they were irritated at me. They then ran upon me with their swords in their hands, and called me a coward.

"And now," I said, "since it is resolved among you that you will die, come on, let us commit our deaths to be determined by lot. He whom the lot falls to first, let him be killed by him who has the second lot, and thus fortune shall make its progress through us all.

They thought that death, if I might but die with them, was sweeter than life; yet I was with left, along with another man, to the last, whether we must say that it happened by chance, or by the providence of God.

Thus I escaped in the war with the Romans, and was led to Vespasian. (*War*, 3.8.6-8)

We are left with various possible interpretations of this account. Either Josephus contrived it entirely in order to tell a compelling story, or by some miracle only he and one other actually survived the siege, or, quite possibly, Josephus secretly rigged the lots to insure his own survival. As it is, the story certainly sounds suspicious, and the only thing of which we can be certain is that the name Yosef ben Mattatiyahu (Josephus son of Mattathias) has from that point in time been a byword for treason in the Jewish mind. The Romans proceeded to raze Yodfat to the ground, the siege of the town having cost some forty thousand Jewish lives.

Josephus would henceforth behave as a Roman lackey, trying to persuade the nation to give up lest they all face a fate similar to the Galileans. His celebrated histories of the Jewish people and the war of liberation they waged would be slanted toward the Romans, and for this reason many of the details they contain must be questioned. We would nonetheless be lost in our knowledge of this period without his voluminous writings.

The question remains: What of the Nazarenes? Where were they and what were they doing during the turmoil that engulfed the land? It is one of the enduring mysteries of this seminal age, which ultimately birthed the three great religions of the west. While some in the scholarly world continue to argue that the Judeo-Christians of this period were deeply involved in anti-Roman agitation, including the revolt itself, the cryptic message of the texts that survive is that they should not only avoid such involvement, but should at an opportune moment flee entirely. They must, like Josephus, have felt warned, perhaps through dreams, visions and holy oracles, that insurrection was suicide. Like Josephus, they too would find themselves branded traitors to the great cause of freedom that, ironically, drove the nation inexorably toward destruction.

Notes

1   It has been maintained that the core of apocalyptic is the concept of 'theodicy', namely affirming hope in divine justice and sovereignty, even when radically contradicted by the blows of history. See A. LaCocque, *Daniel in His Time* (Columbia, SC: University of South Carolina Press, 1988), 59-75.

2   See Eusebius *History* 3.39.1-11.

3   Alternate theories abound, including the idea that ten heads represent the provincial governors under Nero. See David Chilton, *Paradise Restored: A Biblical Theology of Dominion* (Nashville, Dominion Press, 1987).

4   Josephus, *War*, 2.16.380.

5   Robert Eisenman has reached some striking conclusions, namely that the Teacher of Righteousness was James the Just, that the Wicked Priest was the high priest Ananus who was responsible for James' execution in 62 CE, and that the Man of Lies was Paul the apostle. He argues that the Zealot faction was broad enough to have encompassed the early Christians, suggesting that Jesus and his followers were linked with the Zealots. He further suggests that such language as being "zealous for the Law" (Acts 22:3) is applicable to the Qumranites and should equate them with the Zealot party – a controversial inference for many. See R. Eisenman, *James the Brother of Jesus* (New York, Penguin, 1998); *The New Testament Code* (New York, Sterling Publishing, 2006). Eisenman's interpretations have been criticized by many within the scholarly community, though the dismissive tone of

such responses should give us pause for thought. See E.W. Larson, "Qumran and
the Dead Sea Scrolls: Discoveries, Debates, the Scrolls and the Bible," *NEA* 63.3
(2000): 168-71. M. Broshi also disagrees with Eisenman, noting that radiocarbon
tests have dated the bulk of the scrolls to the first two centuries B.C.E. See M. Broshi,
Review of Eisenman 1993, BA 57.1 (1994): 62-3. It should be noted, however, that
defensiveness is often the response when the status-quo is challenged.

6   No less an authority than Solomon Zeitlin declared that the Essenes consisted
of Hasidim, who rose in response to the Antiochan persecution. See S. Zeitlin,
"The Propaganda of the Hebrew Scrolls and the Falsification of History," *JQR* 46.3
(1956): 209-58. It has been argued that the Essenes may even have derived their
names from the Hasidim and that they arose from a quietist, pacifistic stream of
the Pious of an earlier period. Josephus dates their origin to the reign of Jonathan
(*Antiquities*, XIII, 171). See M. Grant, *The Jews*, 42, n. 12. However, Lawrence
Schiffman (*Reclaiming*, 89) asserts, in light of 4QMMT (the "Halakhic Letter"),
that earlier theories which link the Dead Sea sect with the Hasidim (as well as the
Essenes) must be abandoned. Schiffman's own hypothesis, claiming a Sadducean
origin for the sect, is nonetheless just as problematic, in light of the sect's clear
rejection of the Jerusalem Temple. In any case, one need not assert that the Dead Sea
sect was a direct offshoot of the Hasidim to demonstrate strong pietistic influence
on the content of the Scrolls themselves.

7   See Cullmann, "Significance," 213-26.

8   Flusser (*Judaism*, 483-4) asserted that a "new sensitivity" developed during
Second Temple Judaism, emphasizing unconditional love and the solidarity of
humankind. While Flusser saw the Dead Sea sectarians as reacting to this new
sensitivity by developing a theology of hatred toward the "sons of darkness,"
he acknowledged passages in the Scrolls which are in line with it, such as 1QS
10:17-18: "To no man shall I return evil for evil, I shall pursue a man only for
good."

6

The Lady and the Dragon

ROPHECY IS CONSIDERED BY MANY A DIVINE GIFT THAT HAPPENS to have made the Israelites unique among all people. It is true that surrounding cultures had their sorcerers, their wandering shamans, their oracles and soothsayers, but only Israel had an entire class of writing prophets whose ethical messages of social consciousness, couched in elaborate poetry, have resounded through the ages. When Martin Luther King led his great marches for social justice, it wasn't just Gandhi he quoted, it was Isaiah. How odd, that most modern critical scholarship is almost embarrassed at the role played by the ancient prophets.

There has been wide acknowledgment that the New Testament book of Revelation references in surprising detail the events of the Great Revolt against Rome. But its oracles had to have been written, declare most critics, long after the fact, because of course there is no such thing as "true prophecy." Nonetheless, there are a number of other ancient sources that, like Revelation, contain "predictive" passages directly relating to the Great Revolt. We have already seen such "prophecies" in the Dead Sea Scrolls, and we have also noted Josephus' "night dreams," that he claimed made clear to him the course of future events as well as the futility of the rebel cause.

Josephus, regardless of his "treason" in defecting to the Romans, is an endlessly fascinating character. Having willingly surrendered to the Roman enemy, he claims to have played the prophet once more, this time predicting to Vespasian that he, the pragmatic Roman general, was destined to become the emperor of all Rome. It was no small prophecy, and while we cannot be sure that Josephus was telling the truth, we can know that, being deemed a traitor in the eyes of his own people, he would henceforth serve as Rome's faithful lackey.

In any case, when it came to the horrors that lay ahead, even the heavens could not maintain silence, bearing witness of extremity, calamity and what appeared to many to be the "end of days." Josephus as well as the Roman historian Tacitus told of various signs and portents that seemed to herald Jerusalem's doom, some manifesting themselves even before the revolt broke out. A bright star shone upon the city as if it were a sword prepared to strike. A comet also appeared in the sky, lasting an entire year. When the people were assembled for the Feast of Unleavened Bread, a brilliant light enveloped the altar in front of the Temple, illuminating the holy sanctuary for half an hour. While the people perceived this to be an omen of good fortune, the priests told them the opposite. Then, as though nature had taken leave of her senses, a cow was reported to have given birth to a lamb in the Temple courtyard. Furthermore, the inner courtyard's massive eastern gate, which required a team of twenty men to move, suddenly flew open of its own accord in the middle of the night.

Wormwood

Of even greater concern, in the year 67 the usual winter rains were, as if by some inexplicable divine agency, held back. By summer of that year the relentless heat had scorched the earth and turned the holy land into a holy hell. Josephus recorded that in the center of the country the sect of Samaritans, who had been considering joining the revolt, were struck particularly hard, many dying of thirst and many others defecting to the Romans. Was this what the book of Revelation was referring to when it relates the following?

> A great star burning like a lamp fell from the heaven, and it fell on the third part of the rivers and on the fountains of waters. And the name of the star is called Wormwood, and a third part of the waters became wormwood. And many men died from the waters, because they were made bitter. (Revelation 8:10-11)

The Nazarenes, while sitting on the sidelines, had to have been paying keen attention to these catastrophes to have made such vivid reference to them in their great apocalyptic text. We can only imagine that they must have been planning their next move, which had to be executed at precisely the right moment.

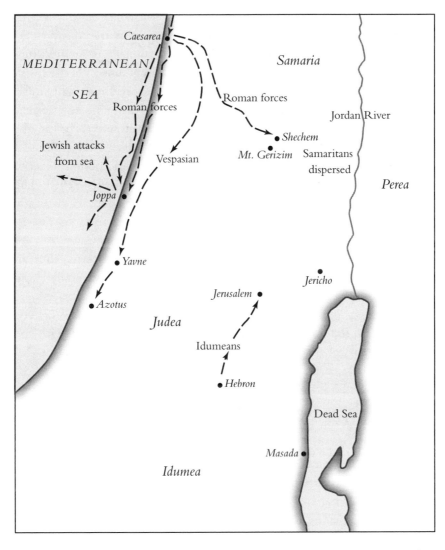

As if the extremity of this situation were not bad enough, Josephus relates that his new lord, Vespasian, next decided to subdue the port of Yafo (Joppa) on the Mediterranean coast. Its inhabitants rushed in terror down to the sea, boarding a small fleet of ships, imagining that they had saved themselves. But nature itself seemed to do battle against them, as a fierce wind called a "Black Norther" tore into the vessels the following morning, dashing them upon the reefs. Those who escaped drowning and who managed to struggle back to shore were hacked to pieces by their adversaries, so that the sea turned red with the blood of over four thousand corpses.

Similar horrors ensued at a place called Magdala, on the Sea of Galilee, which, nearly four decades earlier, had been home to a very famous "Miriam" – the Magdalene – of whom so much has been written and speculated. Whatever became of this Miriam will remain in the realm of mystery, but her home town became a refuge of sorts for a small multitude of insurgents who fled there, and the focus of Vespasian's next assault. As at Yafo, they boarded boats, which they pushed out onto the great lake to escape the marauding Romans. Remaining in range, they continued to attack Vespasian's troops, only to find the Romans assembling a fleet of rafts, which they launched in relentless pursuit of the hapless rebels. The stones hurled by the Jewish freedom fighters merely rattled off the heavy armor of the Romans, who returned volleys of arrows and long lances, killing many.

The legionaries next made their way onto the rebel vessels, hacking their victims to pieces, severing heads or hands which desperately clung to the sides of the boats. Those who managed to escape the carnage were butchered as soon as they reached land, so that the shore became littered with over six thousand seven hundred corpses, intermingled with the broken remains of the rebel fleet. Josephus describes a "terrible stench" that polluted the entire district, noting that "the lake was red with blood." Once again the book of Revelation employs language that seems to hauntingly depict these events, as if in warning to the Nazarenes in the Galilee and Judea:

> And the second angel sounded, and as it were a great mountain burning with fire was cast into the sea. And the third part of the sea became blood. And the third part of the creatures in the sea, those having souls, died; and the third part of the ships was destroyed. (Revelation 8:8-9)

Soon thereafter, Vespasian had the survivors of this melancholy engagement rounded up in the stadium at Tiberias, where 1,200 of the aged and infirm faced a bone-chilling edict. Dare we imagine the victorious general barking orders to his minions. "Execute them!" Six thousand of the strongest and healthiest would be among countless Jewish captives to find themselves in the capital of the empire to die as gladiators for the pleasure of the bloodthirsty crowds. But even this was not enough retribution. Vespasian decided to sell another 30,400 as slaves, most of whom would be worked to death.

The last bastion of resistance in the north of the country was a rocky precipice that rose in the high country to the east of the Sea of Galilee. Shaped like the hump of a great camel, *gamal* in Hebrew, it was known as Gamla. An almost impregnable fortress, its Jewish defenders fought heroically against the advancing Romans. Many of Vespasian's soldiers took refuge on the roofs of the houses that lined the steep slopes of the hump-like rocky outcropping. The houses, however, could not bear the weight of so many heavily armored troops and literally collapsed underneath them, cascading down the hillside and burying great numbers in the mass of rubble. The Romans, however, were like an army of ants who, in spite of staggering losses, simply continued their advance, undaunted and unstoppable.

Making matters worse, a fierce storm rose without warning, blowing directly in the faces of the Jewish defenders. As if the heavens were fighting on Vespasian's side, the winds carried the Roman arrows with great force but slowed down those of their opponents. The legionaries quickly scaled the "camel's back," surrounding and slaughtering over 4,000 inhabitants, men, women and children, even flinging infants down the slopes to their doom. As at Yodfat, the rebels resorted to suicide, a tactic that had always been unthinkable in Jewish eyes. As if possessed by some maniacal power mixed with misguided messianism that propelled them to abandon all reason, they flung themselves in large numbers – some 5,000 – from the escarpments to the valleys below. Josephus curtly reports: "Thus Gamla fell."

Dynasty – The Torch Is Passed

At some point during this distressed and fragmented period, the Nazarenes managed to designate a new leader, who would replace the fallen Yaakov. It would be a pivotal moment in the development of Yeshua's dynasty, for it would mark the passing of the spiritual torch, from one member of the Heirs to another. The New Testament, not surprisingly, says nothing of this, since it prefers to keep its focus on Shaul. Consequently, it is by no means easy to affix a date to this transition of power. Some theorize that it came early after Yaakov's death, while others believe that there was a considerable delay due to the outbreak of the great revolt and perhaps lasting through it. Given the silence in our ancient sources, one guess is as good as another.

We do, however, have testimony from outside the New Testament that the disciple known as Shimon (Simeon/ Simon) son of Cleophas/ Clophas took the helm of the movement at this critical juncture. While he is often depicted as Yeshua's cousin, we may speculate that he was in fact another of his physical brothers. Not to be confused with that other Shimon, also called Petros (Peter), the "Rock," he may have been hoary-haired and well advanced in years by the seventh decade of the Common Era. We might ask: Under Shimon did the character of the movement change? Did it become less observant of Jewish law, less "Hasidic"?

We need only look to the Hasidic dynasties that thrived for centuries in Europe to realize that the spirit of one "rebbe" continued to guide and energize succeeding generations in a dynastic tradition from rebbe to rebbe. As if to confirm this authority, healing gifts were also manifested, from generation to generation, so that all would know that the Shekhinah, the Divine Presence, had placed its seal on the dynastic line. The rebbes of Europe also occasionally received prophetic warning of trouble on the way, of anti-Semitic violence that threatened property and life. They sometimes courageously led their flocks of disciples to new locations, other cities and if need be other countries, in order to preserve their lives. The new Nazarene leader, Shimon, would have inherited unquestioned authority and also supreme responsibility for the welfare of the beleaguered sect, nestled, as they were, in the midst of the raging storm.

Josephus relates that at some point during the revolt, at the feast of Pentecost, the priests ceremonially crossed the threshold of the Temple's inner sanctuary only to hear a cacophonous sound, followed by a great multitude of haunting voices that declared in unison, "We are leaving this place; we are leaving this place!" Could this supernatural phenomenon, recorded by the ancient Jewish historian, represent written record of what we can otherwise only guess at, via the book of Revelation and the records of the early Church Fathers? Could it be cryptically telling us of the decision of Shimon and the entire Nazarene community (along with whoever else sensed that the time was right) to abandon the city of Jerusalem and flee to safer territory? The identity of these voices is never confirmed by Josephus, but the numbers of the Nazerene community must have been substantial by this point, and their departure must surely have been felt. The population of the city, which had become increasingly radicalized during the course of the revolt, may well have labeled them traitors, defectors from the cause of freedom just as Josephus had been. But as Yeshua himself once said, "Wisdom is vindicated by her children" (Luke 7:35).

Perhaps the time had finally come when Shimon and his flock recognized the portents, which, like the changing of the seasons, beckoned them to flee. Had not Yeshua delivered a chilling imperative that warned of the difficult times ahead and admonished his followers to flee? There is a particularly haunting passage from the Gospels, that most have taken to refer to the "end of days" but that in fact seems to presage the time of trouble in which the nation was now engulfed:

> And immediately after the tribulation of those days, the sun shall be darkened and the moon shall not give her light, and the stars shall fall from the heaven, and the powers of the heavens shall be shaken... Now learn a parable of the fig tree. When its branch is still tender and puts out leaves, you know that summer is near. So you, likewise, when you see all these things, shall know that it is near, at the doors. Truly I say to you, this generation shall not pass until all these things are fulfilled. (Matthew 24:29, 32-34)

Those who are familiar with the history of this period may recognize in the imagery of the falling stars a coded reference to the Jewish aristocracy and priesthood of Jerusalem, who were dislodged from their dominant positions and supplanted by a core of radical Zealots. Since the ruling class represented divine authority, it was indeed as if the powers of heaven were shaken. Nevertheless, modern scholarship tends to reject the idea that the Yeshua of history ever uttered such words, because they are such an accurate portrayal of the tragedy of the Great Revolt. How could anyone have foreseen these things decades before the fact? they reason. The entire passage must have been added by later editors of the text. But do we really have to be so dismissive of the prophetic oracle? Why not look at such verses as reflective of a deep tradition among the Nazarenes that bid them to exit from the eye of the storm and that saved them from certain extinction? It is a conclusion bolstered by yet another passage from the book of Revelation, commonly taken as an eschatological reference to the end time but that in fact dovetails with the Gospel oracle:

> And when He had opened the sixth seal, I looked, and behold, there was a great earthquake. And the sun became black as sackcloth of hair, and the moon became like blood. And the stars of heaven fell to the earth, even as a fig tree casts her untimely figs when she is shaken by a mighty wind. And the heaven departed like a scroll when it is rolled together. (Revelation 6:12-14)

Whoever wrote this had to have been familiar with the imagery of the High Holy Days, especially *Yom Kippur* (the Day of Atonement), when, according to Jewish tradition, a great scroll in heaven containing the names of those recorded in the "Book of Life" is closed, determining the fate of all humanity for the coming year — who will live and who will die. If Yohanan (John) the Beloved, Yohanan the Revelator, were in fact from a Jerusalemite priestly family, this would explain much about the literary flavor of the New Testament apocalypse. And if the intended readers of these oracles were in fact the Jerusalemite community of Nazarenes under the leadership of Shimon, we can imagine the impact of a particularly strident directive found elsewhere in the book:

> And he cried mightily with a strong voice, saying, Babylon the great has fallen, has fallen! And it has become the dwelling-place of demons... And the kings of the earth have committed fornication with her. (Revelation 18:2-3)

Another ancient Jewish book not included in the biblical canon, known as the Sibylline Oracles, paints the picture with similar images, depicting the idolatrous empire of Babylon as Rome:

> And from heaven a great star shall fall on the dread ocean and burn up the deep sea, with Babylon itself and the land of Italy, that has caused many of the Hebrews to perish, holy and faithful, and the people of truth.... Woe to thee, thou city of the Latin land, all unclean, thou maenad circled with vipers, thou shalt sit a widow on thy hills... Thou saidst, "I am alone, and none shall despoil me." Yet now shall God who lives forever destroy both thee and thine.... Abide thou alone, thou lawless city, wrapt in burning fire. (Sibylline Oracles IV: 159-179)

We must, however, wonder whether the image of Babylon has been transposed to Jerusalem, which, under the radical Zealots has become just as corrupt and unclean as the city on the Tiber.[1] If so, the following verse from the New Testament apocalypse contains the most chilling admonition of all:

> And I heard another voice from Heaven, saying, Come out of her, My people, that you may not be partakers of her sins, and that you may not receive of her plagues. (Revelation 18:4)

And again we ask, is this about Rome, or did the intended recipients of this oracle not understand it as a directive to come out of Jerusalem? Is this not one more link in a well established textual tradition that testifies to the flight of the Nazarenes at this critical juncture? And while much modern scholarship scoffs at the idea of prophetic oracles, we still have to come to grips with certain passages such as the following, from the second century apocryphal text known as Pseudo-Clementines:

> Every one who, believing in this Prophet who had been foretold
> by Moses, is baptized in his name, shall be kept unhurt from the
> destruction of war which impends… (Recognitions 1:39:3)

Were such words fabricated long after the events of those days, prophesying, as it were, backwards, or are they recollections of genuine traditions of warning that motivated the Nazarenes to leave the land of Israel entirely if revolt should break out?

The Beast is Dead, Long Live the Beast

However these words of warning came to be recorded, there is no mistaking the fact that by 68 - 69 CE, Jerusalem was indeed surrounded by armies. All of the Galilee had been overrun by marauding Roman forces, and the commanding general of the legions, Vespasian, had hastily returned to Rome in the wake of Nero's demise. The senate, as if in fulfillment of the "oracle" of Josephus, finally tired of the emperor's mad antics and formally declared him a public enemy. Before the Praetorian Guard could capture him, he chose suicide.

Rome immediately descended into chaos, as three more emperors came forward, Galba, Otho and Vitellius, each in turn to meet a quick demise. Total anarchy was averted only when Vespasian arrived, establishing order and ushering in the Flavian dynasty, the first not directly descended from Julius Caesar. It was the name Josephus would subsequently take as his own. The book of Revelation weighs in on this as well:

> The beast that you saw was, and is not, and is about to ascend out
> of the abyss and go into perdition. (Revelation 17:8)

The Apocalypse in coded fashion records not only Nero's death, but the struggle for the throne that ensued after his suicide:

> The seven heads are seven mountains, on which the woman sits. And there are seven kings; five have fallen, and one is, and the other has not yet come. And when he comes, he must continue a short time. And the beast that was, and is not, even he is the eighth, and is of the seven, and goes into perdition. (Revelation 17:9-11)

Again we find mention of Rome's seven hills, along with a mysterious woman. Of course the woman symbolizes Rome, but she is also a sort of "anti-Mary (Miriam)" image, deliberately selected by the author to be a perversion of holy matriarchy. The five fallen kings correspond with Julius Caesar through Claudius. The king who "now is" can only represent Nero. Being the sixth emperor, this is one more clue to his identity as "666." The one who "has not yet come" refers to Galba, who was designated by the senate as Nero's replacement. But he was destined to rule only for "a short time," being assassinated in 69 CE. The eighth beast refers to Otho, who replaced Galba, only to commit suicide when Germany rose in revolt and selected a general of its own as ruler.

Another detail of the Revelation passage is of great interest:

> The beast that you saw was, and is not, and is about to ascend out of the abyss and go into perdition. And those dwelling on the earth will marvel — those whose names were not written in the Book of Life — when they behold the beast that was, and is not, and yet is. (Revelation 17:8)

The hidden key to understanding this passage has to do with an aspect of traditional Jewish liturgy, as practiced to this day in synagogues. At the conclusion of every service, the congregants extol the Eternal, "...who was, who is, and who is to come, in glory." As with the so-called "mark of the Beast" – a perversion of the practice of wearing phylacteries (wrapped on the left arm, close to the heart) – this oracle regarding Nero represents a similar corruption of the heart of Jewish liturgy. Whereas Israel's deity "was, and is, and is to come," Nero, the "anti-God" / "anti-Christ," in committing suicide, "was, and is not, and yet is." The Dead Sea Scrolls hint at the same perversion of the Jewish credo, by a dastardly enemy known only as the *Kittim*:

> They lean on that which is not and shall not be. To the God of Israel belongs all that is and shall be. (*War Scroll*, col. XVII)

But how could Nero, whose ignominious demise effectively ended the dynasty of the Caesars, somehow come again? History tells us that the rumor had spread in Rome that Nero had not in fact committed suicide, but had instead escaped, with the intent to return to power some day. There is yet another way that Nero would come again, for his reign was about to be "reincarnated" in the form of the new Flavian dynasty. To be sure, with Nero's death and the ensuing power struggle, the entire fabric that was imperial Rome might have come to an end, the whole empire being plunged into civil war and rent asunder. But as Josephus had predicted, that was not to happen. Elsewhere the book of Revelation relates:

> And I saw one of its heads as having been slain to death, and its deadly wound was healed. (Revelation 13:3)

Josephus recounts that Vespasian's own troops declared him emperor and beseeched him to rescue the beleaguered empire. Thus, the pragmatic general returned to the city on the Tiber, leaving his son Titus to finish off the Judean rebels. This Titus did with all due haste. Little did anyone know that the worst of the carnage still lay ahead.

The Great Tribulation

Meanwhile, the moment of decision had come in Jerusalem, especially as word reached them that all of the Galilee lay in ruins. The small community of pietists known as the Essenes, nestled on the northwest shore of the Dead Sea, had been overrun with some survivors being tortured to death (while happily rendering up their souls to God) and others apparently fleeing south to the rocky fortress of Masada, which continued to defy the Roman legions. As the forces of Titus turned toward the capital of the nation, the Nazarenes may well have been inspired by another oracle that had either been directly uttered by Yeshua or placed in his mouth by subsequent editors. We find it in two of the Gospels:

> And when you see Jerusalem compassed with armies, then know that its destruction has come. And let those in Judea flee to the mountains. And those in its midst, let them go out. And those in the open spaces, let them not go into her. For these are the days of vengeance, that all things which are written may be fulfilled. (Luke 21:20-22)

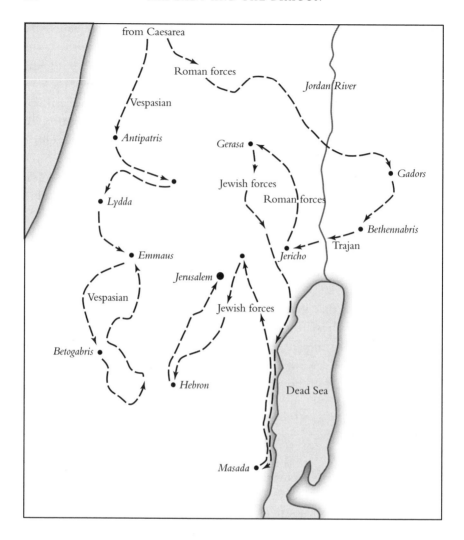

But pray that your flight is not in the winter, nor on the sabbath day; for then shall be great tribulation... (Matthew 24:20-21)

For the next twenty centuries there would be endless speculation about the "Great Tribulation" as referring to the "last days" of human history, mostly among those whose knowledge of the first century is lacking. But for those caught up in the rush of events surrounding the Great Revolt, there was no doubt that the "last days" had already arrived with a vengeance. Early rabbinic sources mention the concept of the "pangs of the Messiah" (*hevlei mashiach*), a time of trouble that will consume the world like the travail of birth prior to the dawn of universal peace when the lion lies down with the lamb.

Many modern Hasidic Jews expect the return of the deceased rebbe, Menachem Mendel Schneerson, at the end of this age. For Shimon and the Heirs there must have been a general anticipation of the supernatural reappearance of Yeshua, a nonviolent form of messianism just as fervent as the militant messianism of the Zealots, which had by now turned into a frenzied mania.[2] Josephus wrote that civil strife was rampant in the holy city and that one faction fought against another, as though a mad beast were devouring its own flesh. Another oracle from Matthew's Gospel captures these turbulent events:

> And many false prophets will rise and deceive many. And because iniquity shall abound, the love of many will become cold. (Matthew 24:11-12)

Yet, for the *ma'aminim* the blows of history were not random. This was all part of the divine order, and it called for their precipitous withdrawal from the city and from the land of Israel itself. They decided to flee eastward, through the wilderness of Judea, across the Jordan River, and on to an immense plateau known from ancient times as the Mountains of Moab.[3]

Transjordan had long been a place of refuge for those who, for whatever reason, found it necessary to find a safe haven. It was the location of Petra, a vast city carved into the rock face of the limestone cliffs. By now, this "exodus" was the only hope of salvation for the Nazarenes, who would otherwise be trapped in Jerusalem during the inevitable siege that lay ahead. There was no time to spare, as in the days of the first "exodus" out of Egypt. The only difference was that this journey took them away from the Promised Land, not toward it.

Josephus recounts that during this time, a number of fugitives, who had fled before the advancing Romans, spread alarm throughout the countryside by declaring that Caesar's legions were on the march. A great multitude immediately rushed to Jericho, where they hoped to find refuge. We recall the flight of Yaakov and the first *ma'aminim* after the stoning of Stephanos and subsequent riot on the Temple Mount. This time, however, the refugees were pursued by their Roman adversaries, whereupon they attempted to ford the Jordan River and make their way to safety.

Crossing the Jordan can be a risky proposition. For much of the year, the river is shallow, little more than a stream, and fairly easy to traverse.

But during the rainy season from October through April, sudden downpours can turn the river into a raging, uncontrollable torrent. This was the meaning of the oracle, "Pray that your flight is not in the winter..." For these woebegone fugitives, streaming to the river from the storied city of Jericho, there would be no redemption. The Roman cavalry relentlessly pursued them, driving a vast horde of hapless humanity into the cascading watercourse. In great numbers they were carried off by the stream and drowned, one more tragedy in an episodic series of calamities to befall the seed of Abraham.

We can only imagine the anxiety and sheer terror that must have befallen the Nazarene community as they turned themselves into one more group of fugitives departing the city, most likely from the Essene Gate, and trudging in the direction of Jericho and the same river that would either give them safe passage or sweep them all away. Indeed, the previous exodus of the wounded Yaakov and his disciples from Jerusalem to the city of palms prefigured this even greater migration, so that Shimon's departure was not without precedent. For Yaakov, however, it had only been a matter of convalescence while for the Nazarenes under Shimon this was to be a permanent relocation from which there would be no return.

It must have been an incredible sight, as this sizable sect, several thousand strong, abandoned their homes and marched en masse away from the city at this most critical time. What would have been the response of the rest of the city's population, maddened as it was by the promises of the Zealots? If they called Josephus a traitor and a defector, what would they have called these Nazarenes, who had no stomach for battle and who appeared to be interested only in saving their own skins? Charged by their compatriots with both treason and cowardice, it is surprising that they were not massacred by their fellow Jerusalemites as they departed. Fate, however, seems to have befriended them.

There was, moreover, another group of pacifists in the city who had traditionally been allied with the Nazarenes – the Pharisees. They had chosen to remain in the holy city, at least for the time being, but they must have been inspired by the sight of this exodus, and at least one of their leaders would in his own way follow suit. His name was Yohanan ben Zakkai, and he would at a later time feign death, instructing his disciples to carry him out of the city in a coffin, whereupon he leaped out and secured safe passage to a city near the coast (Yavne). There he would establish a new "center" for Pharisaic Judaism, in the wake of the total destruction of Jerusalem.

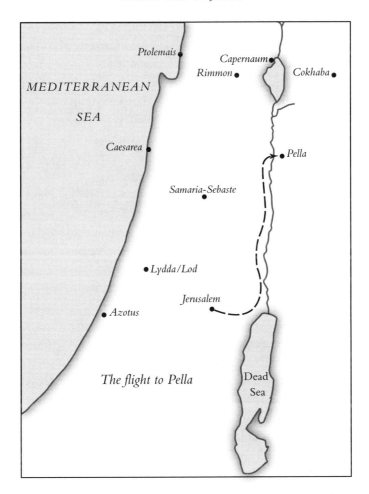

The flight to Pella

The Bones of Yaakov

The *ma'aminim* may well have exited via the Essene Gate, into the Hinnom and Kidron Valleys. The road down to Jericho would have been familiar to them, but they may have avoided it in favor of a more secluded route down through the chalky hills. After all, so many things could have gone wrong. They might have been attacked by roaming bands of Zealots, who still patrolled the region and who would have considered them deserters. They might have encountered the Romans, who were mustering their forces for the final assault on the Jewish capital. Yet, as if by some miracle, they traversed this territory unmolested. Pietists of Hasidic orientation were of course no strangers to miracles, which they believed were in evidence in their daily lives. Descending through the twists and turns of the desert wadis, they would have come to the point where the trail branches off toward Jericho and points north in one direction, and toward what was left of the little community of the Essenes, Masada and points south in the other. Shimon and the Nazarenes took the northern route, but they did not stop at Jericho, as Yaakov had three decades before, nor did they rush headlong toward the River Jordan like the hapless fugitives being pursued by the Romans. They followed the Jordan Valley, keeping the river to their right and passing through the region of Samaria.

The landscape is barren and lifeless and the air hangs heavy, being nearly 1,200 feet below sea level, the lowest spot on earth. This road through hell would have been a journey of several days for these pilgrims, who had to worry about sufficient provisions and finding shelter for sleep, especially for their little ones. Fortunately, the river provided a source of fresh water even in the most unforgiving desert. We have no documents to detail the specifics of their journey, but multiple sources agree on their destination, including the early church historians and a mysterious text found at Nag Hammadi, known as the First Apocalypse of James.

This latter document, part of a huge cache of some fifty-two texts stumbled upon by an Arab peasant in the mid-twentieth century, reflects some of the earliest traditions of the Nazarene movement, including the fact that its titular head was not Shaul (Paul) but Yaakov (James). It also declares that Yaakov subsequently fled to Transjordan, to Pella.[4] While historians like to see this source as authentically historical, the obvious problem with it is that Yaakov (James) was long dead by the time the revolt broke out and the great exodus transpired. One possible way to reconcile the inconsistency is to suggest that Yaakov's younger brother Shimon dutifully carried his bones in an ossuary all the way to Pella. Such an idea is not without precedent, since the book of Genesis tells us that the great patriarch Joseph, who brought his people down to Egypt in ancient times, asked that his bones be carried back to the Promised Land by a later generation. Of course if the now-famous "James ossuary" turns out to be authentic, then the idea that his bones were transported to Transjordan may be fatally flawed. One possible scenario, however, is that the bones were taken to Pella, leaving the bulky limestone box behind. It is one more mystery among many.

In any case, when the pilgrims had traveled halfway through the length of Samaria, they decided to make an eastward turn, to cross the treacherous waters of the Jordan. This was their "moment of truth." Would the Hasidic faith that had sustained them thus far also bring them safely across their own version of the "Red Sea"? Or would holy pilgrimage turn to unholy disaster? In some of the most powerful imagery to find its way into the New

Testament canon, the book of Revelation cryptically but vividly depicts the way it transpired:

> And there appeared a great sign in the heavens, a woman clothed with the sun, and the moon was under her feet, and a crown of twelve stars on her head, and having a babe in womb, she cries, being in travail, having been distressed to bear. (Revelation 12:1-2)

The woman is a symbol of the *ma'aminim* themselves, the faithful Israel, who would "give birth" to the Messiah. But she also brings to mind the hallowed matriarch of the Nazarene movement, Miriam, of whom we have heard nothing since the crucifixion of Yeshua and reports of his resurrection. It is one more historical gap in the canonical New Testament. Yet her memory was deeply cherished by the Heirs. The fact that she is again depicted in this vision, surrounded by celestial symbols, including twelve stars, representing both the original apostles and the tribes of Israel, suggests her continuing influence among the *ma'aminim*. Moreover, the child she carries represents not only the infant Jesus, but the dynasty who came forth from her womb – the *Desposyni*. Her pain and anguish in childbirth reminds us of the story of how King Herod ordered the slaughter of the innocents in Bethlehem at the time of Yeshua's birth in an attempt to snuff out anyone who might challenge his throne. But it also gives us pause to consider the "great tribulation" at the time of the anti-Roman revolt, which might have extinguished all of Miriam's progeny had they remained in Jerusalem.

The Dead Sea Psalms Scroll contains hauntingly similar imagery that seems to depict a messianic figure coming forth from anguished childbirth, some kind of horrible tribulation that would convulse the earth:

> "...like a woman in travail with her first-born child, upon whose belly pangs have come and grievous pains, filling with anguish her child-bearing crucible. For the children have come to the throes of Death, and she labors in her pains who bears a man. For amid the throes of Death she shall bring forth a man-child, and amid the pains of Hell there shall spring from her child-bearing crucible a Marvelous Mighty Counselor; and a man shall be delivered from out of the throes. When he is conceived all wombs shall quicken, and the time of their delivery shall be in grievous pains; they shall be appalled who are with child. And

when he is brought forth every pang shall come upon the child-
bearing crucible." (*Psalms Scroll*, col. III)

Could it be that such poetic imagery of messianic deliverance out of "the
throes of death" had circulated beyond the Dead Sea Sect (the Essenes)
and given hope to the radical Zealots who were driving revolt? Could it,
in a different way, have inspired the Nazarenes, who sought deliverance,
not by fighting, but by fleeing? Some researchers have suggested that the
Dead Sea Sect and the Nazarene movement under Yaakov (James) and the
Heirs were one and the same, an unlikely conclusion given the striking
differences between the Scrolls with their militant apocalypticism and the
Hasidic bent of Yeshua and the Heirs. But we dare not ignore the powerful message that tribulation is in the divine economy equivalent to "birth
pangs" ushering in a messianic child of promise. For the Nazarenes this
"child" was a dynasty, consisting of the Heirs themselves.

The prophetic oracle next envisions the menacing enemy of the woman and the child:

> And another sign was seen in the heavens. And behold a great
> red dragon, having seven heads and ten horns and seven crowns
> on his heads! And his tail drew the third part of the stars of
> heaven, and cast them onto the earth. And the dragon stood
> before the woman being about to bear, so that when she bears
> he might devour her child. And she bore a son, a male, who
> is going to rule all nations with a rod of iron. And her child
> was caught up to God and to His throne. And the woman fled
> into the wilderness, where she had a place prepared by God...
> (Revelation 12:3-7)

The seven-headed dragon is of course Rome, with its "seven Caesars,"
which had an alliance with the ten Parthian kings of the east. There was
also a legend that the deceased emperor Nero would be revived and come
back to power in the company of ten Parthian satraps. The number ten
also reminds us of the Tenth Legion that was to be permanently stationed
in the land of Israel in the aftermath of the conflict.

The stars again represent the Jewish aristocracy, who were targeted for
destruction. Historically, the Romans in their advance on Jerusalem deliberately tried to apprehend those of Davidic descent, lest another Jewish
king attempt to rise to power. Assuming that Yeshua's family was, as the

Gospels recount, from the house of David, then all of the *Desposyni* would have been prime targets for execution.

The "man-child," reminiscent of both the infant Yeshua and his "Heirs," would thus be devoured by the dragon. An ancient Jewish legend told of the Messiah being spirited away immediately after birth, and another legend about Yohanan (John) the Baptist relates that his mother, being convinced that he was to be the Anointed One, escaped to a mountain that opened up to shelter them when Herod's soldiers were slaughtering Bethlehem's babies.

This male child who will rule the nations certainly reminds us of Yeshua, whose ascent to the divine throne in the heavens must have been firmly believed by the Heirs, a belief that was a driving force behind their movement and their dynasty. Fortunately for them, the oracle relates that the woman managed to escape into the Judean Desert and beyond, heading toward Pella where she would be protected and nourished. But she was not to be left unmolested.

The Red Dragon

The oracle goes on to describe war in heaven, not in the elaborate imagery of Milton, but to declare that the malevolent, anti-God power of the spiritual realm had now been cast down to earth. For the ancients there was a deep-seated belief that what happens on earth is a reflection of a higher reality, mirroring events that take place in the highest heavens. Consequently, when "Israel below" teetered on the brink of annihilation, there must, they believed, be some great upheaval going on in the spiritual world. In what may have amounted to a desperate attempt to make sense of the chaos going on around them, the oracle relates:

> And when the dragon saw that he was cast to the earth, he persecuted the woman who bore the man child. And two wings of a great eagle were given to the woman, so that she might fly into the wilderness, into her place, where she is nourished for a time and times and half a time, from the serpent's face. And the serpent cast out of his mouth water like a flood after the woman, so that he might cause her to be carried away by the river. (Revelation 12:13-15)

While the language here is visionary, it reflects a strong tradition, grounded in history, that the dynasty of Yeshua did in fact flee to the Jordan

River. An ancient parable speaks of a great dragon dwelling in the Jordan River, who spews water out of his mouth during the winter months, causing the river to swell torrentially, but who closes his mouth during the dry season, whereupon the river shrinks and shrivels. The community of Nazarenes were, in a real sense, at the mercy of nature, especially the power of water. Would the Jordan be kind or vindictive, a mighty torrent or a gentle stream? The ma'aminim could do little more than pray and prepare for rain.

The oracle of Revelation mystically conveys the miraculous "help" given by the elements to the beleaguered sect:

> And the earth helped the woman. And the earth opened its mouth and swallowed up the river, which the dragon cast out of his mouth. (Revelation 12:16)

For whatever reason, perhaps because of a return of the drought conditions of the year 67, the River Jordan was low enough to ford, and the ma'aminim, presumably with Shimon at their helm, made their way across with haste and determination. We are reminded of the false prophet Theudas who claimed to have the power to dry up the Jordan, only to be beheaded on orders from the procurator Fadus. But such ignominy would not befall these pilgrims. They must have felt like Joshua of old, who, according to the Torah, crossed the Jordan River on dry land while the waters piled up as though dammed. As they first set foot on the eastern bank of the river, they must have breathed a collective sigh of relief. The arid calm of this region of Transjordan, known as Gilead ("the hill of witness"), must have seemed almost Edenic after suffering the scourge of war.

Centuries before, the prophet Jeremiah had plaintively queried, "Is there no balm in Gilead?" Indeed, Shimon and his flock had found Gilead's sweet emollient. They had not, however, reached their final destination. They would continue to trek a short distance to the east, though still in the Jordan Valley, to a small city called Pella, a site with a long history that had been inhabited without interruption since the Neolithic age and that was mentioned in Egyptian inscriptions going back to the nineteenth century BCE. At this time, however, the city was one of the ten centers of Greco-Roman culture known collectively as the Decapolis. The Decapolis contained a predominantly non-Jewish population but had nonetheless been visited by the piously observant Yeshua during his travels. We are not told whether Yeshua ever visited Pella per se, but his one-time presence in this area may have been a source of inspiration for the Nazarenes, who would henceforth call Pella their home. It must have been a strange sight for Pella's inhabitants to behold a large group of Jewish pilgrims descending upon the city to take up permanent residence. We should remember, however, that wars naturally create refugees, and that Pella was probably not the only city of Transjordan that suddenly found itself inundated by people fleeing the carnage on the other side of the river.

It is also possible that this community of *ma'aminim* was augmented in those days by other groups of Nazarenes and/or Ebionites, who had been living in other parts of the land of Israel, especially the Galilee.[5] We have already seen that the "Jesus movement" had for some time been growing exponentially across ancient Israel and that various expressions of it were alive and well and very much a part of the character and fabric of the Judaism of those times. The book of Revelation hints that even after the Nazarenes abandoned Jerusalem, other communities of *ma'aminim* still found themselves imperiled:

> And the dragon was enraged over the woman, and went to make war with the rest of her seed... (Revelation 12:17)

Might the rest of the seed of the "Jesus movement" all have ended up in this single city of the Decapolis? We should point out that the site of Pella, as uncovered in archaeological excavations, is ample to support a refugee population, with a sufficient water supply provided by a natural spring. It is also possible, as one scholar suggested, that the flood of pilgrims might have occupied caves in the vicinity if Pella alone could not accommodate them.[6] It is nonetheless uncannily popular in the world of scholarship to cast doubt on long-held traditions of the past, and the account of the flight to Pella is no exception. Archaeologists are quick to point out that the location of this ancient settlement has in the past decades been well-excavated and that nary a shred of evidence has surfaced in the archaeological record of any presence of "Judeo-Christians" in this city. But does the lack of solid archaeology genuinely disprove the presence of the sect in this location? Are traditional Christian paraphernalia such as crosses and symbols of "the fish" (*Ixthus*) being sought in the rubble of Pella? Perhaps the archaeologists simply don't know what they are looking for. Again, the absence of evidence is not evidence of absence.

The Puzzle of Pella

There are objections to the account of this great migration that cannot be ignored. History tells us that prior to the great revolt, after the Jews of Caesarea had been slaughtered by its gentile inhabitants, the city of Pella was sacked by other Jews in wild revenge, which in turn culminated in the butchery of many of its non-Jewish citizens. Is it conceivable that Jewish *ma'aminim* would have gone to a city where the gentile survivors would themselves have been bent on revenge? But as valid as these objections are, it is still important to recognize that war changes everything, and no one dare make glib presumptions about how people in the midst of a cataclysmic upheaval of untold proportions (such as the gentiles of Pella) would have reacted or should have behaved, especially given the fact that a pious Hasidic group, such as the *ma'aminim* likely were, shared nothing in common with the murderous Zealots aside from ethnicity. The citizens of Pella had to have known this, and were hardly in a mood for more bloodshed.

Furthermore, while the stately Hellenistic columns that rise from the archaeological site shed no light on the possible presence of Nazarenes/ Ebionites in those fateful days, there are multiple ancient sources outside of the book of Revelation that do. The Church historian Eusebius wrote:

> But the people of the church in Jerusalem had been commanded by a revelation, vouchsafed to approved men there before the war, to leave the city and to dwell in a certain town of Perea called Pella. (History of the Church 3:5:3)

> The whole body, however, of the church at Jerusalem, having been commanded by a divine revelation, given to men of approved piety there before the war, removed from the city, and dwelt at a certain town beyond the Jordan, called Pella. (Eusebius, 3:5)

Elsewhere, Eusebius records another important detail:

> After all those who believed in Christ had generally come to live in Perea, in a city called Pella of the Decapolis of which it is written in the Gospel and which is situated in the neighborhood of the region of Batanaea and Basanitis ... Ebion's preaching originated here after they had moved to this place and had lived there. (*Panarion* 30:2)

Who was this Ebion? According to the Church Father Irenaeus, he was the founder of the sect known as Ebionites (in Hebrew *evionim*, the "poor ones"), who, as we have seen, were in serious conflict with Shaul but who held Yaakov in high esteem. It may well be that there never was a historical character named Ebion, but that he was invented in order to account for the existence of the Ebionite sect. Some have suggested that Pella was a kind of "magnet" for the *ma'aminim*, who came from the Galilee as well as Judea and consisted of various groups, from Nazarenes to Ebionites, who only there delineated their differences and crystallized their identities.[7]

Additional testimony about Pella and another city called Chochabe is offered by the fourth century Church historian, Epiphanius:

> The Nazoraean sect exists in Beroea near Coele Syria, in the Decapolis near the region of Pella, and in Bashan in the place called Cocaba, which in Hebrew is called Chochabe. That is where the sect began, when all the disciples were living in Pella after they moved from Jerusalem, since Christ told them to leave Jerusalem and withdraw because it was about to be besieged. For this reason they settled in Peraea and there, as I said, they lived. This is where the Nazoraean sect began. (Panarion 29:7:7-8)

> For when the city was about to be captured and sacked by the Romans, all the disciples were warned beforehand by an angel to remove from the city, doomed as it was to utter destruction. On migrating from it they settled at Pella, the town already indicated, across the Jordan. It is said to belong to Decapolis. (On Weights and Measures 15)

> Their sect began after the capture of Jerusalem. For when all those who believed in Christ settled at that time for the most part in Peraea, in a city called Pella belonging to the Decapolis mentioned in the gospel, which is next to Batanaea and the land of Bashan, then they moved there and stayed. (Panarion 30:2:7)[8]

The long-silent ruins of Pella have emerged from obscurity in recent decades, but while excavations have been ongoing for many seasons, they have yet to reveal their secrets. Perhaps they will someday yield conclusive evidence of the presence of the Nazarene and/or Ebionite movements. Even if the remnants of this ancient site remain eternally elusive, and even if the spade of the archaeologists never turns over a scintilla of evidence to establish the presence of the Heirs of Yeshua in this region, it is nonetheless difficult to ignore the multiple textual traditions that testify to the sect's pilgrimage from Jerusalem and the jaws of death, across the Jordan's blue torrent to the vast refuge of the east.[9]

The world of archaeology is in constant flux, and one never knows what will surface next. In June, 2008, new evidence came to light from a site in Jordan east of Pella known as Rihab, where the slumbering remains of a first century Judeo-Christian place of worship unexpectedly surfaced. An ancient grotto beneath the church of St. Georgeous (itself considered the oldest "proper" church in the world) appears to date to the period between 33 and 70 CE. According to a mosaic inscription found in the floor of the church, it was most likely the sanctuary of a group of seventy Nazarene refugees from the besieged city of Jerusalem. The place was dedicated to the "seventy beloved by God and the Divine" and was used for the practice of certain rituals that predate even the ancient church. Central to the shrine was a circular area used for worship, surrounded by stone seats with living quarters adjacent. A tunnel led down to a cistern that supplied water to the inhabitants. Pottery items and a nearby cemetery confirm that the descendants of this lost branch of the Jesus movement continued in this region through the seventh century. These new findings may not be a "smoking gun" that "sets in stone" the migration of the Nazarenes to Transjordan, but they certainly help establish it as something more than clever folklore. Written records, though often compelling, are always subject to dispute; but when the stones speak from long ago, even the knees of skeptics are inclined to bow.[10]

Even if it can never be established that Pella was the final destination of these refugees, it is clear that the Nazarenes of those days did not remain in beleaguered Jerusalem. The horrors to which the great City of David succumbed are beyond the power of words to express. By the time it was over the majestic Temple that adorned Jerusalem's holiest hill was reduced to a smoking ruin and the city itself was leveled to its foundations. The toll in human life was incalculable. It has been noted that of all the factions and sectarian movements competing for adherents during the Second Jewish Commonwealth, only two survived the Great Revolt of 66 - 70 CE, the Pharisees and the Nazarenes (Judeo-Christians). But had the ma'aminim not fled the city when they did, it is a good bet that only one sect would have survived, and it would not have been them. As it turned out, however, another generation of Desposyni would continue to thrive and to rule a reorganized "Sanhedrin" for decades into the future.

Notes

1   According to the Dead Sea Sect, all human beings are unclean, and only the elite members of the sect may be cleansed by initial baptism (ritual immersion) coupled with avoidance of all members of the unclean world. See M.H. Gottstein, "Anti-Essene Traits in the Dead Sea Scrolls," *VT* 4.2 (1954): 141-7.

2   It has been argued that militant Davidic messianism (inspired by Ps. Sol. 17) developed in the late Hasmonean period and became a dominant ideology during the subsequent Herodian age. It is also argued, however, that the later Hasidim stood in stark contrast with this militant approach. See K. Atkinson, "On the Herodian Origin of Militant Davidic Messianism at Qumran: New Light from Psalm of Solomon 17," *JBL* 118.3 (1999): 435-60.

3   The exact timing of this exodus is debatable. Some place it in 66-67 CE, after the Jewish victory over Cestius Gallus. Others suggest that it occurred after Vespasian left the region to attend to the volatile situation in Rome, in 68-69 CE. See A. Harnack, *The Mission and Expansion* II, 79 ff.; Arnold A. A. T. Ehrhardt, "The Birth of the Synagogue and R. Akiba," *The Framework of the New Testament Stories* (Manchester: Manchester University Press, 1964), 112. Lietzmann and Jocz hypothesize that the flight may have occurred soon after James' execution, around the year 62 CE, as implied by ancient traditions connected with this event. This, however, appears too early a date for many scholars to accept, especially since Josephus relates that Jewish rebels attacked the city in 66 CE and would likely have killed such a group of "deserters" of the cause. See H. Lietzmann, *A History of the Early Church.* B.L. Woolf, trans. (reprinted; London: Lutterworth Press, 1961), I, 178. See also Jakob Jocz, *The Jewish People and Jesus Christ* (London: SPCK, 1954; reprint, Grand Rapids: Baker, 1980), 165.

Pella was one of the subjects taken up by Hans Joachim Schoeps, who in 1949 produced a seminal volume tracing the origins of Jewish Christianity (Judenchristentum), focusing on the so-called Ebionites. Also known as Nazaraeans and Symmachiani, he stresses the esteem in which they held James (the brother of Jesus) and Peter, while villainizing Paul. He records their presumed flight to the pagan city of Pella in Transjordan, noting that they spoke Aramaic as well as Greek. While they were dominant in much of the Transjordan and eastern Syria, they attempted to be both Jews and Christians, succeeding only in being rejected by both. See H.J. Schoeps, *Theologie und Geschichte des Judenchristentums* (Tuebingen: J.C.B. Mohr, 1949), 188-255.

4   Additional light has been shed on the Nazarenes through an Arabic treatise dating to around 1000 CE, discovered by S. Pines. See "Judaeo-Christian Materials in an Arabic Jewish Treatise," *AAJRP* 35 (1967): 187-217. This text reflects the ideas and traditions of a Judaeo-Christian sect, distinct from the Ebionites and very likely identical with the Nazarenes mentioned by the Church Fathers.

5   It was entirely possible for a moderately sized group to have taken up residence in Pella, without having had much interaction with others, aside from occasional sojourns to the nearby spring. See J. Julius Scott, *Jewish Backgrounds of the New Testament*, (Grand Rapids: Baker, 2000), 366-7. This could easily have been the case if they had resided in caves, as Schumacher theorized. See G. Schumacher, *"Pella" in Abila Pella and Northern 'Ajlun* (London: Palestine Exploration Fund, 1885-90).

6   J.E. Taylor insists that Jewish-Christianity did not consist of a diverse strand of heterodox sects all sprouting from the community in Jerusalem, via Pella, but rather that the sects rose in independent fashion, involving churches which were ethnically Jewish. There was, moreover, no recognizable theology through which all these groups may have been integrated. See J.E. Taylor, "The Phenomenon of Early Jewish-Christianity: Reality or Scholarly Invention?," *VC* 44.4 (1990): 313-34.

7   J. Verheyden, noting the early testimony of Eusebius and Epiphanius that the Christians of Jerusalem fled to Pella during the Great Revolt, points to certain New Testament passages which also reflect this tradition. These include Mk. 13:14-20 and Rev. 12:6,14. Eusebius' remarks further shed light on the theorized Jerusalem origin of the Nazaraeans and the Ebionites, who came to reside in Transjordan. However, Verheyden assumes the flight to Pella to be legendary. He argues that Epiphanius borrowed this account from Eusebius, who (he supposes) added it to a revision of his history. Nonetheless, Verheyden fails to explain why Pella was chosen as the place of escape, and he summarily dismisses the real possibility that Eusebius came across this tradition at a later time and appended it to his work. See J. Verheyden, *De Vlucht van de Christenen naar Pella. Onderzoek van het Getuigenis van Eusebius en Epiphanius* (Brussels: Paleis der Academien, 1988), 28-40.

8   See R.A. Pritz, *Nazarene Jewish Christianity from the End of the New Testament Period until its Disappearance in the Fourth Century* (Jerusalem: Magnes Press, 1992), 48-70. While Pritz's conclusions are based on limited sources, such as fragments of the Gospel of the Nazarenes quoted by Jerome, he does much to demonstrate the authenticity of the early traditions regarding the flight to Pella.

9   Eusebius (c260 CE - c340 CE), in his *History of the Church* (c325 CE), Epiphanius (c315 CE - 403 CE), the Bishop of Salamis in his *Panarion* (c374 CE - 376 CE) and *On Measures and Weights* and the so-called *Pseudo-Clementines* (c 4th century CE) all testify of the sect's flight to Pella.

10   See Rula Samain, "Archaeologists Unearth 'First Church in the World' in Rihab," *The Jordan Times*, June 10, 2008.

7

The "Lost Gospels" of Pella

HE ANCIENT GREEK WORD DIASPORA MEANS "DISPERSION," and the Jewish people were not unaccustomed to such transplantation. The great patriarch Abraham had himself turned nomad, leaving the land of his birth and his father's house to become a stranger in a strange land. His descendants found themselves in Egyptian bondage, to be rescued by their great deliverer Moses and ultimately led into the promised land of Canaan. In the sixth century BCE the people would find themselves in exile again, "by the rivers of Babylon." Their corporate lament is picked up by the psalmist in a poetic dirge: "We hanged our harps upon the willows… For there they that carried us away captive required of us a song… But how shall we sing the Lord's song in a strange land?" (Psalm 137:2-4).

For Shimon (Simeon) and the Nazarene community, the Transjordanian city of Pella must have seemed no less alien than the rivers of Babylon. They must all have been acutely aware of the vast wasteland to which Jerusalem and the whole of Israel had been reduced, the most cruel blow of all being the total destruction of the Temple, the geographic center of Israel's faith. The end of the Great Revolt was for Jerusalem's inhabitants nothing short of a holocaust. The lucky ones fell by the sword while those less fortunate perished from slow starvation. Those who tried to flee the city were apprehended by the Romans and crucified en masse in a huge concentric circle surrounding the city's battered walls.

Yohanan ben Zakkai, the mild-mannered sage of Pharisee persuasion, who, like Yaakov, had determined to flee the besieged capital, hatched his

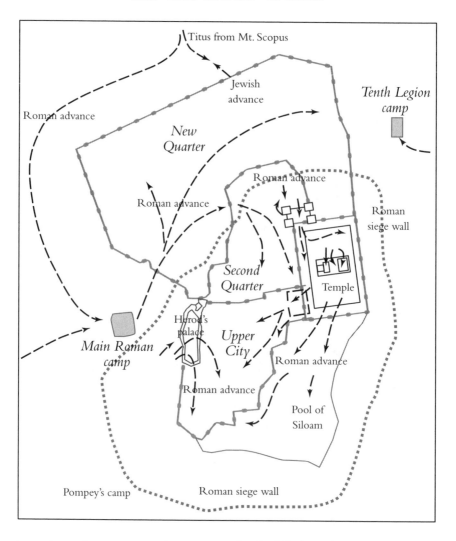

Titus from Mt. Scopus

Jewish advance

Tenth Legion camp

Roman advance

New Quarter

Roman advance

Roman advance

Roman siege wall

Roman advance

Second Quarter

Temple

Herod's palace

Upper City

Main Roman camp

Roman advance

Roman advance

Pool of Siloam

Pompey's camp

Roman siege wall

ingenious plot to escape the tortures that befell the other deserters from the city. Having feigned death, he had instructed his disciples to tell the Romans that they simply wanted to bury their master, who had from the beginning avoided any involvement in the insurrection. When the coffin lid opened ben Zakkai explained that he only wanted safe passage to the Mediterranean city of Yavne, where he would continue to teach his disciples the peace-loving precepts of the Torah.

There were thus two groups of exiles from Jerusalem in those days, the Nazarenes under Shimon, who journeyed northeast to Pella, and Yohanan ben Zakkai and his Pharisaic disciples, who headed west to the coastal community of Yavne (Jamnia). Both communities, in their respective places of exile, were to set up rabbinic "dynasties" of sorts, as well as respective Sanhedrins, for adjudicating everyday matters of life, human relationships and ritual observance. These two movements, the Nazarenes and the Pharisees, were the only two sectarian groups (out of scores that had populated the landscape of Second Temple Israel) to survive the devastation of the Great Revolt. All others perished, including the mighty Sadducees, who, without a Temple over which to preside, quickly became extinct. Far from being adversarial, far from representing two emerging religions, the disciples of ben Zakkai and Shimon were in fact cut from the same cloth, having determined as separate yet kindred communities, to be "pursuers of peace" (*rodfei shalom* in Hebrew). It would take additional decades before their emerging ideological differences would bring them into conflict.

A Curse on Their Heads!

The immediate burden, however, was to provide a structure of authority. Under the auspices of Yohanan ben Zakkai the first version of a rabbinic academy was established. The task ahead was daunting, if not staggering. Ben Zakkai and his disciples had to formulate a whole new basis for the faith in an age when the Temple was no more. When despair permeated the Jewish population, when wandering bands of ascetics

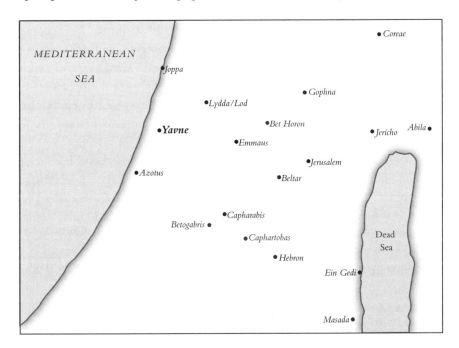

known as *Avlei Tzion* ("mourners of Zion") uttered a collective "woe" and lamented life itself in the absence of their sacred shrine, the disciples of Yavne held out hope. The story is told that one day ben Zakkai and a group of his followers returned to what was left of Jerusalem. As they all stared gloomily at the pile of broken limestone that used to be the grandest temple complex in the entire near east, possibly in the world, his disciples queried, "With no Temple and no sacrifice, what shall be our atonement?" Ben Zakkai responded with a single statement that was audacious if not revolutionary. "Acts of loving-kindness!" he declared. "They shall be our atonement."

There was no vindictiveness here, no call to get even with the Roman despoilers of the holy city, not a trace of anger. In this single statement of creative innovation, the great sage of Yavne had singlehandedly saved his people from what might otherwise have been sure extinction. The unmitigated despair into which the nation had fallen on the heels of the Roman destruction might well have tolled the death-knell for the entire faith. With no religious identity to galvanize them, the Jews might well have suffered the same fate as many other conquered peoples of the ancient world, assimilation and disappearance. But here was a message of hope, encouragement and optimism that opened the door to a whole new definition of the faith that didn't require the shedding of the blood of animals, that didn't require a Temple at all.

In building on what the Pharisees had already advocated for generations, ben Zakkai shifted the focus from ritual observance by the priesthood to ethical behavior on the part of every individual. The message was liberal, progressive and humanistic. It is not on the basis of creeds and proclamations of faith that humanity is judged, he proclaimed, but by deeds involving ethical behavior, the actions of each person toward his or her fellow.

However, in a Temple-less nation, in which the priesthood had been obliterated, who was to specify what those deeds would entail? Everything was up for review, and it would be in a real sense like reinventing the wheel. Aspects of religious observance that were previously in flux would be standardized, codified. The language of prayer would be set in stone, in spite of the myriad of debates over what to pray, when to pray and how to pray. Rituals, from welcoming the Sabbath to observing the major festivals such as Passover and the Day of Atonement, to purification laws such as the washing of hands, would all be fixed so that there would be one practice and one mode of observance. In spite of the Temple's destruction life would go on, though certain practices would be instituted to remember the desolate sanctuary. For example, musical instruments would now be banned on the Sabbath, even while joyous song would, more than ever, fill the synagogues. One small corner of every Jewish home would remain unpainted as a sign of perpetual mourning for Jerusalem, and during the most joyous ceremony of all, the wedding, a glass would be broken in remembrance of the Temple.

All of this required a steady hand of authority, and to that end ben Zakkai began a practice that continues to this day in Judaism, the formal ordination of rabbis. He would stretch out his hands to confer such ordination, a practice known down to the present by the term *smichah* ("stretching"). In so doing he would mark the beginning of a rabbinic "dynasty" whose authority would be felt in every corner of the Jewish world.

The task of the newly ordained sages of Yavne would, over the coming decades, be nothing short of monumental. Their council, their "Sanhedrin," was charged with what amounted to the most significant task ever undertaken by a religious authority. Around the year 90 CE, some twenty years after the Temple's destruction, they convened an assembly to determine formally the "canon" of the Bible, an authorized list of books deemed "holy writ." By contrast they would determine which books would be excluded from the collection of thirty-nine texts now known as the *Tanakh*: the Torah, the Prophets, and the Writings. Such books as Enoch, quoted, as we have seen, in the book of Jude and apparently considered "canon" by the *ma'aminim* of Yaakov's day, were not deemed worthy and so were excised.

The Council at Yavne had to decide not only which books were "kosher," but which Jews were "kosher" as well.

There is good reason to believe that while the headquarters of the Nazarene movement may have moved to Pella, significant numbers of *ma'aminim* continued to populate the land of Israel. Some scholars have reasoned that many of the Nazarene refugees from the Great Revolt later returned to their homes both in Jerusalem and in the Galilee in the years and decades thereafter. Moreover, they seem to have been fairly well tolerated by their fellow Israelites, growing in number at an astonishing rate. Some of the best evidence for this is archaeological, at the town of Capernaum on the Sea of Galilee. Excavations there have revealed an impressive ancient synagogue resting on foundations that go back to the first century. Capernaum was the town Yeshua had chosen to call his home

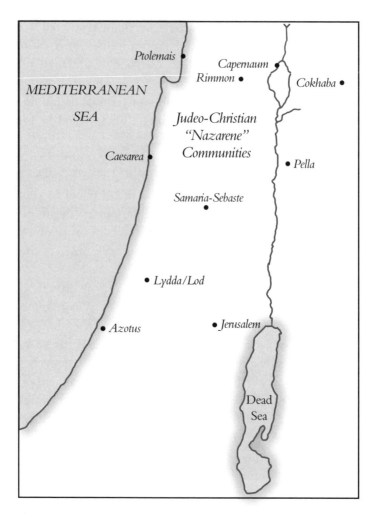

after he left Nazareth, and this was the synagogue where, according to the Gospels, he had once healed a man possessed by a demon.

Within easy walking distance of this well-preserved edifice archaeologists have revealed the remains of an early Byzantine church, resting on what had been an authentic house from the first century. Ancient Aramaic graffiti found on the walls of this house suggest that this may well have been the original home of none other than Shimon, whom the Gospels call Peter. Clearly, this site was revered not just by pilgrims from abroad but by home-grown Israelite *ma'aminim*, as the Semitic inscription indicates. The shrine's proximity to the synagogue also suggests a relatively symbiotic relationship between what we may from this point on call "Rabbinic Judaism" (as it developed during those formative decades) and the Nazarene Jewish sect. There is certainly nothing to indicate hostility between the two groups or the persecution of one group by the other.

Back in Yavne, however, there was the increasing sense that the Nazarene sect was becoming so dominant across the land that they might swamp and overwhelm the entire authority structure that had been so carefully crafted since the accession of Yohanan ben Zakkai. As groups of these Nazarenes returned to live in upper and lower western Galilee, they not surprisingly found themselves in conflict with the rabbis of Yavne. At some point the long-established *modus vivendi* between Pharisees and Nazarenes came to an end. The rabbinic sages therefore took the unprecedented step of formulating Jewish prayer that targeted "heretics" and assorted dissidents. There is debate about whether this prayer specifically mentioned the Nazarenes, but it must certainly have included them. According to Talmudic tradition, Rabbi Gamliel II had asked if anyone can compose a benediction against the "*minim*" ("sectarians"), and Rabbi Samuel the Small responded by composing one of the so-called Eighteen Benedictions recited to this day. Interestingly, the Hebrew *minim* sounds suspiciously like the word *ma'aminim* – "believers" – which some scholars argue was an early designation for Jewish Christians.

At some point, as the Judeo-Christian movement grew ever larger, the prayer's language was made even more specific. A very early text of this benediction, found around the turn of the twentieth century in the attic of a synagogue in Cairo, reads:

> May no hope be left to the Nazarenes [Hebrew *Notzrim*]; but may wickedness perish as in a moment; may all Thine enemies be soon cut off, and do Thou speedily uproot the haughty and shatter and humble them speedily in our days. Blessed be Thou, O Lord, who strikest down enemies and humblest the haughty.[1]

While this harsh language hardly amounted to bona-fide persecution (a tactic employed by Sadducees, *not* Pharisees) it nonetheless represents a low point in the development of Rabbinic Judaism, a hallmark of which was tolerance. Rabbis, after all, were out to regulate behavior, not belief. Oddly enough, however, the notorious curse on the *minim* provides clear evidence that the Nazarene sect was still considered fully Jewish, for the simple reason that the rabbis were not about to curse some other, non-Jewish religion, only movements within Judaism that they deemed "un-kosher." It is also worth pointing out that this infamous curse on the Nazarenes was, for all its bluster, completely ineffectual, and that the word "Nazarenes" was in subsequent generations completely expunged from the twelfth benediction. "The Eighteen" (*Shmone Esrei* in Hebrew) are still recited today, but in place of the word "Nazarenes" we find the term "slanderers" (*malshinim*). It is equally important to note that the curse did not arrest the spread of the Nazarene movement. Ironically, it took Christianity itself, as it evolved into a separate religion with its own increasingly rigid orthodoxy, to do that. The orthodox hierarchy would in time assure that not a solitary trace of the Nazarene movement, composed of Hasidic oriented Jewish *ma'aminim*, remained intact.

Dueling Dynasties and Vanished Gospels

It is tempting for many to conclude that the animosity of Yavne toward the Nazarene movement must have involved the latter group's suspending many of the regulations of the Torah in favor of a more relaxed approach to Jewish observance. Many have glibly determined that the Nazarene sect was by now well on the way to becoming a new religion, distinct from Judaism, and that in the wake of the Temple's destruction they were more inclined than ever to view the death of Yeshua as their "once-and-for-all" sacrificial atonement. But what is the basis for this conclusion? Isn't this one more example of historical anachronism, looking at what western Christianity became and transposing this paradigm backwards onto its origins? While Shaul in the west had contributed, wittingly or unwittingly, to the final schism between Judaism and what would come to be called Christianity, are we to assume that the *Desposyni* completely ignored Yeshua's own teaching, that "until heaven and earth pass away, not a single letter of the Torah shall be altered" (Matthew 5:18)?

The more likely reason for the ill-will of Yavne toward the Nazarenes had nothing to do with the question of atonement or the relaxation of the provisions of the Torah, but with the early Pharisee attitude toward the Hasidim such as Yeshua and his family, who had always evinced a bit too much hutzpah in their approach to God and in their sometimes audacious expression of faith and dynastic authority. What we have in the Nazarenes amounts to a Jewish "sister movement" opposite Yavne and the rabbinic sages, shepherded by a ben Zakkai counterpart, such as Shimon and those who followed, and like ben Zakkai, interpreting *halakha* (Jewish law) in a post-Temple environment.

Were they developing a systematic theology that pictured Yeshua as the only atonement for all of humanity? Did they declare Yeshua to be not only the "son of God" but God incarnate, foreshadowing the theological concept of Trinity? Did they have any developed "Christology" at all, in terms familiar to modern theologians? The answer to all of these is certainly not.[2] The very word "Christ," being Greco-Roman, had not reached them at all, and they continued to think of Yeshua as a human being, not a god, born in ordinary fashion to Yosef and Miriam. They probably did think of him as God's "adopted" son, but this was by no means a claim to divinity. Such a construct would have fractured the very essence of monotheism and would have been anathema to any observant Jew.

What is likely is that the Nazarenes made strong messianic claims on behalf of Yeshua. Given that he was a descendant of the house of David, this is quite a plausible scenario, especially in light of the fact that Hasidic Jews down through the ages have often carried a messianic torch. Messianism in a Jewish context implied regal sovereignty from King David, not godhood. The challenge for the Pella community was to maintain a "kosher" tradition about Yeshua in the face of many heterodox ideas about who and what he represented. In spite of the authority structure that Pella seems to represent, researchers have, during the past several decades, reached the unmistakable conclusion that there was never anything approaching a unified Christianity in those early days. Contrary to earlier models, depicting a single faith that later became splintered, the reverse is more likely the case. There were multiple incarnations of the faith, from the original Nazarenes of Yaakov, to the Ebionites, to the western congregations under Shaul, to multiple expressions of gnostic Christianity whose adherents disparaged the physical world and sought to find a higher knowledge by transcending it. Pella, according to this theory, was the place where the Jewish Nazarenes delineated their differences from the other groups in an attempt to preserve the purity of Yeshua's teaching and lineage.

Part of that attempt involved setting down in writing an accurate account of the life and work of Yeshua himself. While little evidence of such accounts has survived, there are vestigial remnants of alternative "gospels," anonymously composed, that floated around the ancient near east and were subsequently quoted by the Church Fathers in the west. In addition to the Gospel of the Ebionites, we have fragments from a mysterious text known as the Gospel of the Nazareans. There is also reference among the Church Fathers to a book called the Gospel of the Hebrews, which has prompted scholars to question, whether this, the Gospel of the Nazareans and the Gospel of the Ebionites represent three separate works or whether they are different designations for a single text. Nevertheless, the Church

Father Epiphanius draws a clear distinction between the Nazarene Gospel and that of the Ebionites, since the Ebionites were regarded as heretics by the western Church, while the Nazarenes were not — at least not yet.

The Gospel of the Nazareans is one of the truly amazing early Christian texts for a number of reasons. Today we know it only through the writings of church fathers such as Eusebius and Jerome, who quoted it in the Greek of their own writings, though only for the purpose of disparaging it. Both Jerome and Eusebius maintained that the gospel was originally written in the Hebrew language, and Jerome in particular declares that it was used by both Nazarenes and Ebionites. Its date of composition was also remarkably early, toward the end of the first century. It must therefore have originated not in the Pauline communities to the west, but in the land of Israel itself and therefore within the circles of Shimon's *ma'aminim*. Unfortunately, only fragments of the text survive, because as the church grew to the west, it not only severed itself from Judaism, but became increasingly anti-Semitic in tone, suppressing texts such as this gospel that maintained too much of its Jewish identity. Moreover, since few western Christians could read Hebrew, it was considered suspicious at best.

Perhaps the most significant thing about the Gospel of the Nazareans is that it does not contain an account of Yeshua's miraculous birth. While it generally parallels the stories about Yeshua found in Matthew's Gospel, any reference to the Nativity story from the first two chapters of Matthew is curiously absent. Is this because the Nazarenes as a sect, including Yeshua's physical Heirs, never regarded him as a divine being, an idea that would come to dominate western theology, but as an ordinary human, who was "anointed" messianically, because of his righteous deeds?[3]

The Gospel of the Nazareans contains other details slightly at odds with the canonical Gospels. Whereas Matthew's Gospel relates the story of Yeshua's encounter with a "rich young ruler," the Nazarean Gospel depicts two rich men, along with additional concerns regarding ethics. It also relates that at the time of the crucifixion, it was not the veil before the Temple's Holy of Holies that was rent asunder (Matthew 27:51), but rather an enormous lintel that cracked and split, a detail found also in the writings of Josephus. Additionally, in the famous "Lord's Prayer" (Matthew 6:9ff.), the Nazarean Gospel depicts Yeshua as saying, "Give us this day the bread of tomorrow," a rendering popular among many modern commentators.

Of equal significance, the Gospel of the Hebrews, as quoted by Jerome, reveals special interest in Yeshua's brother Yaakov (James). Unlike the canonical Gospels, Yaakov was the first person to lay eyes on the resurrected Yeshua, according to this text. Yaakov was also said to have been with Yeshua at the Last Supper, where (according to Jerome's citation) we read that Yeshua "... took bread, blessed it, broke it, and handed it to James the Just, saying, 'Eat this bread, my brother, for the Son of Man has risen from those who sleep'" (author's translation). In another detail, Yaakov is identified as the unnamed disciple who, along with Clophas, encountered the resurrected Yeshua on the road to Emmaus (Luke 24:18). There is also specific emphasis on the feminine in particular, as we read in the citation of Cyril of Jerusalem, "The power came into the world and was known as Mary, and the Christ was within her womb for seven months" (author's translation).

When it came to the Gospel of the Ebionites, there was widespread condemnation among the Church Fathers. Epiphanius called it a "forged and mutilated" version of Matthew's Gospel. Why had it, like the Gospel of the Nazareans, omitted the Nativity stories? Simply because the Ebionites considered Yeshua to have been elevated to the position of God's son at his baptism, rather than at birth. It was then that the divine *Ruakh*, the Holy Spirit, united with his human soul to make him the "anointed one." While this is consistent with Jewish ideas about the Messiah, it was heresy to the developing orthodoxy to the west. In any case, while the Ebionites and Nazarenes differed on a number of points (such as Ebionite vegetarianism and complete rejection of the Temple), they likely shared this perspective regarding Yeshua's true identity. It was a perspective that would come to have no place in Christian orthodoxy.

One More James

For the time being, however, the Patriarchs of Pella had their own "Sanhedrin" and their own orthodoxy. We should again stress that this concept of a "dynasty" of descendants of Yeshua's family is well attested in the earliest Christian records. The "father of Church history," Eusebius, makes reference to what he called "the throne of the bishopric of the Church in Jerusalem," to which Yaakov had been elected. Since Eusebius never refers to a bishop's "throne," it is likely that the Nazarenes looked upon the *Desposyni* as "royalty," even attaching Davidic status to the Heirs. Eusebius also describes Shimon as a son of Clophas, who elsewhere is called a brother of Yosef (Joseph), Yeshua's father.[4]

Eusebius' source was another ancient historian of the church, name-ly Hegesippus, who recorded that Shimon remained at the helm of the

Jerusalem congregation until persecutions broke out during the reign of the Roman emperor Trajan (98-117 CE). At that time, when he was one hundred twenty years old, he suffered torture and crucifixion, as both a descendant of David and a leader of the Judeo-Christian sect. His successor, according to Hegesippus, was another Nazarene Jew named Justus, though Eusebius is unclear as to whether he was also a member of Yeshua's family.[5]

In any case, Eusebius adds an additional account regarding the grandsons of Yehuda (Jude), "the brother, humanly speaking, of the savior." Once more crediting Hegesippus, he relates that the emperor Domitian (81-96 CE) commanded that the royal descendants of David be rounded up, in fear that they might employ Jewish messianism to foment insurrection. But when these grandsons of Yehuda, namely Sokker and Yaakov (yet another James), were hauled in front the emperor, he mockingly dismissed them, since they were only rude peasants with rough and calloused hands:

> There still survived of the kindred of the Lord the grandsons of Judas, who according to the flesh was called his brother. These were informed against, as belonging to the family of David, and Evocatus brought them before Domitian Caesar: for that emperor dreaded the advent of Christ, as Herod had done. So he asked them whether they were of the family of David; and they confessed they were. Next he asked them what property they had, or how much money they possessed. They both replied that they had only 9000 denaria between them, each of them owning half that sum; but even this they said they did not possess in cash, but as the estimated value of some land, consisting of thirty-nine plethra only, out of which they had to pay the dues, and that they supported themselves by their own labour. And then they began to hold out their hands, exhibiting, as proof of their manual labour, the roughness of their skin, and the corns raised on their hands by constant work. Being then asked concerning Christ and His kingdom, what was its nature, and when and where it was to appear, they returned answer that it was not of this world, nor of the earth, but belonging to the sphere of heaven and angels, and would make its appearance at the end of time, when He shall come in glory, and judge living and dead, and render to every one according to the course of his life. Thereupon Domitian passed no condemnation upon them,

but treated them with contempt, as too mean for notice, and let them go free. At the same time he issued a command, and put a stop to the persecution against the Church. When they were released they became leaders of the churches, as was natural in the case of those who were at once martyrs and of the kindred of the Lord. And, after the establishment of peace to the Church, their lives were prolonged to the reign of Trajan.[6]

With a little bit of detective work, it is well within the realm of possibility that Yaakov (James), brother of Sokker and grandson of Yehuda (Jude), authored an encyclical "open letter," originating in Pella and addressed to Jewish *ma'aminim* scattered across the ancient near east. This letter would subsequently become known as the New Testament book of James.[7] This comes as a surprise if not a shock to most readers of the Bible, who glibly adhere to the tradition that this James was the physical brother of Yeshua. But a little textual sleuthing immediately reveals the problems with this. The text as we have it makes almost no mention of Yeshua himself and shows no sign of the personal familiarity that we might expect from his physical brother. Certainly, someone who had grown up with Yeshua and who had known him all his life would never have written in such a detached fashion.

The text does begin, however, with the superscription identifying James (Yaakov) as the author. Modern scholars are inclined simply to dismiss this as an invention by a later editor who wanted to lend the epistle more weight, by falsely ascribing it to Yeshua's brother. But another attractive possibility presents itself, namely, that the superscription is authentic and that the Yaakov in question was not Yeshua's brother but his grandnephew, the grandson of Yehuda. Scholars also point out that the letter is written in good Greek and is thoroughly Jewish in tone, but at the same time Hellenistic. This makes perfect sense assuming that the letter was written in Pella, generations removed from Yeshua. Pella, being a city of the Decapolis, was, after all, a Hellenistic/ Greek community.

But in spite of its good Greek, the essential Jewishness of the letter has hardly gone unnoticed by the scholarly community.[8] Researchers have long recognized the lack of distinctively Christian elements in the epistle of James. Not only is Yeshua a marginal character at best, being referenced in only two verses (1:1 and 2:2), but the letter as a whole is full of ethical admonitions that are almost entirely found not in Christian texts, but in parallel Jewish works. In one of the passages where we do find reference to

Yeshua (2:2), we also find the meeting place of the *ma'aminim* designated a "synagogue."[9] The other characters alluded to, including Abraham, Rahab, Job and Elijah are exclusively Jewish, as are the congregations to whom the text is addressed, "the twelve tribes in the Dispersion." This opening line is exactly what we would expect from a Jewish "circular letter."

The very concept of an "epistle" isn't Christian in origin, but Jewish. For centuries throughout antiquity it was a custom that the central religious authority of the Jewish people would dispatch open letters to Jews living across the Diaspora, as the center of the Jewish world moved from Jerusalem to Yavne, to Tiberias in the Galilee, and ultimately far to the east, in Babylonia. The practice continued, as new political and social realities demanded new formulations for Jewish life and observance. Our epistle of Yaakov (James) should rightly be seen within this context. Moreover, the fact that it addresses Jewish *ma'aminim* in the Diaspora hints at just how far the Jewish branch of the Jesus movement had spread.

Some have speculated that from Pella it branched as far as the Tigris and Euphrates Rivers in Babylonia, an intriguing notion given that the headquarters of Judaism ultimately moved to precisely this area, in order to get as far away as possible from the yoke of imperial Rome. It was there that later generations of rabbis set up great academies of learning, in such otherwise obscure cities as Sura, Pumbedita and Nehardea, and it was there that they eventually set in writing what we call today the Babylonian Talmud. There is evidence suggesting that the Nazarene community continued to live in this relatively safe area, preserving their uniquely Jewish traditions.

Eventually the rabbis established an entire genre of literature, known as *responsa*. It consisted of a series of questions and answers having to do with the application of Jewish law and ethics in changing conditions. We don't know exactly when the tradition of writing *responsa* began, but traces of it are preserved in the Talmud, and by the third century, letters containing rabbinic rulings and admonitions were regularly being dispatched from Judaism's new Babylonian "headquarters" back to the land of Israel. The epistle of Yaakov might similarly be seen as an early example of ethical *responsa* literature, addressing burning social issues of the day. But what were the specific issues that prompted him to write this particular letter? To understand Yaakov's motives, we need to take a step back and come to grips with the general religious tension in those days between east and west.

Dueling with Dualism

Make no mistake, the Nazarene movement in the Greco-Roman territories to the west continued to define itself and be defined by others as a Jewish sect, even though its membership was becoming dominated overwhelmingly by non-Jewish God-fearers. The question of how to behave, especially with regard to ritual observance, whether to become circumcised, whether to keep the Sabbath and Jewish festivals, whether to abstain from certain foods, never ceased to perplex them. As long as Shaul was present with his heavy hand of leadership, there was a central authority vested in one man to provide guidance, albeit autocratic. His own versions of *responsa* circulated across the Mediterranean, becoming over time a written "constitution" of sorts. As a Jewish movement composed largely of non-Jews, its very nature was paradoxical, constantly begging clarification.

Shaul was able to hold it all together by the force of his own personality as he continued to write his encyclical letters through the sixth decade of the Common Era. After his execution at the hands of the emperor Nero, he achieved martyr's status, but the movement he established was already splintering in multiple directions. Judaism was ever-popular in the Roman empire, even after the disastrous revolt of 66 - 70 CE. While the revolt decimated the Jews of Israel, it did not touch the Diaspora communities, who had neither joined in it nor supported it. The Church Fathers indicated that there continued to be attempts by Diaspora Jews to nudge the Nazarene sect in the west toward full conversion to Judaism. And why shouldn't they, given that Judaism was such an attractive option for so many non-Jews who had tired of the multiple and competing deities of the pagan west?

On the other hand, the western Nazarenes were lured even more by the multiple sectarian groups of the Hellenistic world, who sought "higher knowledge," the Gnostics. Though Shaul, or perhaps some anonymous writer, had strongly cautioned against such groups, charging them with seeking "what is falsely called knowledge" (1 Timothy 6:20), their appeal grew exponentially after the great apostle's martyrdom. Before long there were multiple gnostic gospels and gnostic epistles, flooding the western churches like a veritable papyrus deluge and perpetrating ideas, some of which were not just un-Jewish, but anti-Jewish, what we would today call "anti-Semitic."

Though later effectively suppressed by the western Church orthodoxy, an enormous cache of gnostic documents was found at Nag Hammadi in

Egypt. They have opened for us a window on what gnostic Christians truly believed and taught. The Gnostics taught that God should be conceived not as the preeminent divine being, but rather as the "divine fullness," the totality of deity. They referred to this "holy essence" as the Pleroma, who acted in consort with an "emanation" of the Divine, who was female yet male, Mother yet Father, known as Barbelo. Together, they "emanated" as it were, fragments of the divine essence known as aeons, including the Holy Spirit, female in nature, and the Primordial Christ, pre-existent from the beginning of the world. This pair later emanated Jesus in the physical realm, born to the Virgin Mary.

There was, however, another aeon, the lowest of them all, known as Sophia, who sought secret knowledge forbidden to her and was therefore exiled from the Divine Presence. Her fate was to wander throughout the cosmos, seeking a way by which she might return to the Pleroma. Having no partner of her own, she brought forth a single monstrous offspring referred to as the Demiurge, whom she wrapped in a cloud out of shame. The Demiurge, knowing nothing of the higher reality, stole power from Sophia and proceeded to create the material world, including the progenitors of all humanity, Adam and Eve.

The physical world as we know it, including all who inhabit it, is therefore equally alienated from the higher spiritual reality. What is the role of Jesus in such a world? To help people find their way back, via spiritual enlightenment, to the true reality of the Pleroma. But the path to enlightenment is not so easy, for the Demiurge also brought into existence certain powers and principalities known as Archons, who stand as obstacles between fallen humanity in a corrupt world and spiritual "salvation," which consists of enlightenment regarding the higher reality of the Pleroma. The Gnostics shared certain commonalities with Pauline teaching, especially the idea that all of humanity is born in sin, that the flesh is therefore evil, and that "salvation" consists, not of doing the right thing, but of a spiritual awakening, being "born again," and discovering the truth/ wisdom.

What do you have to *do* to be saved? Nothing, since you have to recognize that you can't "do" anything in the first place that will be pleasing to the Divine. It certainly sounds Pauline, for it was Shaul who famously wrote, "For by grace you are saved through faith, and that not of yourselves, it is the gift of God, not of works, lest anyone should boast" (Ephesians 2:8). Was Shaul perhaps influenced by gnostic thought, even while condemning the Gnostics themselves? Various Gnostic groups certainly lay hold of these ideas, ultimately equating the God of the Hebrew Bible with the Demiurge, whom they now referred to as Yaldabaot.

When the first century rolled into the second, a prominent theologian came to the fore named Marcion, who, while not a Gnostic himself, reformulated the ideas of the Gnostics to express not the strict monotheism of the Jews, but a kind of "dualism." According to Marcion, there were really two deities. There was the God of the Hebrew Bible/ Old Testament who, though the Creator of the material world, was nonetheless stern of character, harsh and judgmental, condemning humanity on the basis of the Law. The God of the New Testament, by contrast, was full of grace, mercy and love. This was the God represented by Jesus. These ideas, Marcion believed, were in sync with the writings of Shaul.

While Marcionism, like gnosticism, was condemned as heretical by Christian orthodoxy, many ideas from both movements silently slipped into the fabric of what Christianity ultimately became. Moreover, it is no exaggeration to say that the western Nazarene movement, as it slowly morphed into something else, consisted of a polyglot cauldron of competing sects, marked by a diverse mixture of Jewish and Hellenistic philosophy. The response of the Jewish Nazarenes to the east, especially among the *Desposyni* (the Heirs) at Pella, must have been nothing short of shock and revulsion. What was at stake here was more than various notions about the messianic identity of Yeshua m'Natzeret. The paramount issue for all Jews was now on the table, the very unity of God.

The position that Yaakov would take, setting it down in writing in his famous epistle, would be to dig in his heels, reasserting the values of traditional Judaism, adding his own Hasidic angle. While a pure heart is the greatest sign of Hasidic piety and devotion to God, the ultimate measure of this piety is behavioral, ethical, and intimately linked with performing the *mitzvahs*, the "commandments" of the Torah. This was no time to mince words; Yaakov had to confront the teachings of Shaul head on.

Keeping the Faith

The conflict is not particularly evident at the outset of the epistle, the first chapter of which raises a whole litany of issues, ranging from temptation and struggle to persecution, steadfastness and doubt:

My brothers, count it all joy when you fall into different kinds of temptations, knowing that the trying of your faith works

patience. But let patience have its perfect work, so that you may
be perfect and entire, lacking nothing. (James 1:2-4)

The focus here has nothing to do with Pauline logic, but goes back to
Yeshua himself. The emphasis on being "perfect and entire" smacks
strongly of Yeshua's message, to be "perfect, even as your Father in heav-
en is perfect" (Matthew 5:48).[10] Being perfect sounds like a tall order to
most modern readers of the text. But when we read through the Greek
and place the message in a Hebrew / Semitic context, the word "perfect"
becomes *shalem*, which means "whole" and is related to the shalom (peace)
through wholeness.

Of course the letter speaks of being strong in the face of suffering and
persecution, but was this persecution the result of being members of a new
and distinct Christian faith? The fact is, all Jews in that era had to deal
with persecution, the Romans being relentless in subjugating any who
opposed them. After the crushing blows from the Roman legions, they
even convened a council in the city of Lod, which happens to be the location of modern Israel's international airport – a virtual suburb of today's
Tel-Aviv – in order to determine how far to go in their resistance to persecution. It was decided that if, for example, a pagan should demand, on
pain of death, that you break the Sabbath, you should break it so that you
might live to keep it next week. But if it he demanded that you worship
an idol, be prepared to "die and not transgress."

These were the kind of practical issues that *responsa* of the period dealt
with. For Yaakov, the key to strength in the face of such trials is simply
faith. The Greek word for "faith" is *pistis*, which implies a mental condition that Christians have long equated with deep and sincere belief. But
if we look beyond the Greek to the Semitic context of the passage, we
discover that "faith" meant something else entirely. Ancient Hasidic Jews,
such as Yeshua m'Nazeret, would tell you that faith was all about being
steadfast in action and behavior. As Winston Churchill once quipped,
"Never give in, never give in, never give in!" Faith meant dogged determination to do the right thing.

Yaakov's epistle next admonishes against "doubt" and being "double-
minded." But again, while the letter is composed in good Greek, its context is Hebraic, and scholars have long suspected that the Greek here is
parroting a Hebrew expression, *lev levav*, "double-heart."[11] Elsewhere, the
Hebrew Bible uses this exact expression to refer to men of war:

...who had understanding of the times, to know what Israel ought to do... who could keep rank. They were not of a double heart. (1 Chronicles 12:32-33)

Understood Hebraically, "doubt" is no more a mental condition than "faith," but rather an inconsistency of action, an inability to "keep rank." Yaakov was admonishing his community to be "culture warriors," in the face of Roman oppression and a desolated homeland. In other words, faith is not "belief" but rather hutzpah! As a "Hasidic" sect, however, the Nazarenes were not to be militant or arrogant as "spiritual warriors." These, after all, were the people who had left Jerusalem rather than take up arms in company with the rebels. On the contrary, Yaakov teaches that the greatest attribute of all is humility:

But let the humble brother rejoice in his exaltation; and the rich one rejoice in his humiliation, because he shall pass away as the flower of the grass. (James 1:9-10)

In typical Jewish/ Hasidic fashion he appeals to the wisdom of past sages, specifically the great and venerable Hillel, from the first century BCE, who found his strength precisely in his humility:

Go two or three seats lower and take your seat, until they say to you "Come up," rather than that you should go up and they should say to you, "Go down" ... and so Hillel used to say, "My self-abasement is my exaltation ..." (Lev. Rab. 1:5)[12]

Hillel was apparently among those whose messianism was mild, not militant, who expected the Redeemer to come not on a white horse of conquest, but, as the ancient prophet Zechariah had declared, on an ass.[13] It is not an exaggeration to say that pietists down through the ages have always erred, for better or worse, on the side of humility. The Hasidic master known as the Baal Shem Tov, who lived in Poland in the 1700s, was a man whose life was marked, not by great learning, but deep humility, combined with wondrous good deeds, including many divine healings. The greatest Hasidic sage of the twentieth century, Brooklyn's Menachem Mendel Schneerson, was, for all his great wisdom, humble enough to stand on a street corner weekly and pass out dollar bills, so as to establish a tradition of giving to those in need. Compassionate help to those less fortunate was therefore a hallmark of Hasidic Judaism dating back to ancient times. The epistle of Yaakov fits perfectly in this context, so much so that it ought to be viewed, not as a "Christian" book at all, but as a manual of sorts for Jewish Hasidim.

"Become doers of the Word," Yaakov declares, "not hearers only."[14] This isn't abstract theology, which traditional Jews have never spent much time pondering, but practical instruction that in a "rabbinical" context has to be coupled with down-to-earth examples. "Suppose a rich man comes into your assembly," Yaakov writes (2:2). As noted, the Greek word for "assembly" used here is *sunagoga* (synagogue). Yaakov points out that if you observe this person dressed in fine clothes and wearing gold rings, you may promptly give him the best seat in the synagogue, while to a poor man dressed in ragged clothes you might say, "Go sit over there, or have a seat on the floor." And we're immediately reminded of Broadway's "Fiddler on the Roof," where our protagonist, Tevye, wistfully imagines, "If I were a rich man... I'd have the time that I lack to sit in the synagogue and pray, and maybe have a seat by the eastern wall!"

Yaakov seems to have calculated his words to produce guilt, an emotion quite different from Tevye's and near, if not so dear, to the Jewish psyche. He follows up with his classic definition of "true religion":

> Pure religion and undefiled before God the Father is this, to visit orphans and widows in their afflictions, and to keep oneself unspotted from the world. (James 1:27)[15]

Modern western readers, unfamiliar with Jewish thought, are somewhat stunned by all of this. Where is the theology here? Where is the list of doctrines, tenets of faith? The things one is supposed to "believe"? If we take Yaakov at his word, it isn't really important what we believe, but what we do, morally and ethically. And while classical Christian theology, as we know it today, is curiously absent, Yaakov's link with his distant uncle, Yeshua m'Nazaret, is striking. In an archetypal parable about the final judgment, Yeshua spoke of those who approach him on that final day, saying "Lord..." quite possibly a Jewish euphemism for "messiah." While their declaration may have been pleasing on a theological level, they are rebuffed and set aside for judgment. Yeshua defined faithfulness in terms of feeding the hungry, taking in the homeless, clothing the naked, and visiting the sick and those in prison.[16] To this the "theologians" of the day object, "Lord, when did we see You hungry, or thirsty, or a stranger, or

naked, or sick, or in prison, and did not minister to You?" Yeshua's re-
tort is as timeless as it is biting: "Truly I say to you, inasmuch as you did
not do it to one of the least of these, you did not do it to Me" (Matthew
25:44-45).

It took the likes of Shaul to turn "salvation" into a set of precise creeds,
built on a "systematic theology," to be given unflinching assent to. But for
Hasidim like Yeshua and his Heirs, it was not about creeds, but deeds.[17] The
same Yeshua had said elsewhere, "Let your light so shine before men that
they may see your good deeds and glorify your Father who is in Heaven"
(Matthew 5:16). He also declared that "whoever speaks a word against the
Son of man, it shall be forgiven him. But to him who blasphemes against
the Holy Spirit, it shall not be forgiven" (Matthew 12:32; Luke 12:10). In
other words, one might speak against Yeshua with impunity, denying him,
his message and his messiahship (assuming he ever made this claim), but that
isn't what's important. It is the *ruakh*, the Spirit, that energizes the "kingdom
of heaven" through miraculous good deeds.

Battling Shaul – The Full Broadside

By far the most recognizable call to action issued by Yaakov is the following classic declaration:

> But will you know, O vain man, that faith without works is
> dead? Was not Abraham our father justified by works when
> he had offered Isaac his son upon the altar? Do you see how
> faith worked with his works, and by the works faith was made
> complete? And the Scripture was fulfilled which says, "Abraham
> believed God, and it was imputed to him for righteousness, and
> he was called the friend of God." You see then how a man is
> justified by works, and not by faith only. (James 2:20-24)

Yaakov is in this passage specifically quoting a verse from the book of
Genesis, that has also been translated, "[Abraham] believed in God, and
He counted it to him for righteousness" (Genesis 15:6). Suffice it to say
that the story of Abraham, especially his near-sacrifice/ murder of his
miraculously born son Isaac, has been perplexing at best to traditional
Jews throughout the long history of biblical interpretation. The very idea
of child sacrifice, as practiced by the pagan Canaanites, was in Jewish eyes
monstrous. How, then, could the champion of faith, the "friend of God,"
Abraham, even consider such an act, much less be prepared to go through

with it? Never mind that he had heard it as a direct command from God. He should have responded to the Divine, saying: "I will not! Kill me if You like; I will not kill my son!" Instead, he sheepishly consents to do the unthinkable. One is reminded of Alfred Lord Tennyson's famous "Charge of the Light Brigade," where he elegaically wrote, "Theirs not to reason why, Theirs but to do and die…"

Jewish exegesis provides no pat answers for this dilemma, but "believing in God" was certainly not what "justified" Abraham. The Hebrew verb here, translated "believe" is *aman*, a derivative of which has come down to us as the word "Amen." Its root meaning is "steadfast," "immovable," "unflinchingly determined." While belief may be a motivating factor, its true measure is in action. Is intellectual doubt possible while nonetheless remaining steadfast? Absolutely. And Jewish folklore, as recorded in the Talmud and other ancient sources, speculates that Abraham must have been racked with doubt, questions and vacillation regarding God's grotesque command. He nonetheless remained steadfast in his behavior, and this is what made him just.

For Yaakov, the analogy fit, given that he had also addressed doubt, which he called being "double-minded," and which he would likely have defined as "duplicity," not of thought but of action. Modern folk would call it hypocrisy. But perhaps the most intriguing aspect of this whole passage of the epistle is that the "proof text" in Genesis was also quoted verbatim by none other than Shaul, who used it as a springboard to develop his own systematic theology. Shaul famously wrote in the book of Galatians:

> Even as Abraham believed God, and it was counted to him for righteousness. (Galatians 3:6)

The question for us is whether Shaul and Yaakov quote the same verse by mere coincidence or whether Yaakov was aware of the Pauline epistle, the teachings of which were by now seriously undermining the essential Jewishness of the whole Nazarene movement in the west, and delivered a deliberate broadside against him.

The Monk from Wittenburg

Well-meaning religious folk have always been disinclined to look for conflict in the pages of the Bible, and they are willing to go to great lengths to smooth out inconsistencies and to view everyone as belonging to "one big happy family" of faith. Rather than admitting the obvious, that Yaakov is thoroughly opposed to Shaul's notion that all that counts is what a person "believes," the theological "spin doctors" attempt to reconcile the two sides: Yaakov (James) doesn't really mean that works are more important than faith. He is only saying that if faith/ belief is sincere, works will follow. But unfortunately this approach skirts the issue, namely, that the fundamental arguments of Shaul and Yaakov are, at the bottom line, like oil and water. They don't mix. Sometimes it takes a bit of brazen honesty to recognize the obvious.

In the early 1500s in a town called Wittenburg, Germany, a monk of rather feisty temperament stepped out of obscurity to challenge the view that works can be reconciled with faith, that Yaakov can be reconciled with Shaul. And in so doing, he rocked the whole of Europe on its foundations. His name was Martin Luther.

Up until this point the Roman Catholic Church had taught that good deeds, as well as faith, are an essential component of righteousness, and therefore the basis for divine judgment. Luther denied this by claiming that faith alone is the basis of all divine favor. One day while doing penance in Rome, by crawling up a staircase on his knees, a scripture flashed before his eyes from the ancient prophet Habakkuk (2:4): "The just shall live by faith." Little did he realize that the word "faith" in Hebrew (*emunah*, another derivative of the root *aman*) doesn't refer to a state of mind, as the Greek word for "faith" (*pistis*) certainly does, but rather to steadfastness, action, behavior.

This was unimportant to Luther. He went on to declare virtual war against the authority of the pope, unintentionally sparking what came to be called the Protestant Reformation. It was more than spiritual and quickly developed into a political revolution, which would spark multiple wars that would take countless lives, send a third of Germany's population to the grave, and rage on in places like Northern Ireland almost to the current day. On a theological level, however, Luther correctly understood what was at stake. To be consistent with this "radical" theology of faith alone, he could not co-mingle it with the teaching of Yaakov. He could not mix oil and water, faith and works. He chose the systematic and complex theology of Shaul, utterly excoriating the teaching and admonitions of Yaakov (James). The book that bears the latter's name he referred to as "the straw epistle," and he openly advocated ripping it out of the New Testament canon.

To be sure, Luther shared much in common psychologically with Shaul himself, being feisty, temperamental, complex and argumentative. It shouldn't surprise us that he sided with his ancient counterpart, his "knight of faith." He was, by anyone's estimation, brutally honest, even if he was fundamentally wrong regarding the meaning of the word "faith." We can speculate that if Yaakov had had his way at the end of the first century of the Common Era, he would have ripped the writings of Shaul out of the developing New Testament canon. History, of course, is written by the victors.

Notes

1   See E.J. Bickerman, in *HTR 55* (1962): 171, n. 35. Solomon Schechter pointed to an early text that was specifically aimed at Judeo-Christians; see Schechter, *JQR* 10 (1987/98).

2   L.E. Elliott-Binns found a linkage between the epistle of James and the phenomenon of Galilean Christanity, which in his view had four characteristics: a focus on Jesus' teaching as opposed to teaching about him, an undeveloped Christology, the lack of a doctrine of redemption, and a close relationship to Judaism and the Hebrew Bible. He further asserted that those who fled to Pella included both Galilean and Judean Christians, that they delineated their differences there, and that some returned to their Galilean homes after the Great Revolt, establishing churches which persisted until the Arab conquest. Elliott-Binns concluded that a brand of Jewish Christianity, distinctly different from what prevailed in Jerusalem, may be discerned in the epistle of James (along with Mark, the Q source, and some Matthean material). It was Galilean in origin, its readers consisted of Galilean Christians, and it was distinct from Paul's Gentile Christianity. He placed all this in the context of what he depicted as the considerable friction between the liberty-loving Galilean Jews and the tradition-oriented Jews of Judea. See L.E. Elliott-Binns, *Galilean Christianity* (Chicago: Alec R. Allenson, Inc., 1956).

3   See Bart D. Ehrman, *The New Testament and Other Early Christian Writings* (New York; Oxford: Oxford University Press, 1998), 137.

4   Eusebius, *History* 3.11.

5   Eusebius, *History* 3.32, 35.

6   Eusebius, *History* 3.19-20; *cf.* S.L. Harris, *The New Testament* (Mountain View, CA: Mayfield, 1998), 248.

7   Schoeps argued in Excursus I of his text (*Theologie*, 343-9) that a Christian of Jewish descent – who was not an Ebionite – wrote the letter of James in the early

second century. Its purpose was to oppose the antinomianism of Paul. It has been pointed out that Jerusalem must have been a locus of Greek learning in the first century CE, inasmuch as Josephus (*Letter of Aristeas*) declares that the translators of the LXX were Jerusalemite priests. This would explain the mastery of Greek by James, Paul etc. See S. Safrai and M. Stern, *The Jewish People in the First Century*, Vol. 2 (Philadelphia: Fortress Press, 1987), 1054-5.

8   It has long been recognized that the book of James strongly rests on the language of the Hebrew Bible. Nearly a century ago S.J. Case (1911: 101-2) observed that the first half of James draws largely on the language of the Pentateuch while the second half takes inspiration from the Prophets and the Psalms. See S.J. Case, "The New Testament Writers' Interpretation of the Old Testament," *BW* 38.2 (1911): 99-102. It has also been theorized that every element of the letter of James is Jewish in character and that its author may in fact have been a Jew writing in the first century CE. See F. Spitta, *Zur Geschichte und Lieratur des Urchristentums* (Gottingen: Vandenhoeck un Ruprecht, 1893), 382-91. Massebieau took a similar position, notwithstanding James' apparent reliance on the Sermon on the Mount. See L. Massebieau, "*L'Eptre de Jacques. Est-elle l'oeuvre d'un Chretien?*," *RHR* 32 (1895): 249-83. Both advanced the theory that James was a Jewish work that was later Christianized by a twofold reference to Jesus (1:1; 2:1). This view is challenged by Ropes, who maintained that the epistle is closer to a Hellenistic diatribe than to the Jewish Wisdom tradition. See J.H. Ropes, *A Critical and Exegetical Commentary on the Epistle of St. James* (Edinburgh: T&T Clark, 1916), 6-24. Ropes' skepticism, however, should not overrule the bulk of sound scholarship, including Deissmann, who argue convincingly for the correlation between James and the many tracts of ancient Wisdom literature. See A. Deissmann, *Bible Studies: Contributions, Chiefly from Papyri and Inscriptions, to the History of the Language, the Literature, and the Religion of Hellenistic Judaism and Primitive Christianity* (Winona Lake, IN: Alpha Publications, 1979), 52-5. For an excellent discussion on various positions relating to the dating of James, see P. Davids, *The Epistle of James: A Commentary on the Greek Text* (Grand Rapids: Eerdmans, 1982), 2-5, 21-22.

9   See Ehrman, *New Testament,* 276.

10   See J. Licht, *Thanksgiving Scroll: A Scroll from the Wilderness of Judaea* (Eilat, Israel: Bialik Institute, 1957), glossary. See also Y. Yadin, *The Scroll of the War of the Sons of Light against the Sons of Darkness* (Oxford: Oxford University Press, 1962), 291, 327. It should be observed that in Matthew, the term "perfect" shows considerable affinity with sectarian thought. Note Mt. 19:21, which links "perfect" with the term "poor": "If you want to be perfect, go, sell what you have and give to the poor..." I would argue that Jesus was generally at odds with sectarian thought (especially on the matter of the exclusivity of the *Yahad* in separating themselves from the "Sons of Darkness"), but that when it comes to matters of personal probity and integrity, he agrees with the "pietistic" aspects of the Qumran corpus. The word "perfect" additionally appears in the book of Hebrews and in Paul's Epistles (2 Cor. 12:9): "And He said to me, My grace is sufficient for you, for My power is made perfect

in weakness." See also Flusser, *Judaism*, 36.

11 It has been observed that the Septuagint fails to render this Hebraic expression, found in 1 Chr. 12:33. See Oscar J.F. Seitz, "Relationship of the Shepherd of Hermas to the Epistle of James," *JBL* 63:2 (1944), 131-40.

12 D. Flusser suggested that Hillel's proverbial meekness was in fact a sign of his strength and self-awareness, an attribute similar to that attributed to the pietistic Jesus. See Flusser, *Judaism*, 512. S. Libermann's assertion that Hillel is speaking about God rather than himself is unwarranted in light of Hillel's other sayings. See Libermann, *Tosefta*, 124.

13 Zech. 9:9 "Behold, your King comes to you. He is righteous and victorious, meek and riding on an ass, even on a colt, the son of an ass."

14 James 1:22

15 For a thorough discussion of the common policy advanced by ancient Near Eastern literary traditions with regard to the protection of widows, orphans and the poor, see F.C. Fensham, "Widow, Orphan, and the Poor in Ancient Near Eastern Legal and Wisdom Literature," *JNES* 21.2 (1962): 129-39. It is noteworthy that such concerns were a crucial element in the sections of the Torah dealing with the covenant between God and Israel. "You shall not afflict any widow or fatherless child" (Ex. 22:21).

16 Matthew 25:35-36.

17 It has been observed that religion of an ethical type (James being an example) brings about a moral union with God, involving a unity of purpose. It brings about a life of action, striving to right the wrongs of humanity. This is in turn equated with 'salvation.' Adherents of such religion come to appreciate, not the abstract "good" of philosophy, but the good deed as well as the good intention that accompanies it. See F.A. Starratt, "Ethical and Mystical Religion," *BW* 46.6 (1915): 363.

8

The Great Dissolution

WHO AMONG ALL THE HUMAN FAMILY DOES NOT WANT TO be restored when ailing? Anthropologists have estimated that in ancient Judea, up to one quarter of the total population was afflicted with some sort of illness or disease, and in such an environment, the gifts of healing were prized and healers were beloved.

Such was the environment in which Yaakov wrote his great epistle. It shouldn't surprise us that the final section of the letter deals with the subject of healing:

> Is any among you afflicted? Let him pray... Is any sick among you? Let him call for the elders of the congregation, and let them pray over him, anointing him with oil in the name of the Lord. And the prayer of faith will cure the sick, and the Lord shall raise him up. And if he has committed sins, it will be forgiven him. Confess faults to one another, and pray for one another, that you may be healed. The effectual, fervent prayer of a righteous one avails much. (James 5:13-16)

The segment of the population of ancient Israel that produced healers was the same sector that produced Yeshua and the Heirs – the pious Hasidim. They were the ones who daily experienced the Divine Presence in their lives. There had been many such pietists before Yaakov, and many would follow him. In the decades following the destruction of the Temple – about the same time that the epistle of Yaakov was composed – one of the disciples of the illustrious Rabbi Akiva named Hanina ben Dosa gained a reputation for bringing about miraculous healing by the power of prayer. The story is told that when Akiva's son fell ill, Hanina was summoned and, following much entreaty before God, the child miraculously recovered. Though Akiva was considered to be one of the greatest sages ever to grace the land of Israel, he was utterly astonished at the spiritual dynamic of his Hasidic disciple. He declared, "I might have prayed all day, and it would have done no good!" He went on, saying, "The difference between Hanina and me is that he is like the bodyguard of a king, who has unlimited access to him at all times, while I am like a lord before the king, who has to wait his turn."[1]

Another story relates that when the son of the great Jewish patriarch Gamliel II became sick, he prayed for healing from a distance. When he finished he announced to the patriarch's messengers that the child's fever had left him. "I am no prophet, nor the son of a prophet," he explained, quoting the ancient prophet Amos, "but I have learned that whenever my prayers flow freely from my mouth, it is a sign that my requests have been granted." The messengers recorded the exact time that Hanina made this declaration, and when they returned to Rabbi Gamliel II, they found that the child had indeed recovered, exactly at the hour that Hanina had prayed. The story reminds us of the famous account of Yeshua, recorded in the gospel of John, that he was once asked to pray on behalf of the son of an official in Capernaum, who was grievously ill. When the official approached Yeshua, the Hasidic healer replied, "Go, your son will live!" Upon his return home, his servants met him and announced that his son had recovered – as it happened, at the exact hour that Yeshua had prayed.[2]

Cleaving to God – "Woe to the lizard!"

Since most of the history of the Jewish Nazarene movement was suppressed by the western church orthodoxy, we can only guess at what it must have been like, but stories in ancient Jewish sources regarding the miracle-working sages of that day must have had strong parallels among the Nazarenes at Pella and beyond. Prayer for healing and miraculous recovery must have been central to their communal experience. Observance of Jewish law was at the heart of their daily lives and they taught that righteous conduct and ethical behavior was the basis for the "good life" in the here-and-now, and for life in the world to come. But there was another level of life that went beyond the mere performance of good deeds.

Later generations of Hasidic Jews, who populated central Europe from the Middle Ages on, would call it *d'vekut*, "cleaving" to God. Just as

Adam "cleaved" to Eve and the two became one flesh, so must the Hasid cleave to God, becoming one spirit with the Divine Presence. The word itself means not just "cleaving," but being "glued," cemented one to another. It was a discipline developed generation after generation among the Hasidim. It was said of Hanina ben Dosa that he was so concentrated in his prayer that even when he was bitten by a lizard, he was not dissuaded, but only continued in his devotions. "I didn't even feel the bite!" he later declared, whereupon his disciples exclaimed, "Woe to the man bitten by a lizard, and woe to the lizard who bites Hanina ben Dosa!" After this episode it was said, "Compared to Hanina, even the prayers of the high priest are of no avail!"

Centuries later, in the heart of central Europe, the Hasidic sage known as Baal Shem Tov would regularly retreat into the mountains to devote himself to prayer and meditation. Like his ancient Hasidic predecessors, he was not the most learned of sages, but he so "cleaved" to God that he experienced the Divine Presence intimately in his life on a moment-by-moment basis. And like his ancient counterparts it wasn't long before he began to manifest the gift of healing, effectuating the miraculous recovery of all those around him who were afflicted with disease or stricken with illness.

As in ancient times there were detractors galore, including the famed rabbi, Elijah ben Shlomo Zalman, known popularly as the Vilna Gaon, who decried what seemed to him like so much Hasidic hysteria. His emphasis was on learning, on devouring the Torah, and the resulting conflict between study and miraculous good deeds precisely mirrored that of ancient Judea. The Hasidic teachings of the Baal Shem Tov and his growing band of pietistic disciples were ultimately banned by the rationalistic rabbis of central Europe, and the Hasidim responded in kind, with counter-bans. It all seemed to verify the old adage, that when there are two Jews together, there are at least three opinions. The controversy was finally smoothed over, at least to some extent, when the Hasidim developed academies of their own. These were ultra-orthodox rabbinical yeshivas, where pious d'vikut was combined with arduous Torah study.

It was a paradigm similar to what developed over time in ancient Judea, for the academy of Yohanan ben Zakkai spawned many others, such as the study house of the illustrious Rabbi Akiva, the very rabbi whose son was healed by the Hasidic miracle-worker, Hanina ben Dosa. While the good deeds of Hanina were remembered for posterity, Rabbi Akiva nonetheless asserted that the study of the Torah takes precedence over all. Study versus good deeds, *mitzvahs*, was, as always, the underlying tension. Hillel (in the first century BCE) had emphasized study, Yeshua good deeds. Akiva stressed study, Hanina good deeds.

When it came to study, Akiva's knowledge of the scriptures became so detailed and his exegesis so sophisticated that Moses himself – who according to one story miraculously appeared one day in the midst of the study house – was unable to understand it. It was said that Akiva not only analyzed each letter of the Torah seeking to determine its deepest significance, he even studied the decorative "spurs" that often embellished the tops of the letters, believing that they carried some kind of mystical message. Indeed, Akiva found a message that was at once mystical and messianic. He found the Messiah, God's "anointed" vessel, who would deliver Israel from Roman servitude.

Lion or Lamb?

There were, as we have already seen, two conflicting thoughts in ancient Israel about the Messiah, which mirrored the conflict between the preeminence of study and the performance of good deeds. Some believed that since the root of the messianic concept was the notion that this "anointed one" would restore the throne of David that had long since been abandoned, he must therefore come as a conquering hero. They imagined a militant Messiah, who, with sword in hand, would crush the Roman legions and give the Israelites the freedom they desired most.

Others embraced a very different view, that true liberation comes from the inside out, that judgment starts at home, with the house of Israel, and that only when Israel becomes obedient to the commandments, the *mitzvahs*, would national redemption bud. Taking up the sword is not necessary, for Rome will crumble of its own accord, and a day of glorious liberation will dawn by itself.

The exact nature of the Messiah was a tension mirrored in the ancient Israelite prophets themselves, who sometimes wrote of the Messiah as a triumphant liberator and sometimes as a humble servant. The Messiah would come as a conquering lion, though perhaps he would come as a lamb. Both views are curiously embodied in the words of the prophet Zechariah:

Behold, your King comes to you. He is righteous and victorious, meek and riding on an ass, even on a colt, the son of an ass. (Zechariah 9:9)

Among those who advanced the latter image of the "meek Messiah" were Israel's pietistic sages, the Hasidim, whose determination not to take up the sword had already been tested during the Great Revolt of 66 - 70 CE. Their teaching had certainly been borne out as correct in light of the terrible devastation that befell the land as a consequence of the ill-conceived war of liberation.

However, the greatest rabbinic mind of the age, Akiva, whose endless study of the Torah led him to conclude that a militant Messiah was indeed the divine will, disagreed. As far as he was concerned, the "anointed one" would come on a white horse, "conquering and to conquer." His arduous study of the biblical text had led him to this undeniable conclusion. He examined, for example, the celebrated story of Balaam, who long ago, after the Israelites had left Egypt in their great "exodus," was sent to curse them as they sojourned in the Sinai desert, only to be contravened by divine agency and forced to utter a blessing instead.

Balaam's blessing, "How lovely are your dwelling places, O Jacob" (Numbers 24:6), was wildly popular in ancient Israel, and became the source of Akiva's speculation. As Balaam of old continued his prophetic proclamation, he exclaimed:

> I shall see him, but not now. I shall behold him, but not near. There shall come a Star out of Jacob, and a Scepter shall rise out of Israel and shall strike the corners of Moab and destroy all the sons of tumult. (Numbers 24:17)

As it happened, the Hebrew word for "star" (*kokhav*), became the seedbed for Akiva's messianic speculation. It didn't mean much by itself, but it suddenly took on a new significance, at least in Akiva's mind, when he encountered a gruff, though charismatic, Judean military commander who, like the Nazarene leader who took up residence in Pella, was also named Shimon (Simeon). He was from the little known Judean town of Coseba, and hence he was called Shimon ben Coseba ("Simeon son of Coseba"). He was an ancient "Braveheart" who looked at the ongoing foreign occupation of his land and determined that Israel could and should be free. The Tenth Roman Legion, with the idolatrous carved eagles atop their standards, were an affront to the people and an insult to the one and only God. He had had enough of the Roman boot and the imperial iron fist. If the Great Revolt had ended in ignominious defeat, it was only because the people were bitterly divided with one faction fighting another. If only they could stand together as one force, they could take on any foe and bring them down. They could even vanquish the might of Rome, if only, with God's help, they willed it so.

Rabbi Akiva was taken with this message of hope, so much so that he determined that this must in fact be the dawn of the messianic age. The bold commander Shimon ben Coseba was no ordinary tactician, he was the "anointed one" for whom they had all been waiting. Suddenly, Balaam's prophecy came to mind, praising the "star" who shall come out of Jacob. Akiva meditated on the fact that the Aramaic version of *kokhav* ("star") is *kokhba*, a word that sounds curiously like Coseba, Shimon's home town. The great rabbi next took a blind leap of faith, declaring that Shimon ben Coseba should henceforth be called Shimon bar Kokhba ("Simeon son of the star").

Akiva's pronouncement provided the impetus for what would soon become a second great revolt against Roman domination of the land of Israel that would break out in the second century of the Common Era. Details surrounding it are somewhat scant, because the great Jewish historian Josephus Flavius was by now long dead, and we must fill in the gaps in our knowledge by piecing together various comments from other historians of the period, such as Dio Cassius. What we know for sure is that the "Bar Kokhba Revolt," as it came to be called, had a number of causes, not the least of which was the fact that the Roman emperor of that day, Hadrian, made life hell for his Jewish subjects. Hadrian was fundamentally different from his predecessor Trajan (who by force of arms expanded the empire to its greatest geographic extent) because he was not a conqueror but a consolidator. Since he had no interest in conquering any more territory, he decided to imprint Roman culture firmly on the provinces he already ruled.

Liberty or Death?

When he first came to power in 118 CE, he was sympathetic to his Jewish subjects, even allowing them to rebuild their fallen temple. Soon, however, he came to realize what a stubborn and rebellious lot these Judeans were, and he decided to put them in their place. He rescinded his decree allowing the Temple to be rebuilt, insisting that it be moved to some other locale. Fearing further rumblings of revolt, he began deporting Jews to North Africa. This only fueled the cause of a new generation of rebels, who began building secret sanctuaries in the desert caves and organizing a guerilla force. In the year 123 CE they initiated a series of

surprise assaults on the Roman forces, frustrating the emperor-consolida-
tor to no end with an orchestrated campaign of terrorism.

Hadrian responded in the only way he knew, with an iron hand and
by force of arms. He personally led the Sixth Legion to Judea to join
the already overtaxed Tenth. He also set a new man in charge, Tinneius
Rufus, to be governor of the region. Next, he took the unprecedented
step of repressing Judaism, which he perceived as a "foreign" religion.
This action was more than unusual for Rome, which, as a pagan society, was remarkably tolerant. Paganism had, throughout human history,
evinced tolerance and diversity, wherein the concept of religious persecution was virtually unknown. But Hadrian the "consolidator" felt different
about religious and cultural diversity. He resented the Jews all the more,
since they had enjoyed a special status within Roman culture, and had
been granted formal immunity from emperor worship. He issued an imperial edict forbidding the ritual of circumcision.

For Hadrian this strange Jewish custom amounted to nothing less than
genital mutilation. But for Jews the order was more than an outrage, This
was an issue of life or death. The questions debated at Lod came front and
center. For which commandments must one be willing to lay-down one's
life rather than transgress? Was circumcision such a commandment? For
most Judeans of that day and age, it was indeed. Circumcision had been
established in the days of Abraham as an eternal "sign" of belonging to
the community of Israel. It was the distinctive mark of the Covenant that
set Jews apart from every other people. It had been central to the debate at
the Council of Jerusalem, when Shaul had stood against Yeshua's brother
Yaakov and prevailed, claiming that his non-Jewish "God-fearers" should
not be required to be circumcised in order to become members of the
Nazarene movement. Of course the observance of Jewish law had never
been incumbent upon non-Jews, and for this reason Yaakov and the Heirs
relented. It was, however, implicit that the Jewish ma'aminim would continue to observe the whole of the Torah, including circumcision. This was
never in question.

Suddenly, however, Jews were to be forced to relinquish the Torah
by imperial fiat. By a single edict the Jewish people, who had survived
against all odds in the face of the random blows of history, were to be
made extinct. Decades before, when the Great Revolt had broken out,
there were endless questions about whether a course of violence, even for
the cause of liberty, was justified. Granted, the Romans were often cruel
oppressors, but Jews could still express their ethnic identity. They still

had their "immunity." Now, however, all such talk evaporated, and the Judeans responded to the anti-circumcision edict with one voice, "This will not stand!"

There is nothing as effective as persecution to solidify faith and turn ordinary citizens into zealots. Needless to say, the Jewish population adamantly rejected Hadrian's edict and continued to circumcise their male infants, as commanded by the Torah, on the eighth day after birth. It would not have been difficult for Roman authorities to punish any number of individuals deemed guilty of breaking Hadrian's order, but when a whole population ignored it, there was little to be done. Hadrian, not to be dissuaded, decided to add insult to injury by building a new city on the ruins of Jerusalem. But this was not to be Jerusalem. It would be a pagan city, on the order of a Greco-Roman *polis* ("city-state"). It's new name would be Aelia Capitolina, a combination of the name of the Roman deity Jupiter Capitolinus and Hadrian's own name. On the site of the Temple itself he would erect a shrine to Jupiter, the ultimate desecration of the most sacred site in the Jewish world. Tinneius Rufus performed the foundation ceremony of Aelia Capitolina in the year 131.

It should have been cause for celebration, but the response of the Judeans was again overwhelming. "This will not stand!" As far as they were concerned, it amounted to "ploughing up the Temple." When Rabbi Akiva, who had found his messiah in Shimon Bar Kokhba, convinced the Sanhedrin at Yavne to support the growing clamor for revolt, the moment seemed ripe for action. They would take care to avoid the mistakes of the previous century's revolt by planning their strategy in great detail. It would begin in the town of Modi'in, to the north, on the border of Samaria, where the first honored set of Jewish freedom fighters, the Maccabees, had once staged a successful revolt against the Syrians and given Jews a full century of freedom until the Romans quashed their budding kingdom in 63 BCE. From there they would fan out across the land and cut off Hadrian's garrison in Jerusalem.

It was a good plan with a just cause, backed by the most venerable rabbi of the age. But who would risk life and limb and the wrath of the empire to join? The Jews of the Diaspora certainly would not, for they had already suffered ignominious defeat at the hands of the emperor Trajan, who put down a Jewish insurrection that flared up in Mesopotamia, Cyprus, Cyrene and Egypt. They no longer had the stomach for war.

What about that other sizable religious sect among the Jews, the Nazarenes (*Nozrim*), who had their own Sanhedrin across the Jordan in

Pella? How much did their Jewishness mean to them? Were they prepared to fight the good fight in the name of the unity of God? The *ma'aminim* were certainly alive and well in the days of Rabbi Akiva, and they could not have been unaware of the great sage's messianic "mania." Moreover they had to have known of the anti-circumcision edict and the desecration of Jerusalem's Holy Hill. Who was in charge in those fateful days, and how far had the movement spread?

The Church Father Eusebius recorded a list of fifteen "bishops of the circumcision." With approximate dates attached, they may be identified as:

1) James (Yaakov), until 62 CE

2) Simeon (Shimon), 67?-107 CE

3) Justus, 107-113 CE

4) Zacchaeus (Zakkai – not to be confused with Yohanan ben Zakkai), 113-? CE

5) Tobias (Tuvyah), ?

6) Benjamin (Binyamin), ?-117 CE

7) John (Yohanan), 117-? CE

8) Matthias (Mattitiyahu), ?-120 CE

9) Philip, ?-124 CE

10) Seneca, ?

11) Justus II, ?

12) Levi, ?

13) Ephram (Ephraim), ?

14) Joseph (Yoseph), ?

15) Judas (Yehuda), ?-135 CE.[3]

These names were probably traditional in Yeshua's family, but none was ever named after Yeshua himself. The early Christian chronicler, Hegesippus, declared that after Shimon's (Simeon's) martyrdom, a Jew named Justus was selected "from among the thousands" of Judeo-Christians. His choice of language suggests some regret, as though the line of *Desposyni* / Heirs had by his time come to an end.[4]

We have in fact other evidence to indicate that the family line of Yeshua continued for generations, even centuries beyond the first Great Revolt and the destruction of the Temple. That they and their followers represented a sizable sect among the Jewish population in those days is a real possibility, and their participation in Bar Kokhba's great cause could have been vital for its success. The response of the Nazarenes would not, however, be favorable.

Messianic Muddle

At the center of Nazarene identity was the firm conviction that Yeshua, the Hasidic sage from Nazareth, was in fact the *Mashiakh*, the "anointed one." Rabbi Akiva's candidate for the title, Shimon Bar Kokhba, was unacceptable even though Akiva employed the very methods of manipulation of Scripture to "prove" his choice for Messiah that the Nazarenes used to substantiate their claims on behalf of Yeshua. Each camp had devised complex exegetical systems for uncovering secret clues hidden in the Scriptures, in order to bolster their viewpoint. Akiva, like many of his earlier Pharisee counterparts, pointed to Scriptures that seemed to indicate a conquering, militant messiah who would wield a scepter and sit on David's throne.

The Nazarenes identified with the portrait of a meek, humble messiah, riding astride a donkey. They were transfixed by the classic fifty-third chapter from the prophet Isaiah that speaks of a suffering servant who would be martyred on behalf of the people.[5] Scholars have pointed out that Isaiah 53 was never intended by its author to be messianic, any more than the story of Balaam's prophecy with its mention of a star coming forth from Jacob. Isaiah's suffering servant might well be an emblem for Israel as a whole, or perhaps even the prophet himself, who suffered grievous persecution in the days of the evil king Manasseh. But for the Nazarenes it could only refer to Yeshua.

Moreover, following a course of revolt fundamentally contradicted the Hasidic message. In the modern nation of Israel there is endless controversy regarding the Hasidim,[6] who enjoy all the rights and privileges of citizenship in the Jewish state but who do not serve in the military or risk their lives in Israel's wars. Some are ardent Zionists, but believe that it is better to pray and study the Torah than to take up arms, since, they believe, God alone is the sole deliverer of the nation. There are some Hasidic groups, however, who are far more radical, declaring that since modern Israel is a secular state, it is not God's nation. They therefore choose not to recognize Israel as sponsored by God. In their view a new Jewish state with a resurrected throne of David can only be established in the messianic age.

Then as now, the Jewish world was a house divided. The Nazarenes as a whole were divided from Bar Kokhba's rebels, and the eastern Nazarenes remained divided from those in the west, who had taken the Pauline epistles to their logical conclusion and increasingly divorced themselves from the Jewish cause. The conventional scholarly opinion is that the Bar Kokhba Revolt represents the decisive point at which Christianity broke from Judaism.

But what of Hadrian's infamous edict forbidding circumcision? We should again recall that Shaul had never counseled Jewish Nazarenes to abandon the mark of the covenant, and when it was discovered that one of his disciples, Timothy, had a Jewish mother, he personally circumcised the young man. By the turn of the second century, however, there were fewer Jewish Nazarenes in the west, simply because once Shaul had opened the door to non-Jews entering the movement, the Jewish component found itself overwhelmed. Shaul's admonitions about not following Jewish law were increasingly applied not just to the God-fearers, but to Jews as well. Those who continued to follow Jewish practices were increasingly unwelcome in western churches, for they were, after all, "Judaizers." For most western congregations circumcision was simply a non-issue.

The east, however, was a different story. While the Heirs had no affinity for Bar Kokhba and his rebels, we have every reason to believe that they were not only still Jews, but piously observant Jews. Did the *ma'aminim* of the east sheepishly assent to Hadrian's prohibition of the one ritual at the core of their Jewish identity? Did they at this point cease to be Jews altogether and become adherents of Christianity, the new and distinct western religion that had now been formally birthed? It is tempting to assume along with the "party line" of Christian scholarship for the past two millennia, that the bulk of them did just that, deciding that circumcision is simply not an issue worth dying for. This would indeed have been the moment of the "great schism" between Christians and Jews.

Is it, however, not possible that twenty centuries of Christian scholarship has committed the sin of transposing what Christianity ultimately became on what it was then – of assuming that the final split with Judaism was an inevitability and that the Bar Kokhba Revolt simply drove the nails in the coffin of a single, unified, monotheistic faith? In point of fact, had the muddle over the quasi-messiahship of Bar Kokhba amounted to the de-facto "end" of the Jewish-Nazarene movement, we would also expect the dynastic line of the Heirs of Yeshua to have faded into oblivion at precisely this juncture.

But history tells us that this was not the case, that the dynasty of Yeshua persisted in the east at least into the fourth century. This means that they did not acquiesce to Pauline Christianity, nor did they throw up their hands

in despair at the ill-fated messianic pronouncement of Rabbi Akiva and relinquish their Jewish identity. Like most Jews across the empire, they would
simply not obey Hadrian's edict against circumcision. As Andrew Jackson
once said of Chief Justice John Marshall, "He has made his decision; now let
him enforce it!" They would not accept the Pauline logic that all *ma'aminim*
are "circumcised in the heart" and therefore require no outward sign. And
Eusebius, who dutifully recorded the names of the fifteen "Jewish bishops
of Jerusalem," also observed, doubtless to his considerable chagrin, that they
were all "of the circumcision." They and their followers would continue to
keep Sabbaths, festivals and holidays. Their diet, like the rest of their lifestyle,
would continue to be strictly kosher.

They would not, however, join ranks with what was soon to become
a second disastrous war against the imperial eagle. The Nazarene community in Pella must have continued to provide guidance to other communities of *ma'aminim* scattered across the region, including the Galilee,
Yeshua's place of origin. Historians have long noted that during the first
Great Revolt against Rome, the Galilee was a hotbed of anti-Roman resistance and was strategically integral to the cause of the Zealots.

When Bar Kokhba began his revolt, however, the Galilee stayed on the
sidelines, even while many Jews from abroad, as well as some non-Jews,
volunteered to serve with the resistance. Could this be connected with
the fact that late in the first century CE, substantial numbers of Nazarenes
began returning from their exile in Transjordan to reoccupy the Galilean
homes they had abandoned during the devastating conflict? Might they
have grown substantially in number, in such places as Capernaum, which
had been the hub of Yeshua's career as a teacher/ healer? Might the presence of a large, peace-loving Hasidic-oriented population of Nazarenes in
the Galilee have so changed the complexion of the region that it would
under no circumstances take up the sword, even against the tyrannical
Hadrian? It is difficult to known how large the Jewish Nazarene community was in the Galilee and elsewhere because the Church Fathers don't
want us to know. But just as they saved themselves during the first revolt
by fleeing to the east, they saved themselves again by hunkering down in
pious Galilee while a horrific war raged to the south.

War is Hell

Bar Kokhba did enjoy some degree of initial success on the battlefield,
trouncing with fury the notorious Tinneius Rufus, along with the general
and governor of Syria, Publus Marcellus, who had been dispatched by

Hadrian to subjugate the resistance. Under Bar Kokhba's leadership and Akiva's inspiration, the rebels overran some 50 Roman strongholds and captured 985 villages and towns, encircling them with walls and building underground defensive tunnels. With the slogan "For the freedom of Israel!" they managed to conquer the greatest prize of all, Jerusalem.

In celebration they struck coins depicting the outlines of a Jewish Temple. Is it possible that Shimon Bar Kokhba obliterated the beginnings of Hadrian's temple to Jupiter and established a new Jewish Temple on Jerusalem's holy hill? This is unlikely in the midst of a cataclysmic war against the world's mightiest army. What is likely is that Bar Kokhba not only accepted his messianic designation he "proved" it by orchestrating the resumption of animal sacrifice on the Temple Mount. Even though the Temple itself continued to lay in ruins, this new "deliverer" of the Jews would make sure that no pagan shrine occupy the site. He would even restore "kosher" Jewish sacrifice. Who else but the Messiah could bring about this "miracle"?

However, the Nazarenes remained unconvinced. Had they finally accepted the "orthodox" Christian position that Yeshua was the eternal, once-and-for-all sacrifice and that no further sacrifice was needed or acceptable? Certainly not, for Christian theology as we think of it today had by no means reached them. All such theologizing was, after all, distinctly Pauline and more than a little un-Jewish. They may well have cheered the resumption of animal sacrifice, but they would not have cheered the "messianic pretender" offered them, a man who was leading the nation not to glorious liberation but ruinous calamity.

The calamity would come swiftly, like a plague of locusts, borne by a wind from the north. At the helm of the invading army was Julius Severus, who came in from Britain in the company of the governor of Germania, Hadrianus Quintus Lollius Urbicus, to orchestrate the defeat of the rebels. In due course a total of twelve legions descended on the land of Israel from Egypt to Syria and parts beyond to put an end to Bar Kokhba's "messianic mania." The rebels were too numerous to engage openly, so the strategy would be to attack them in their fortresses and choke off food and other supplies until all resistance collapsed.

We can only wonder how the Nazarenes must have felt as word reached them of the fate of their compatriots in Judea, misguided though they were. The once proud citizen army that had stood up bravely to Hadrian's legions was now reduced to a band of brigands hiding in caves. From one such cave, in a place today called Nahal Hever along the Dead

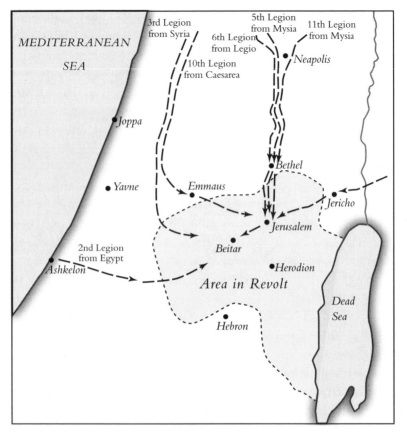

Sea's western shore, Bar Kokhba himself commanded what was left of his forces. His collected correspondences haphazardly scribbled on parchment scraps were hastily deposited in a leather pouch, which remained in the caves long after its inhabitants fled.

Discovered in the mid-twentieth century not long after the Dead Sea Scrolls first came to light, the pouch and its contents, known today as the Bar Kokhba Letters, have given us an uncanny eyewitness glimpse into the tumult of that time. Bar Kokhba conveys in his own words the increasing desperation of the rebel cause. Indeed, the ill fortunes of Israel's erstwhile Messiah must have appeared in the eyes of the Nazarenes to have been "proof" of his fraudulent claims, as well as the futility of the whole militant view of messianism. By the same token they must have felt considerable sympathy for their fellow Jews, who were once again receiving the full brunt of Rome's wrath.

The revolt was doomed to fail, with all 50 rebel fortresses and 985 villages crushed one by one. As with the first Great Revolt, the Judean defenders had no inclination to surrender, fighting in most instances to the last man. Their last stand was at a Judean fortress called Beitar, a name that even today resonates among Israelis as a symbol of freedom and defiance.

The Romans being masters of siege warfare, it was only a matter of time until all resistance was crushed. The fortress was surrounded and on the ninth day of the month of Av – the date set aside to mourn the destruction of the Temple – the Romans battered down its walls. Every Jew in Beitar, including Shimon Bar Kokhba, was slaughtered. The Talmud recounts that the Romans "went on killing until their horses were submerged in blood to their nostrils."[7] Many more in the surrounding countryside were sold into slavery.

One of the captives was identified as none other than the venerable Rabbi Akiva, whose pronouncement on behalf of Ben Coseba / Bar Kokhba helped precipitate the whole disastrous conflict. Akiva would not die mercifully. He was stretched out on the rack, whereupon metal tongs were sadistically employed to tear the skin from his body. In his death agonies he was nonetheless able to utter one final defiant proclamation. "Hear, O Israel," he chanted in Hebrew, "the Lord our God is one." Legend has it that as the word "one" passed from his lips, his soul departed and he breathed his last.[8]

In the aftermath of the carnage, the entire city of Jerusalem was plowed under, and the pagan city of Aelia Capitolina grew up on its ruins. Jews were forbidden to live inside the city on pain of death and were only allowed to enter on the ninth of Av, to stand at the Western Wall, the last vestige of the once glorious Temple Mount, to mourn and weep. Hadrian determined to wipe every vestige of Jewish presence from the land itself, which he now renamed *Syria Palestina* / "Palestine," symbolically resurrecting the ancient land of the Philistines.

This was the final ignominious conclusion to Judea's last and best hope for freedom. While hope may have died at the siege of Beitar, the Jewish people themselves had no intention of being consigned to the ash heap of history. The realities of the day had fundamentally changed. The results of this war were so horrific that the land itself could no longer sustain a population of any substantial size. Even the victorious Romans had been deeply wounded by the carnage. While it was the custom for the emperor to deliver an annual report to the Senate, prefaced with the phrase, "I and my legions are well," Hadrian at the conclusion of the Bar Kokhba revolt in the year 135 conspicuously deleted the phrase, for it was clear that the legions were not well.

As the bulk of the surviving population of Judea fled slowly eastward to Babylonia, Yavne, the seat of Jewish learning, was forced to flee with its Sanhedrin to find residence elsewhere. A new rabbinical center was subsequently established to the north in the Galilee at a place called Usha.

Sects in the Shadows

A dynastic patriarchate of rabbis would soon rise in Usha, endeavoring in the midst of Roman oppression to keep hope alive. They would, ironically, find themselves living in close proximity with the Nazarenes, the very sect that the previous generation of sages had formally cursed. For both groups the Galilee represented a relatively safe haven, though both rabbinic Jews and Nazarenes still had to contend with Hadrianic intolerance that sporadically expressed itself in outright persecution. In such an environment, who had time for curses? Hadrian targeted all expressions of Judaism, rabbinic sages and Nazarenes alike.

Clearly the Romans still did not consider the Nazarenes to be a new religion, and we can only assume that even after the Bar Kokhba revolt, its members continued to be observant of the faith, practicing all of the things that Hadrian now expressly forbade: circumcision, Torah study, Sabbath observance, feasts and holidays, ritual washings (which western Christians came to call "baptism"), gathering in synagogues and Jewish courts. We should bear in mind that up until this time, a Jew would be loathe to go to a secular Roman court for the resolution of a conflict or any type of grievance. The Bet Din, or Jewish "Judgment House," was the place for all conflict resolution. That Nazarenes had similar "Houses of Judgment," essentially Jewish in character, was an important aspect of their life and practice as alluded to by Shaul:

> Do any of you dare, when you have a matter against another, to go to law before the unjust, and not before the saints? (1 Corinthians 6:1)

To deny all Jews, including Nazarenes, this expression of autonomy must have been a particularly cruel blow. We can nonetheless assume that the Nazarene Sanhedrin continued to function in its Pella headquarters, but that pockets of Nazarene communities took root and sprouted across the region. Sources from the period indicate that communities claiming to have stemmed from Yaakov's leadership sprouted up from Damascus to Arabia and remained alive and vital in the second and third centuries.[9]

There is some confusion as to whether these were Nazarene or Ebionite communities. Differences between the two groups must have remained over such issues as vegetarianism, which was championed by the Ebionites. We will assume that in spite of their differences they must have coexisted peaceably, alongside the growing rabbinic orthodoxy.

Indeed, it must have been hard to tell Nazarene Jews and "traditional" Jews apart in their personal lives as well as in their liturgical observance. Except for their belief in Yeshua as the Messiah, there was nothing to distinguish them from their fellow congregants in the synagogues of the Galilee. The common roots of the *ma'aminim* and traditional Jews were evident to everyone. Their religious services were parallel and they shared

the same holy days. On the Sabbath they gathered for readings from the
Hebrew Bible, singing eastern melodies of Jewish flavor. The congregation of one synagogue might listen to its rabbi chant a text from the
Torah, while at a nearby synagogue, another assemblage might join in a
prayer believed to have been uttered by Yeshua.

We can assume that Yeshua's heirs continued to preside from Pella, even
as the rabbinic patriarchate, ensconced for a time in the city of Usha, moved
itself repeatedly to Yavne and back, to Shepharam, Bet Shearim and Sephoris
(all in the Galilee), and by the end of the second century to Tiberias. As long
as Hadrian held sway over the empire, the persecution of all expressions of
Judaism persisted. Over time, however, Jews would reach a *modus vivendi*
with their Roman overlords, since the pagan world was, after all, a largely
tolerant place.

Judaism would nonetheless inexorably turn inward, removing and excluding itself from the whole Greco-Roman world. For the first time, the
land of Israel would no longer be the focal point of Judaism. Its focus would
turn eastward, toward Babylonia, where new rabbinic academies were
sprouting up along the Tigris and Euphrates Rivers in places such as Sura,
Nehardea and Pumbeditha. They would eventually supplant the Galilee as

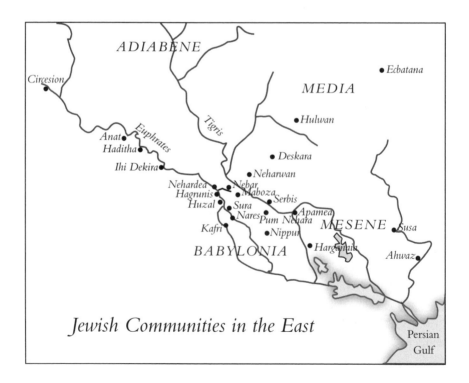

Jewish Communities in the East

the undisputed "center" of the Jewish world. A new body of Jewish literature would grow up in such places, known as the Babylonia Talmud. This literature would serve as an intellectual "fortress," behind which the Jewish people, with their new inward gaze, would seclude themselves.

No longer would Jews seek converts in the non-Jewish world. They would in fact forbid proselytism altogether. It has been said that as a direct result of Israel's two catastrophic and failed revolts against the Roman empire, the Jewish people ironically saved themselves. By systematically disengaging from the Greco-Roman world, they did not suffer slow extinction as it did. Rome would inexorably fall, and the peoples who populated her empire would progressively assimilate into other tribal and ethnic groups. But the Jews, who now established their headquarters far in the east beyond the reaches of Rome's empire, would still survive.

But what of the Nazarenes? It is fair to speculate that they, like the other Jews of this period, increasingly lost touch with the west and likewise disengaged themselves from the Greco-Roman world. Eusebius records that "the bishops of the circumcision ceased at this time."[10] At least as far as the west was concerned they ceased, though the true picture is much more complicated. To be sure, as the Nazarenes distanced themselves from the pan-Hellenic culture in the west, the non-Jewish *Christianoi* ("Christians") increasingly embraced that culture. While Jews, including, we assume, Nazarenes, ceased proselytizing, the western Christians increasingly proselytized, gaining large numbers of non-Jewish converts and becoming an increasingly dominant cultural movement in the west. Though they were in time overwhelmingly outnumbered by western Christians, Yeshua's heirs still maintained their identity and what their lineage represented. As far as they were concerned, they were still the authoritative "voice" of the "Jesus Movement," a position they maintained throughout the third century of the Common Era.

But everything would come to a head after the third century slipped into the fourth. Conflict was, of course, inevitable. Far to the west, the bishop of the city of Rome had long claimed his own dynastic authority, stemming from Peter (Shimon) and of course Shaul. Whoever sat on the chair, or *cathedra*, of Saint Peter was officially designated "Holy Father" (*papa* in Latin) – the pope. Given the general disarray of competing Christian sects in the west, it fell to this pope to exercise strict authority and put them in their place. Since theology, not law, was the basis for western, non-Jewish Christianity, a rigid and systematized standard of belief had to be formulated.

The central question related to the person of Yeshua, now formally called by his Greek name *Christos*, the Christ. Was he human? Was he divine? Was he perhaps a mixture of both? Discussions turned to debate, and debate to theological warfare that was destined to rage for centuries and to shape the course of the western world. Among the many competing sects vying for dominance in the theological cauldron of the era were the Nazarenes from the east. In the year 318 CE, a fateful meeting took place in Rome itself, between the presiding *papa* of the day, Pope Sylvester I and eight Heirs, descendants of Yeshua's family. The pope was supposed to have received his authority in a lineal descent from St. Peter. Imagine, then, his shock to be confronted by another line of descent, a physical bloodline leading directly back to Yeshua's brothers and sisters. Perhaps the pope himself was an illegitimate "heir"!

It is likely that one Yosef (Joses), the eldest of their company, spoke with authority on behalf of all the others, making specific demands.[11] First, they insisted that the confirmation of the non-Jewish Christian bishops of Antioch, Ephesus, Alexandria, and even the holy city of Jerusalem be rescinded and that they be formally defrocked. From this we can be sure that the Heirs continued to rule their Jewish flock from elsewhere, presumably Pella, and that as a matter of course one of their number governed all of the early congregations of the east. This would explain why the appointment of non-Jews would be deemed an affront.

Secondly, they demanded that replacements for these bishops be made from among the Heirs themselves. These were all eastern cities where Jews continued to reside, and on that level it made sense that the leaders of those congregations not only be Jewish but descended from the family of Yeshua.

Thirdly, since the Jews of Jerusalem had been oppressed and beleaguered since the reign of Hadrian, they requested that financial contributions be made to this community in particular, which they still insisted was the "Mother Church." Finally, they urged that the Torah be reintroduced into these congregations, emphasizing the keeping of the Sabbath, new moons and festival days.

What is particularly striking about this meeting is that it took place at all. For, in an age when the mantle of authority had presumably passed to the west, the Holy Father still found it necessary to consult with Yeshua's Heirs from the east. The Heirs were therefore still recognized as a potent force as late as the fourth century. Pope Sylvester had even funded their sea travel, from Palestine to the Roman port of Ostia.

The Long Decline

But if the pope imagined that he was in a position of superiority over the Heirs, he was seriously mistaken, for they unquestionably refused to recognize the whole western Roman authority structure that had now assumed a place of supremacy. To the Heirs it must have seemed ironic that Rome, which had twice decimated the land of Israel and its Jewish population, had now become the seat of authority for the brave little Jewish-Hasidic sect that sprouted from the land that the Roman empire despised. It had been "hijacked" by Shaul, who in turn had co-opted Peter (Shimon) to his side, and it had since become thoroughly "Romanized."

Was Pope Sylvester swayed by the *hutzpah* of the Heirs? Did he acquiesce to their "just" demands? He knew that for the sake of propriety he had to pay them respect; nor could he ignore their considerable pedigree. But he also knew that the western "Church" had become so dominant, even in the face of sporadic persecution, as to make its original Jewish core quite irrelevant. The emperor in those days was none other than Constantine the Great, who not only ended the anti-Christian persecutions of his predecessors, but personally embraced Christianity. The Church was in the process of becoming the definitive face of Rome. Some degree of theological accommodation may have been established by the two sides of the Jesus movement, but Yeshua's Heirs would go home empty-handed, knowing that even in the cities of the east where the Church had established congregations, its leaders would be non-Jews, and Nazarenes would be sidelined and ignored.

Worse still, Shaul's original admonitions to the effect that Torah observance should not be required of non-Jews would now be applied universally to Jews as well. Jewish *ma'aminim* who persisted in circumcision, Sabbath observance, a kosher diet, ritual purification and other observances were looked at askance, as being "under the Law of bondage." Whatever Christianity had become, it was no longer Jewish, and to be accepted, Jews had to relinquish their Jewish identity and completely assimilate into the growing Christian culture. Moreover the gentile Christians had by now created the myth that "the Jews" had rejected Jesus. It was an idea that would resonate for all of history, giving rise to centuries of Christian anti-Semitism in the heart of Europe. The charge became so vicious that the Jews themselves became known as "Christ-killers." These accusations would one day lead to Auschwitz.

In any case, it is clear that the Jews had not *en-masse* rejected Jesus, as demonstrated by the tenacious congregations of Nazarenes. The truth was in fact the reverse, for Christianity had rejected the Jews. Never again would there be open discussion between representatives of the original Mother Church (Jerusalem) and the new Mother Church (Rome). Western Christianity had not yet reached a consensus regarding the "divine nature" of *Iesus* / Jesus, but under Constantine's influence, Pope Sylvester would cloak the structure of Christianity in an imperial Roman garb. In the future all dissent would be squelched, and the Nazarenes would suffer the fate of so many other "heretical" groups, being hunted down as brigands and put to the sword.

In the year 325 CE came the most concerted effort to identify and stamp out "heresy" through the adoption of a formal theological credo to which all Christians were required to give assent. The so-called Council of Nicea was composed of 318 bishops, not one of whom was Jewish, and was chaired (though some would say strong-armed), by Bishop Athanasius. It was he who formally advanced the concept of "Trinity," of God not as one, but as three. Father, Son, and Holy Spirit were to be conceived as separate and distinct "persons," yet of one eternal substance. Such ideas were entirely foreign to the Jewish Nazarenes, who were still stubbornly monotheistic and for whom "anointed one" did not equate to "God."

The council was also charged with the task of regulating Christian holy days, chief among which was the feast of Christ's resurrection, later known as Easter. There was a new determination, fostered by Constantine himself, that this day be divorced from its Jewish association with the Passover. Constantine wrote:

> It appeared an unworthy thing that in the celebration of this most holy feast we should follow the practice of the Jews, who have impiously defiled their hands with enormous sin, and are, therefore, deservedly afflicted with blindness of soul. . . . Let us then have nothing in common with the detestable Jewish crowd; for we have received from our Saviour a different way.[12]

The Sabbath was also changed from Saturday to Sunday, "the venerable day of the Sun." Nicea was not destined to be the only great council of bishops. A subsequent Church council held in Antioch in the year 341 stipulated that Christians were not to celebrate Jewish festivals or engage in other Jewish "impieties" and were no longer to receive gifts from Jews. One might imagine that such attitudes would have been enough to completely extinguish the Nazarene-Jewish movement. Realistically speaking, what choice did they have? They could, in the interest of being "good Christians," abandon their Jewishness entirely and, through assimilation and intermarriage, effectively join the gentile world. Or, they could stubbornly persist in Jewish practice and observance, risking ostracism and even excommunication from ecclesiastical authorities in the west.

Apparently, they chose the latter course, continuing to believe that Yeshua was the "anointed one" while refusing to abandon their cultural heritage. "Faith" for them amounted to nothing more or less than *hutzpah*. And so it was, even late into the fourth century, when the famed presbyter of Antioch, "Saint" John Chrysostom, found it necessary to address those he called "Judaizers," who were still observing Sabbaths, taking part in Jewish festivals, making pilgrimage to Palestine and even undergoing circumcision. Such individuals probably consisted of a mixture of non-Jewish God-fearers (who as a class had still not disappeared) and Jewish Nazarenes.[13] Chrysostum observed that on Sabbaths and holy days, *Christianoi* in great numbers, especially women, still flocked to synagogues where they enjoyed the majesty and solemnity of the services. But the high point of the year was *Rosh Hashanah*, the Jewish New Year, when they would listen to the sound of the ram's horn, the *shofar*, being blown by the rabbi in order to awaken the people from spiritual slumber.

What was Chrysostum's response to all of this? In a series of eight sermons he excoriated Jews and "Judaizers" alike by attempting to force Jewish Christians (Nazarenes) to finally choose between Judaism and the new Christian religion.[14] What is remarkable in all of this is that neither rabbinic authorities nor congregants in the synagogues discriminated against the Nazarenes / *Christianoi* or forced them to leave. The Jews rejected no one while Christian leaders, including Chrysostum and many others, rejected the Jews.

Nevertheless, the moment we are inclined to close the door on the Jewish component of the developing "Christian religion," their presence is discovered in other sources. Such important "pillars" of the western Church as Epiphanius of Salamis and Jerome (who translated the Bible into the Latin Vulgate) maintained that Jewish Nazarenes could still be found in Syria well into the fourth century.[15] The sect of Nazarenes may have grown smaller when compared with the explosive growth of Roman Christianity, but they still maintained their faith. Did Pella still exist as its locus and headquarters? Did the Heirs continue to provide guidance? We cannot be sure, since the silence from the Church historians relegated them to eternal obscurity. The only thing we can know with relative certainty is that Jewish *ma'aminim* existed far longer than has traditionally been imagined.

What ultimately became of them? It is clear that after John Chrysostum's "ultimatum," there would no longer be room for Jews in any expression of Christianity. Like the Gnostics and many varieties of "heretics," they were effectively expunged from Church life. Those who valued acceptance as fellow Christians finally surrendered everything that had made them Jewish. Without the Torah and the law it contained, without circumcision, without festivals and holy days, without a kosher diet or any of the other "trappings" of the Jewish faith, it was only a matter of time until the *ma'aminim* completely disappeared from the landscape of "Christendom."

Others, we can assume, slowly slipped back into the fabric of traditional, rabbinic Judaism, remaining Jews but losing their distinctive form of Hasidic, Yeshua-oriented messianism. But was it really lost? Could it be that certain elements of the "original" faith of Yeshua and his Heirs survived within Judaism, to be expressed over time in a multitude of different ways? May vestigial traces of it even be found today? The answer may be surprising.

Notes

1   Babylonian Talmud, Berakhot, 34b.

2   John 4:46-53.

3   See Eusebius, *The Ecclesiastical History*, Vol. I, 311 (IV, 5.3-4).

4   It has been noted that the early Christian chronicler Hegesippus (see Origen, Contra Celsum, v. 59) attributed the "orthodoxy" of the Judaeo-Christians he had encountered to the fact that they had for the most part maintained a succession of *desposyni* ("kinsmen" of Jesus) as leaders of the Church. H.E. iii. 35 seems to continue this account, describing the successor to Symeon ben Clopas (who was martyred) as being a certain Justus. See W. Telfer, "Was Hegesippus a Jew," *HTR* 53.2 (1960): 143-53.

5   It may be observed that Deutero-Isaiah was a central voice in the evolution of the concept of the "Suffering Servant." While the misery of the Israelites was viewed as proof of their unworthiness, it was now seen, through the aegis of the prophets, as the mark of greatness and of the people's cosmic role in history. The

Suffering Servant theme explicates what had been implicit in the earlier idea of a "saving remnant," namely that all people share in the interdependence of humanity. See R. Gordis, *The Book of God and Man: A Study of Job* (Chicago: Univ. of Chicago Press, 1965), 144-5.

6   The modern Hasidim are also known as *Haredim* - literally, "those who tremble (before God)."

7   Jerusalem Talmud, *Taanit* 4:5.

8   The Babylonian Talmud (*Sanhedrin* 12a) indicates that Akiva's martyrdom occurred after several years of imprisonment. This suggests to some that he was executed before the outbreak of the revolt, since the Romans would have otherwise killed him quickly, without such a delay. Nevertheless, the brutality of his torture does seem to befit a post-revolt environment, and with a paucity of credible records concerning the precise events of those days, much of our recreation of events must inevitably amount to educated guesswork.

9   See Thomas Wright, *Early Christianity in Arabia: A Historical Essay* (London: Quaritch, 1855). Wright appeals to early Latin authorities and offers a complete account of the spread of the Christian sect in the region. It was not until the death of Muhammad that the last sparks of the movement were extinguished. See also Augustus J. Thebaud, *The Church and the Gentile World at the First Promulgation of the Gospel* (New York: Peter F. Collier, 1878).

10   Eusebius, *The Ecclesiastical History*, Vol. I, 311 (IV, 5.3).

11   Malachi Martin, *The Decline and Fall of the Roman Church* (New York: Bantam, 1983), 30–1.

12   Eusebius, *Life of Constantine*, III, 18.

13   See R. Wilken, "John Chrysostom," *Encyclopedia of Early Christianity*, E. Ferguson, ed. (New York: Garland, 1997).

14   See R. Stark, *The Rise of Christianity. How the Obscure, Marginal Jesus Movement Became the Dominant Religious Force in the Western World in a Few Centuries*, (Princeton: Princeton University Press, 1997), 66-7.

15   See J.R. Porter, *The Lost Bible* (Chicago: University of Chicago Press, 2001), 140.

9

Echoes

✦

IDEAS HAVE A TENDENCY TO PERSIST THROUGH TRADITION THAT reinvents itself, generation after generation. It is impossible to know definitively what became of the remnants of the Nazarenes. Some likely did surrender their Jewishness entirely, joining the fabric of the eastern churches, which eventually became known as Eastern Orthodox. But others, perhaps even the majority, including the descendants of the Heirs, slowly became reabsorbed into traditional Judaism. Some may even have rejoined the ranks of the Pious Ones, the Hasidim.

Like a single thread in a much larger tapestry, the strand they represented can scarcely be seen. But Judaism is a faith of action, not "belief," and to this day it is theoretically possible for a Jew to believe that anyone might be the Messiah and remain a perfectly observant Jew. Such a belief should never equate any person with God or ascribe deity to a human being. Moreover, through the centuries various messianic claimants continued to be proposed and even tolerated within Judaism's "big tent." Furthermore, Judaism's "tent" was apparently larger than Christianity's, for when the church councils in the west formally deified "the Christ," they made it impossible for any Jew to remain a Jew and still be a "Christian."

Messiah Son of Joseph

The extent to which messianism was an open and unresolved issue in Judaism is apparent from a difficult and rarely noticed passage tucked away in the Babylonian Talmud. Part of the difficulty lies in the fact that it seems to suggest the existence of not one, but two Messiahs. The text reads as follows:

> The Holy One ... will say to the Messiah, son of David, "Ask
> Me anything, and I will give it to you," for it is written, "I will
> announce the divine decree.... Today I have begotten you. Ask of
> Me and I will give you the nations for your inheritance" (Psalm
> 2:7–8).

God speaks to the Messiah, quoting the book of Psalms, which promises
that this "anointed one" will rule the nations. Next, God appears to make
reference to another Messiah, whose identity continues to mystify readers
of the text:

> But when God sees that Messiah son of Joseph is slain, [the other
> Messiah] will say to Him, "Lord of the universe, I ask of You only
> the gift of life"...God will answer him, "Your father David has
> already prophesied this concerning you," as it is written, 'He asked
> from You life, and You gave him length of days for ever and ever'"
> (Psalm 21:5).[1]

Is the Talmud reflecting some obscure tradition regarding two Messiahs,
the Messiah son of David and Messiah son of Joseph? We know of only
one Jewish sect who maintained such a belief, the Essenes, who lived
along the shore of the Dead Sea and who wrote hundreds of ancient scrolls
that bear the name of this brackish lake. According to their writings, there
will be both a Davidic Messiah and a Priestly Messiah who will come as a
judge at the end of days and bring divine justice to humanity.

From the Talmudic context of this particular passage it appears that
the "Messiah son of Joseph" has died in a great and final battle on behalf
of his people. Afterward, the Davidic Messiah requests from God that
his slain counterpart be brought to life again, and the request is granted.
Many commentators and scholarly sleuths have tried to make sense of this
passage, being saddled with the fundamental problem of what it is doing in
the Talmud at all. How could there be two Messiahs? Who is this Messiah
son of Joseph? Could this somehow be a reference to the prophet from
Nazareth who continued to have adherents within the developing stream
of Talmudic Judaism? Today's Christians might like to think so, imagining that pockets of Torah-true "Nazarene" Jews and members of the Heirs
persisted in a Torah-centered view of Yeshua as the "anointed one." This
may, however, be an example of "the wish fathering the thought."

The fact is, we really don't know what happened to the Nazarene sect or to the Heirs of the "Jesus dynasty" in the centuries after they found themselves ostracized by the western Church. If the bloodline of Yeshua's family continued, it is entirely possible that the descendants of the *Desposyni* forgot their own heritage. Even the name Yeshua, once popular in ancient Israel, would never be used or even mentioned again, except in a pejorative fashion. Yeshua m'Natzeret would henceforth be called Yeshu, an acrostic standing for three Hebrew words – *yimakh shmo v'zikhro* – "May his name and memory be erased." There are in fact some Talmudic passages (subsequently censored or "cleaned up") that excoriate the great Galilean, even judging him worthy of eternal damnation, an understandable, if unfortunate response to increasingly anti-Semitic western Christianity.

Could any group within Judaism, even the physical descendants of Yeshua, have remained intact in such an environment? Is it conceivable that they preserved the tradition, picked up in the Talmud, that a messianic leader would die, only to be resurrected at the request of another messianic figure? Could it be that the remnants of the Nazarenes carried on the tradition of the Messiah son of Joseph and (minus the name Yeshua) helped preserve it for centuries into the Talmudic era? As to the other Messiah, the "son of David," who prayed for the resurrection of the "son of Joseph," might this have been conceived by the Nazarenes as Yaakov (James), who was present at the Master's execution and who carried on his brother's messianic message and heritage into the future?

Recently, some important new light has been shed on the "son of Joseph" passage via an ancient text that has emerged from obscurity. This passage is taken from a stone inscription, dating from the first century BCE and therefore predating Yeshua. It has been tagged "The Gabriel Revelation." There are of course many such engravings that have been found in the land of Israel, but this one is unique. In it we find mention of a Davidic Messiah, and we also find a rough equivalency between him and another mysterious figure known as Ephraim. We find the command, "My servant David, ask Ephraim...." In the Bible, the character Ephraim was a son of none other than the great patriarch Joseph. In other words, this Messiah son of Joseph was in all likelihood a known figure by the end of the first century before the birth of Yeshua.

The Gabriel Revelation also envisions the archangel giving orders to someone, saying that "in three days you shall live."[2] But before getting overly excited about this mysterious and "prophetic" text, we should recognize that the concept of a slain Messiah could not have originally been connected with the Nazarene movement at all. "The Gabriel Revelation" is too early. It more likely had to do with an anti-Roman uprising in Israel in the wake of the death of Herod the Great in 4 BCE. This early revolt was, not surprisingly, crushed by the imperial might of Augustus Caesar, and its "messianic" leadership was exterminated. But from this catastrophe a resurrected Messiah was expected to rise in three days. According to recent scholarship, the "Messiah son of Joseph" amounted to nothing more than Zealot folklore. It was later picked up by the the Heirs of Yeshua and transferred to the story of the Master's death and return to life at the spot marked by an ancient grotto and later by a church called the Holy Sepulcher. While in later rabbinic Judaism such ideas were dismissed, there was remarkably still room to record in the sacred text of the Talmud this otherwise forgotten legend.

Were the remnants of the Nazarenes still scattered among Jewish communities in Babylonia and elsewhere keeping such folklore alive for centuries into the Talmudic age? In truth this tradition likely made its way into the Talmud without any help from the Nazarenes and their remnants. But at least for some time, the most dominant, widespread group to hold and perpetuate the "Messiah son of Joseph" concept must have been the Nazarenes, who would not go quietly into oblivion.

The Movement, the Message, and the Yoke

What we can say for certain is that Yeshua's movement, for all its tenacity, wasn't theologically based to begin with. Its claims for Yeshua as Messiah had to have been loud. However (while it may come as a shock to most theologically-minded modern folk) the message wasn't entirely about messianism. It was messianic in the simple sense that it was about the most basic of Jewish values – life, and how to live more abundantly.

Chief among the tenets of this message was the concept of the "Kingdom of Heaven." The word "Heaven" is itself a Hebraic euphemism for the word "God," whose name is deemed too holy to vocalize. According to most Christian Bibles, Yeshua had declared, "The Kingdom of Heaven is *within* you" (Luke 17:21). But this reading spiritualizes the concept in a way inconsistent with the plain meaning. We should instead read (based on early Syriac versions of the passage), "The Kingdom of Heaven is *among* you," that is, in the midst of the pious among the people, the Hasidim. In fact, had the early *ma'aminim* been called by any name other than Nazarene, they might well have been referred to as the "Kingdom of Heaven movement."

For the Nazarenes, God's reign was not a place, nor a future "event" to come to fruition at the end of the world. It was in the present, finding expression moment by moment in the daily lives of its adherents. It was Hasidic devotion that also found eloquent voice in Yeshua's words, "The Kingdom of Heaven is at hand" (Matthew 10:7). Christian theologians misunderstood the plain sense of these words down through the ages, suggesting that the Kingdom is soon to come, but nonetheless at the end of days. This "spiritualizing" tendency was probably due to the fact that the western Church had become Romanized and that its leaders did not want to imply that God's kingdom might be in opposition to Rome's. But the Hasidic sages rightly grasped what it meant all along, namely, that the "reign" of the Divine is right now and that when it breaks forth in totality, even the might of Rome would be nullified.

This had all along been the teaching of the Hasidim, among whom the Nazarenes were absorbed. Wherever we find the Kingdom of Heaven teaching in rabbinic literature, we may be hearing the echoes of the Heirs. We know from history that the more oppressed the Israelites felt by the "Worldly Kingdom" (Rome), the more those of Hasidic bent anticipated that the reign of the Divine would appear spontaneously in the here-and-now. It was the fervent desire that God would be king over all the earth, that idolatry would be banished, and that the lion would lay down with the lamb, establishing universal peace.

We find this wish preserved in Jewish liturgy, dating back to the earliest form of the so-called *Aleinu* prayer:

> Then all the inhabitants of the earth will perceive and confess that every knee must bend to You, and every tongue confess. Before You, O Eternal our God, shall they kneel and fall down, and unto Your glorious name give praise. So will they accept the yoke of Your kingdom, and You shall reign over them speedily forever and ever. For Thine is the kingdom, and for all eternity You will reign in glory, as it is written in Your Torah: "The Eternal shall reign forever and ever." It is also said: "And the Eternal shall reign over all the world; on that day the Eternal shall be One and His name One." (author's translation)

This prayer came at the very end of the Sabbath service, and before leaving the synagogue, the entire congregation would bow low in prostration while reciting it. While there is no mention of a personal Messiah in the prayer, its ideas were something that the Nazarene remnants, now reabsorbed into Hasidic Judaism, could certainly give assent to. The rabbis even declared that no benediction would be truly effective without some reference to the Kingdom of Heaven.[3]

But as with everything else in Judaism, nothing happens by itself, or even by divine fiat alone. In order for the Kingdom of Heaven to be established on earth, it must first be recognized and accepted by human beings. A saying arose among the Hasidim that before one recites the most important benediction in Judaism, "Hear O Israel, the Eternal is One," one must first personally accept "the yoke of the Kingdom of Heaven." The great medieval mystical tractate called the Zohar transmits the same teaching:

> At the time of the recitation of the *Sh'ma* ("Hear O Israel"), a man has to be prepared to proclaim the unity of the Divine Name and to accept the yoke of the Kingdom of Heaven.[4]

Moreover, just as human beings do this on earth, so do the angels above, when they chant in unison, "Holy, holy, holy, is the God of Armies!" For the Jewish mystics taught that whatever happens on earth in the physical realm is accompanied by a divine occurrence in the supernatural realm (Heaven). There was also the concept, articulated in rabbinic commentaries (such as *Mekhilta*) that when faith in a single God is finally recognized by all humanity, people "... will take upon themselves the yoke of the Kingdom of Heaven as they throw away their idols."[5]

Abraham was said to have accepted the divine yoke, thereby making him king on earth.[6] It was said that when the Israelites crossed the Red Sea, they first sang the praises of the Kingdom of Heaven. It was also declared that they accepted the yoke of the Kingdom when they camped at Mount Sinai. Every righteous proselyte, upon entering the Jewish faith likewise accepts the yoke of God's Kingdom.[7]

But what comprises this "yoke"? Farmers will tell us that beasts of burden such as oxen or horses are driven and controlled by the yoke, a sharpened wooden crosspiece bound to the neck by which a wagon is pulled. For Jews there was no question but that this yoke was the Torah that "trains" humanity in the path of righteousness. The yoke of the Torah was said to grant freedom from all other yokes:

> Whoever takes upon himself the yoke of Torah removes the yoke of the earthly kingdom and the yoke of hard labor. (Mishnah Avot, 3:5, author's translation)

But as we have seen, there is nothing passive about fidelity to the Torah. As oxen pull the wagon via the yoke, so must the Israelites, and by extension the human family, perform the commandments and seek to do all that God requires. It is only then that people begin to experience the miraculous in daily life, what some would call "the abundant life" and what Jews call "the good life." Even though Yeshua's movement was no longer part of the Jewish world, his message remained, being not only tolerated, but embraced. It was all about life (Hebrew *Khayim*) – ever a Jewish value – and life abundant (John 10:10).

Metaphysical Death, Spiritual Life

Even today, in ultra-Orthodox Judaism, there is serious discussion of the Kingdom of Heaven and what it means to take on this yoke. It is taught that the main point of reciting the "Hear O Israel" is to accept God's yoke completely. But this is impossible, modern mystics assert, without first accepting nothing less than a metaphysical "death sentence" from the ancient Jewish legal authority, the *Bet Din*. This biblically sanctioned court was authorized to hand down four types of death sentences: decapitation, burning at the stake, stoning and strangulation. One must accept them all, on a mystical level, following the rabbinical principle that "the laws of the Kingdom are the laws," and all of us have transgressed, as the great prophet Isaiah observed: "All we like sheep have gone astray; we have turned every one to his own way." (53:6).

Modern Hasidic Jews, the spiritual descendants of their ancient counterparts, teach that accepting the yoke of the Kingdom implies accepting this death, whereupon one enters a new world of freedom. When people desperately cling to life in the physical world, they cannot appropriate new life in the spiritual dimension. But when one is willing to relinquish his life in the physical dimension, a new reality opens up. One is no longer bound to the worldly realm. One is no longer a slave to the physical earth or corporeal existence. By allowing the Torah to pass its just sentence, we are set free. By dying we become alive.

It is a message that sounds "Christian," yet it comes from the most orthodox segment of the Jewish world. It would be presumptuous to suggest that this teaching somehow results from the lingering presence of the Nazarene movement across the centuries, but it is not unreasonable to point out the similarity between the words of modern Hasidim and those of Yeshua: "Those who seek to save their lives will lose them, but those who lose their lives will preserve them" (Luke 17:33, 9:24; Matthew

16:25). Yeshua himself would certainly have agreed that the message is more important than the messenger.

The teaching is also echoed in the words of Shaul, who wrote of "... having died to that which held us" (Romans 7:6). Shaul, as we have seen, had his own agenda, namely, that his non-Jewish God-fearers not be required to observe the ordinances of the Torah in order to join what was without question a Jewish sect. But he frequently employed the very teachings of pious Hasidism to make his point. The Hasidim themselves would never have suggested that the Torah's requirements be abrogated, but they did counsel that performing its commandments (*mitzvot*) can be approached not mechanically, out of a sense of onerous duty and responsibility, but with a glad heart, almost effortlessly. It is the ultimate paradox that in dying, we live. Contrary to what most theologians are inclined to believe, this concept is not essentially "Christian" at all, but is in fact Hasidic.

In other words, when the truly pious person accepts the yoke of the Kingdom, obedience to its righteous precepts is no longer burdensome, but joyful. It comes naturally, without even thinking, just as the prophet Jeremiah had declared:

> After those days, says the Eternal, I will put My Torah in their inmost parts, and write it upon their hearts; and I will be their God, and they will be My people. And they will no more teach every man his neighbor and every man his brother, saying, Know the Eternal; for they will all know me, from the least of them to the greatest... For I will forgive their transgressions, and remember their sins no more. (Jeremiah 31:33-34, author's translation)

Indeed, there are parallels to many if not all of the ideas of "Kingdom ideology" ensconced in the multiple collections of rabbinic literature. The exact identity of the Messiah was never the important point, though all agreed that an anointed prince would someday come to occupy the throne of David. Moreover, the idea of a militant Messiah with sword in hand, ready to vanquish the Romans, had forever vanished. In its place the Hasidic-oriented concept of a spiritual Messiah bringing both personal and corporate redemption (a concept quite similar to the earliest Jewish Nazarenes) took hold deeply.

But the rabbis never faltered in their tenacious devotion to a single God, which meant that divine status must never be attributed to any human being, even the "anointed one." Anyone who wavered on this point must be corrected. Once, the Talmudic sage, Reish Lakish, went so far as to declare that when, according to the book of Genesis, the spirit of God "hovered upon the surface of the waters" (Genesis 1:2), this was nothing less than "the breath of the Messiah." His fellow rabbis rebuked him for his insolence in assigning supernatural status to the Messiah, to the point of making him divine. There are not two gods, the divine Father and the Messiah, and there are certainly not (as in western Christian formulation) three.

Sometimes the rabbinic literature does speak of the Messiah in exalted terms, so much so that Professor David Flusser of the Hebrew University of Jerusalem speculated that Christianity's high view of Jesus was actually rooted in ancient Judaism.[8]

Some Talmudic passages elevate the "anointed one" to a surprising level:

> "And God saw the light and it was good." This is the light of the Messiah ... to teach you that God saw the generation of Messiah and His works before He created the universe, and He hid the Messiah ... under His throne of Glory. Satan asked God, Master of the Universe: "For whom is this light under your throne of Glory?" God answered him, "It is for ... [the Messiah] who is to turn you backward and who will put you to scorn with shamefacedness." (Sanhedrin 99a; Berachot 34b; Shabbat 63a)

Elsewhere, the Talmud declares:

> Rabbi Yohanan taught that all the world was created for Messiah. What is His name? The school of Shiloh taught; His name is Shiloh as it is written (Gen. 49:10). (Sanhedrin 98b)

As late as the ninth century, we find Jewish commentaries that proclaim this high view of the Messiah:

> The Messiah shall be more exalted than Abraham... more extolled than Moses ... and be very high; that is higher than the ministering angels ... (Midrash Tanhuma and Yalkut, vol. 2, par. 338)

The great mystical rabbi of medieval Spain, Moshe ben Nachman (Nachmonides) compared the Messiah with the innermost sanctum of the long-destroyed Temple:

This Holy of Holies is the Messiah who is sanctified more than the sons of David.

Rabbi Jonathan ben Uzziel added, "That the 'vision and prophecy' may be fulfilled even unto Messiah, the Holy of the Holies."

Nevertheless, not even these passages go as far as to make the Messiah into a god. They do, however, reveal the intense longing that Jews harbored over the centuries for God's representative to set things right on earth and bring about an end to war, bloodshed and human suffering. Therefore, if the Nazarene Heirs and their descendants were in fact reabsorbed into the fabric of traditional Judaism, they probably felt right at home.

If we put together the puzzle pieces, we see a plausible scenario of what happened to the Nazarene communities. They may well have rejoined the Jewish communities in the region of Damascus and across Arabia as well as Babylonia, where distinct pockets of Nazarenes had previously thrived, while progressively withdrawing from the Greco-Roman world.

At what point they finally ceased to honor Yeshua personally we may never know. They certainly continued to view Shaul as a heretic, but they nonetheless may have shared some of his ideas about the Messiah in a "cross-pollination" with traditional Jews in the east. Their version of messianism postulated that the "anointed one," while generated humanly and naturally, was also a reflection of the "Primordial Adam" – the "Perfect Man" of the heavenly realm after whom the physical Adam was fashioned. This does not make him divine, but it does suggest that he "emanated" from the heavenly realm. This "cross-pollination" would explain why some Talmudic passages proclaim such an exalted view of the Messiah.

In truth such ideas may well be seen as part of mystical Judaism, which came to be known through the centuries as "Kabbalah." As a religious ideology, this mystical messianism employed the imagery of darkness and light and used such language as "sons of light" in the same way as the Dead Sea Scrolls. They appear to have developed the idea of a returning messianic figure who had appeared (as the "Primordial Adam") at specific intervals, such as in the guise of the Melchizedek, the priest-king who suddenly materialized before Abraham (Genesis 14:18-20). This same figure was expected to return, once and for all, at the end of days.

The Kingdom, Kabbalah, and Messiah Sightings

Few serious scholars imagine that the Jewish Nazarenes continued as a distinct movement beyond the first few centuries of the Common Era, but their ideas about the immanence of the Divine Presence expressed in the messianic "kingdom" occur repeatedly in Jewish thought. In the 1500s in the mystical town of Tzfat, nestled high in the hills of Galilee, the kabbalistic rabbi Isaac Luria suddenly asked his disciples to come with him to Jerusalem. When they protested, saying that it was a long trip and that they did not want to leave their wives behind, Luria fired back, "Woe to us! I saw that the Messiah was ready to appear in Jerusalem, and if you had decided to come immediately, we would have been rescued from our exile in the Diaspora."

In the 1600s there was another "Messiah sighting," focused on a charismatic youth whose family had fled from Jewish Spain to Ottoman Turkey. His name was Shabbetai Zvi, and, upon traveling to Palestine and settling for a time in Jerusalem he would foment the most substantial messianic movement since the days of Yeshua. Back in his hometown of Smyrna, on the coast of Asia Minor, he went so far as to celebrate his mystical marriage to the Torah, cradling it in his arms and chanting an old Castilian love song.

Unfortunately for his followers, the "new Messiah" was intercepted on the Sea of Marmara by the Turkish sultan and promptly thrown into prison. Undaunted, he still maintained his messiahship, which he expressed in the most curious ways. While the ancient Hasidim, to whom Yeshua was aligned, were assiduous in their practice of ritual purity, Shabbetai Zvi threw the purity laws overboard. While imprisoned he slew a lamb for Passover and he and his disciples ate it along with the fat, a clear violation of the Torah. He recited the following: "Blessed be God who hath restored again that which was forbidden." Though still revered across the Diaspora, he ultimately converted to Islam and his movement slowly unravelled.

But the embers of messianism continued to burn. One disciple named Jacob Frank not only refused to surrender his messianic faith, but strangely found himself converting to Christianity. Meanwhile, in the midst of the dispute, another kabbalist, ethical writer and poet, named Moshe Chaim Luzzatto, taught the importance of working toward a spiritual redemption, what he called "the healing power of the Shekhinah ('Divine Presence')." He organized a "Society of Seekers of God," whose avowed goal was the study of the great book of Kabbalah that came forth out of Spain, the Zohar. This they did in shifts, day and night, without ceasing in the expectation that the activity itself would hasten the messianic age.

Though the Heirs of Yeshua simply vanished into the proverbial "woodwork," their ideas about the present-tense Kingdom of Heaven and a spiritual, metaphysical redemption continued to flourish. The concepts they championed, that the Messiah is an expression of the "Primordial Adam," continued to find expression. Indeed, there were always Jews who thought and taught as Yeshua and his brother Yaakov had. Perhaps the greatest lesson for modern students of comparative religion is that instead of getting "hung up" on who "believes in Jesus" and who doesn't, the healthy approach is to figure out what Yeshua really meant by his "Kingdom of Heaven" message and discover its applications across religious and denominational lines. Indeed, how could Jesus have been "rejected" by the Jewish people as long as the heart of his message lived on, even in the heart of orthodox and ultra-orthodox Judaism?

One common teaching among the rabbinic sages was that a potential Messiah makes an appearance in every generation. One piece of Talmudic folklore tells of a greatly revered rabbi who approached the gates of Rome one day only to find the Messiah standing there idly. "When will you finally come?" the incredulous rabbi asked. To his amazement, the Anointed One responded, "Today!" The rabbi was overjoyed and eagerly waited the entire day, only to find that nothing happened. He returned the following day with disappointment and puzzlement, asking, "You said the Messiah would come this very day, but he did not! Why the delay?" The Anointed One answered, "Today, if only you will hear His voice…" (Psalm 95:7). Indeed, "The Kingdom of Heaven is within you/ among you," but you have to recognize it. Put another way, the rabbis taught, "Pray as if everything depends on God; live as if everything depends on you!"

Just as in ancient times, the Kingdom of Heaven concept seems to have resided primarily among Hasidic Jews, who were the most earnest in seeking a deep experience with God beyond the performance of *mitzvahs* (commandments) alone. Another proponent of such ideas came out of the shadows of central Poland in the 1700s to foster one of the most dynamic spiritual movements the Jewish world has ever seen. His name was Israel ben Eliezer, also known as the Baal Shem Tov, the "Master of a Good Name."

Like the Hasidic masters of ancient Judea, he wasn't particularly well versed in Jewish law, but he was particularly gifted as a divine healer. As he traveled from town to town through the Polish province of Galicia, he immersed himself in meditation, glimpsing the divine hand in each flower and each blade of grass. Stories about his healing touch circulated widely. Like Yeshua m'Natzeret he never wrote anything down in his own lifetime, but his disciples collected his teachings and recorded the miracles he performed. It was even said that he was once spirited up into the heavens and was privileged to see the Messiah. Upon asking, "When will you come down and reveal yourself on earth?" the Anointed One responded, "When the wellspring of your teaching has been spread throughout the world, when your fountains burst forth to those outside."

This wasn't just a mystical/ kabbalistic approach, but a Hasidic message. Like the Nazarene movement of antiquity, spiritual enlightenment was destined to spread beyond the confines of a single group or sect, becoming the inheritance of all, since everyone and everything is interconnected. As with Yeshua, the teaching of the Baal Shem Tov was designed not to beckon people away from the world but to draw them back into it. The goal was to dissolve inner barriers so as to help people connect with others and with the self. The result is deep humility, peace, joy and love expressing itself in the most minute details of life. At its core it is an "inclusive" way of looking at our humanity, recognizing the infinite potential in each of us to change the world, one *mitzvah* at a time.

The Voice Echoes On

Three centuries later, after the Baal Shem Tov's passing, the distant voice of the ancient Hasidim, by whatever name it is called, still resonates. The descendants of the family of Yeshua, whose movement was once so strong and vital in the land of Judea, may at first glance seem to have vanished. We don't know what became of their lineage, though their genetic fingerprints undoubtedly reside somewhere among the Jewish people of today. There are surely Jews alive in our world whose distant ancestors include Yaakov (James) and his brothers, as well as the line of *Desposyni* who succeeded him. But we can expect that they are unaware that their forefathers were once the leaders of the Nazarene movement. Some of them may even be counted among the Hasidim of today, whose presence is felt as strongly as ever within the fabric of Jewish culture.

"Yeshua-figures" continue to present themselves across the Jewish landscape, sometimes with astonishing impact. In the middle of the twentieth century a kabbalistic rabbi known as the Baba Sali stepped out of obscurity in Morocco and became a legend. He was in the lineage of a family of great Talmudic scholars, but his real claim to fame came as a modern worker of miracles. He was raised to develop the quality of "guarding the tongue," reminiscent of the admonitions of the Nazarenes' book of James ("Whoever thinks he is religious but does not bridle his tongue deceives his own heart," 1:26). The Baba Sali immigrated to Israel along with the entire Moroccan Jewish community, whereupon he gained the reputation of being a true "holy man" and the "praying father" of his people. His wife Precha was not only his soul mate, but a co-laborer in the vineyard of God.

The Baba Sali took up residence near a rabbinical yeshiva in Israel's Negev Desert to the south of Judea where his spiritual presence was such a magnet that the region became a focal point for Jewish renewal. The desert began to bloom spiritually and thousands came to rediscover their own religious roots. The rabbi of the Moroccans quickly became recognized as a leader of world Jewry.

The story is told that a secular ex-soldier in the Israeli army, paralyzed from the waist down in the 1973 Yom Kippur War, came to the Baba Sali as a last resort. Having never seen the man before, the Moroccan sage knew through spiritual discernment that he had never honored the Sabbath or worn Tefillin (little boxes attached with leather straps, containing the declaration, "Hear O Israel"). Did he not know that God gives us limbs in order to render service to the Divine? If he would only agree to become observant, he would receive a complete and miraculous healing. As the penitent paralytic lowered his head and kissed the hand of the "praying father," Precha, the ever faithful wife, urged him to attempt to stand up. In a moment that reminds us of the paralytic healed at the Beautiful Gate of the ancient Temple, when Shimon (Peter) and Yohanan (John) commanded him to "rise up and walk" (Acts 3:6), a flood of supernatural power coursed through the man's lifeless limbs and he stood on his feet and began to walk. The "Kingdom of Heaven" had manifested itself.

The beloved sage and healer died in 1984, his funeral being attended by upwards of 100,000 mourners. His grave remains a site for pilgrimage among modern Israelis and Jews from abroad. To this day pictures of the Baba Sali can be seen, displayed proudly in shops and felafel stands across Israel, especially among the Moroccan community. His influence has been felt worldwide, wherever the seed of Abraham seeks to reconnect with God.

While the legacy of the Baba Sali will not soon be forgotten, the most dominant modern expression of Hasidism and messianism is without a doubt the ultra-orthodox Habad-Lubavitch movement, whose bearded, black-coated adherents stand out for their dress as well as their piety. Headquartered in Crown Heights, Brooklyn, but with an international reach, the organization's basis is a mystical book called the *Tanya*. This collection consists of the teachings of the eighteenth century Hasidic sage

Rabbi Shneur Zalman of Liadi and is said to contain the key to true spiritual awareness.

A veritable dynasty of "Rebbes" followed (not unlike the Heirs), culminating in the seventh and most illustrious of all, Rabbi Menachem Mendel Schneerson. Beginning in 1950, he built Habad (an acronym for the Hebrew words meaning "Wisdom," "Understanding," and "Knowledge") into a movement of unparalleled spiritual dynamic in Orthodox Judaism, emphasizing practical methods to draw close to God. Like the great rabbi of Galilee two millennia ago, Schneerson's approach involved the use of parables and multiple examples in order to understand the innermost psyche and to deal with the challenges of daily life. Moreover, everyone is to understand that there is a purpose in everything and in the universe as a whole, from the creation of the world to the sanctity of each individual life, since the world itself exists only through divine intervention. With this knowledge, received intellectually and through meditation, one may aspire to complete control over one's deeds and actions. Emotion is ephemeral, while through the mind one can control the heart, taking captive one's lusts and desires and steering the soul in the right direction.

The movement's tone tends to be strict and demanding toward the self but moderate and lenient toward others. "Habadnicks" are disinclined to point an accusing finger at anyone else as if to condemn them for not being more "observant." Rather, they encourage fellow Jews to be just a little more observant than they already are, the idea being that "faith," which is still defined by behavior rather than "mental gymnastics," is a simple function of taking "baby steps," which, once joined, become enormous strides forward.

But what about the message to the non-Jewish world? As with Yeshua, who two millennia ago directed his disciples not to go into "the way of the Gentiles" (Matthew 10:5), Habad-Lubavitch is solely for Jews, especially wayward Jews, and is designed to woo them back toward a Torah-true expression of their faith. Habad does proselytize, and even sends out emissaries (in Hebrew, *sh'lichim* – "apostles"), but it does not seek to bring non-Jews into the faith. It does teach, however, that non-Jews are integral in the divine plan for humanity and that they are obligated to keep the much-celebrated "seven laws of the sons of Noah." It is believed that the keeping of this basic set of common-sense ethical requirements by the Gentile nations will hasten the coming of the Messiah.

Again we find echoes of the early Nazarene movement. Interestingly enough, they are the same laws that were condensed into four by the

Council of Jerusalem under the auspices of Yeshua's brother Yaakov, becoming the "door" through which non-Israelites might enter the Nazarene
sect. The difference of course is that the huge sect of "God-fearers," who
used to flock to synagogues in their thousands across the Greco-Roman
world, no longer exists, cancelling any discussion of large numbers of
Gentiles desiring to attach themselves to Judaism or to any Jewish sect.
Nor is there anyone like Shaul who might seek to create new Jewish
sects of non-Jews. Today's Habadnicks have no desire to initiate non-Jews
into their own movement, and, as Jews have traditionally done, heartily
discourage conversion into Judaism. The modern attitude is, "Don't you
have enough problems and challenges already, that you want to become
Jewish too?" Keeping the "Noachide Laws" is more than enough.

Who Wants to Be a Hasid?

In point of fact, the Habad-Lubavitch movement is not a bad analogy for what the Nazarene sect under the Heirs might have resembled.
Anyone, Jewish or not, may visit a Habad synagogue for services. The
Rebbe's presence will certainly be felt, from the moment a visitor walks
in the door, since the visitor will most likely find the Rebbe's picture
displayed prominently on the wall, his piercing eyes looking out with determination beneath the rim of his thick black hat. If the visitor asks about
him, he will be told that this is Menachem Mendel Schneerson, illustrious founder of Habad, who unfortunately died of a brain hemmorhage in
1994. But his stature has not diminished in death. What you will not be
told is that a good many Habadnicks worldwide are not only in "denial"
about the Rebbe's death, but they fervently expect that he will in fact be
resurrected some day. He will come back to life because he was and is in
fact the Messiah.

One might imagine that if such a thing were truly believed by the
Habadnicks, this belief would be the central element of every service,
reproduced in creedal formulas and, as it were, "shouted from the house-
tops" (Luke 12:3). This, however, is not the case. The Rebbe's teaching is
central while his messiahship is a matter of personal conviction. A visitor
will not succeed in discussing with any of the congregants the founder's
possible return. Recall that Yeshua's own messiahship was very much a
"secret," and that he repeatedly ordered those around him not to say too
much ("See that you say nothing to anyone," Mark 1:44). The Habad services themselves follow traditional orthodox liturgy, but a visitor will not
find any direct reference to the Rebbe. There are not prayers offered on

his behalf and certainly no prayers directed *to* him. There has always been harsh criticism directed against the Hasidim, that they engage in nothing short of "rabbi worship." This of course is hyperbole, since Menachem Mendel Schneerson is loved and revered in death as he was in life, but has by no means been deified even though his imminent resurrection is anticipated by many.

Have the Heirs of Yeshua in a sense "survived" among today's ultra-orthodox Hasidim? Is the whole approach of Habad-Lubavitch to the Rebbe a paradigm of sorts for the kind of attitude and even worship practices that would have been familiar to Yaakov and his dynasty of *Desposyni*? What about the argument of Shaul that the movement should be opened to large numbers of non-Jews who professed faith in Israel's God and in Yeshua but chafed at the idea of full conversion to Judaism?

Imagine what it would be like for a non-Jewish visitor to come to a Habad-Lubavitch Sabbath service. Would a "Gentile" be welcomed in such an ultra-orthodox environment? Absolutely. Of course the prayers, which are entirely in Hebrew, would sound like so much gibberish, but the invitation to stay and observe would still be extended. What if the same visitor returned week after week and even began to learn the Hebrew prayers? Would this "Gentile" be invited to join in the prayers with the rest of the congregation? Absolutely. The fact is, any non-Jew would be allowed to participate in the entire service, in all its aspects, save for one thing. A non-Jew would not be allowed to come to the *bima* (the elevated platform in the center of the congregation) and read from the Torah.

What if the returning visitor became so enamored of the Habad brand of Hasidism that he wanted to join the movement? What if he asked, "Where can I purchase my black coat and black hat?" Would this person be discriminated against for being a non-Jew? The answer would be, "Habad discriminates against no one. But you can't come in as a non-Jew and decide that you want to be a member of a Jewish organization. If you insist, there are a few things you have to address, such as *brit milah* (Hebrew for circumcision)." Indeed, it would be absurd for non-Jews to be admitted into a very exclusive Jewish sect without first becoming Jewish. So it is today, and so it seemed to Yaakov and the first *ma'aminim*, who wrestled with this question at the Council of Jerusalem in the middle of the first century.

Imagine the result if today's Habad-Lubavitch suddenly threw open its doors to non-Jews, who in time became so numerous as to swamp the fabric of the movement entirely. Would the whole character of the movement change? Would it become, as it were, a "Schneerson Veneration Society," where the Rebbe was not only honored, but made into a god? Would he come to be seen as co-equal with God Almighty? Would prayer be directed to him personally? Would antiphonal hymns be sung to him? Would any deviation from "Schneerson-worship" be condemned as heresy? And would Hasidic Jews, who pioneered this pietistic expression of faith, be systematically shoved aside, called "legalists" if they did not abandon the observance of the Torah and its precepts, and consigned to hellfire for eternity? Perhaps "echoes" of the movement would survive in small pockets, especially in the land of Israel, where the western megaculture is less dominant. For westerners, the Rebbe would become merely a religious image, an icon of sorts, devoid of any factual "biography." "You mean, he was Jewish?" most would ask, incredulously. Someone else might say, "But didn't he leave Judaism, to start a new faith?" As absurd a scenario as this sounds, it is not unlike the melancholy history of the Heirs of Yeshua as we have reconstructed it in these pages.

Of Rebbes, Lawyers and Lawsuits

There is no one like Shaul today and for this reason Habad is likely to remain Habad. Some, however, would say the movement is already becoming "Christianized." Recently, two branches of Habad-Lubavitch ended up in court over the issue of the Rebbe's "messianism." The Brooklyn headquarters of the movement is controlled by a "radical" group who are convinced that the Rebbe is not only the Messiah, but is in fact still alive. There are signs on display, proclaiming his messiahship, adorning, among other things the "Ark of the Covenant" where the Torah scrolls are kept. An empty seat may be found, exclusively reserved for the Rebbe. But is it really empty, when little children point to it exclaiming that they actually *see* him? At the beginning of services, the congregants form an aisle through which the Rebbe is said to enter, with due pomp and glory, invisible to some but manifest and perceptible to the eyes of others.

An Israeli rabbi wrote an article in 2003 in which he declared that Habad-Lubavitch is, spiritually speaking, Jerusalem and that the Brooklyn headquarters is the Temple. The Rebbe represents the true "Ark of the Covenant," resting on the "foundation stone." It is this holy "Ark," embodied in the Rebbe himself, that is home to the Divine Presence.[9]

The other side in the controversy, the "moderates," claim that such a paradigm, in which worshippers face an invisible human being representing the Divine Presence during prayer is, from the standpoint of Jewish law, no different from a Christian church. In a confrontation that has unfortunately turned violent, the "radicals" defaced a plaque placed on the outside of the building by the "moderates," referring to the Rebbe by a Hebrew abbreviation referencing him as deceased. The whole dispute ended up in court. While the judge decided that he would not intervene in an internal, theological dispute, he nonetheless ruled that the headquarters building itself belonged to the "moderates," the "non-messianist" faction called *Agudat Hasidei Habad.* The problem they face is that a clear majority of those at the headquarters remain committed to the Rebbe's messiahship, though the percentage who hold that he is still alive or is somehow "divine" is harder to assess.

Complicating matters is the fact that many among the "moderates" themselves believe that the Rebbe may one day reveal himself as the Messiah. Moreover, the movement's major educational and communal institutions, as well as its emissaries, appear to embrace the "messianist" approach.[10] Though the court decision may mean that overt reference to the Rebbe will decline at the Brooklyn headquarters, the influence of the "true believers" is far from finished. If we could somehow whisk Yaakov and the Heirs into the twenty-first century to address such issues, one wonders whether they too would denounce the Habad "radicals" for having turned the Rebbe into a demi-god. Now, as in antiquity, contention abounds where there exist religious sects.

Epilogue: "Mythbusting"

What have we learned from this kaleidoscope of religious history? The lessons are multiple, well beyond what we might at first imagine. Few can dispute that religion is in its own right a fairly benign phenomenon, at least as far as the human psyche is concerned. When religious societies form that are "tribal" and sectarian in nature, this personal devotion often turns to group intolerance. The inherently mysterious nature of divinity turns into myth, perhaps needing to be made more concrete for mass consumption. Yeshua, the real man, the historical figure, became Jesus the Christ, morphed by generations of well-meaning religionists into a stained-glass image, unrecognizable to Yeshua himself or any of the people who knew him.

A similar process transformed his mother, Miriam, into a mythologized Mary, ever-virgin and suffused with deity, in stark contrast to the real mother, who might have pointed the way to understanding the great Galilean. Her offspring, Yeshua's brothers and sisters, might have been the clearest link to the Master's original redemptive message that has changed the lives of so many. But because the essential Jewishness of all these people was obcured by western Christendom, those living links were lost. It is important to stress that nothing in these pages is designed to entice Christians to become Jews or Jews to become Christians. History shows that proselytism often diminishes (at least on an ethical level) the very faith intended to be advanced. The real goal of this brief "alternative history" of Yeshua's Heirs is simply to understand and appreciate it *within* the culture that spawned it.

It is in fact possible to cultivate a healthy appreciation of Yeshua and his dynasty as real people, regardless of our own religious and cultural backgrounds. Today's world, while it may have become to all intents and purposes a "global village," is just as diverse and multi-cultural as ever. The healthy difference is that an increasing number of this global village's members are anxious to put narrow stereotypes behind, to actively embrace multiculturalism, and to celebrate diversity. Above all, in small but important "baby steps" we are learning to accept each other along the way. Many are learning that God may be identified by whatever name we choose to call Him / Her.

As one who is no stranger to Judaism, I frequently attend synagogue myself and just as frequently find myself asking, whatever became of the Heirs of Yeshua? I answer myself that, spiritually speaking, they're present in the synagogue, faithfully reciting the prayers of their ancestors along with me. Moreover, the fundamental message of Yeshua, that the Kingdom of Heaven is here among us, is still alluded to in these prayers, and to that extent the "Torah" of Yeshua is as alive in Judaism as it has ever been. Any modern Kabbalist will tell you that the Divine Presence and all of its attendant power to transform, to heal, to make individuals and societies whole again, is accessible to everyone, Jew and non-Jew alike.

It is however, dangerous to reduce this message to "theology." Harmful divisions occur when we denigrate or condemn our fellow travelers on life's journey because their theological understandings differ from our own. The Kingdom of Heaven really is within us and among us. As we connect with the Universe, with God, we just may bring the Messiah into our lives every day.

Notes

1   Babylonian Talmud, *Sukkah* 52a, author's translation.

2   This reconstruction of the wording is the work of Israel Knohl, professor of Biblical Studies at the Hebrew University of Jerusalem. He believes that the original engraving referred to a Jewish rebel leader named Shimon, who led a revolt immediately after the death of king Herod the Great in 4 BCE, only to be killed by the armies of Herod and the emperor Augustus. See I. Knohl, *The Messiah Before Jesus* (Berkeley: University of California Press, 2000), 27–42.

3   Babylonian Talmud, Berakhot 12a.

4   Soncino Zohar, Shemot, Section 2, page 160b–161b.

5   Mek., Beshallah, Amalek, 2; author's translation.

6   Jubilees 12:19; Sifre, Deuteronomy, 313.

7   See Exodus Rabba and Targum Yer. to Exodus 15:19; Sifra, Kedoshim, 11.

8   See Flusser, "Messianism and Christology," in *Judaism*, 246–279.

9   See *"Ekronot be-Olam ha-Hasidut"* at http://www.hageula.com.

10 See D. Berger, *The Rebbe, the Messiah, and the Scandal of Orthodox Indifference* (Littman Library of Jewish Civilization, 2001).

Works Cited

Alon, G., *Jews, Judaism, and the Classical World* (Jerusalem: Magnes Press, 1977).

Atkinson, K., "On the Herodian Origin of Militant Davidic Messianism at Qumran: New Light from Psalm of Solomon 17," *JBL* 118.3 (1999): 435-60.

Berger, D., *The Rebbe, the Messiah, and the Scandal of Orthodox Indifference* (Littman Library of Jewish Civilization, 2001).

Bonz, M.P., "The Jewish Donor Inscriptions from Aphrodisias: Are They Both Third-Century, and Who Are the *Theosebeis?*" *HSCP* 96 (1994): 281-99.

Briggs, C.W., "The Apostle Paul in Arabia," *BW* 41.4 (1913): 255-9.

Broshi, M., Review of Baigent 1991, *BA* 55.2 (1991):107-8.

_____, Review of Eisenman 1993, *BA* 57.1 (1994): 62-3.

Burkill, T.A., "The Competence of the Sanhedrin," *VC* 10.2 (1956): 80-96.

Case, S.J., "The New Testament Writers' Interpretation of the Old Testament," *BW* 38.2 (1911): 99-102.

Chilton, D., *Paradise Restored: A Biblical Theology of Dominion* (Nashville: Dominion Press, 1987).

Clemen, C., "Josephus and Christianity," *BW* 25.5 (1905): 361-75.

Cooper, J.M. and Procope, J.F., *Seneca: Moral and Political Essays* (Cambridge: Cambridge University Press, 1995).

Cross, F.M., *The Ancient Library of Qumran and Modern Biblical Studies* (New York: Greenwood Press, 1958).

Davids, P., *The Epistle of James: A Commentary on the Greek Text* (Grand Rapids: Eerdmans, 1982), 2-5, 21-22.

Deissmann, A., *Bible Studies: Contributions, Chiefly from Papyri and Inscriptions, to the History of the Language, the Literature, and the Religion of Hellenistic Judaism and Primitive Christianity* (Winona Lake, IN: Alpha Publications, 1979).

Derfler, S.L., *The Hasmonean Revolt: Rebellioin or Revolution* (Lampeter, Dyfed, Wales: Edwin Mellen Press, 1989).

Efron, J., *Studies on the Hasmonean Period* (Leiden: E.J. Brill, 1997).

Ehrman, B.D., *The New Testament and Other Early Christian Writings* (New York; Oxford: Oxford University Press, 1998).

Eisenman, R., *James the Just in the Habakkuk Pesher* (Leiden: E.J. Brill, 1986).

_____, *Maccabees, Zadokites, Christians and Qumran: A New Hypothesis of Qumran Origins* (Leiden: E.J. Brill, 1983).

Elliott-Binns, L.E., *Galilean Christianity* (Chicago: Alec R. Allenson, Inc., 1956).

Enslin, M.S., "Paul and Gamaliel," *JR* 7.4 (1927): 360-75.

Feldman, L.H., Review of Efron, *Studies on the Hasmonean Period*, 1997, *JAOS* 114.1 (1994): 87-8.

Fensham, F.C., "Widow, Orphan, and the Poor in Ancient Near Eastern Legal and Wisdom Literature," *JNES* 21.2 (1962): 129-39.

Finkelstein, L, *MGWJ* 76 (1932): 525-534.

_____, "The Pharisees: Their Origin and Their Philosophy," *HTR* 22.3 (1929): 185-261.

Flusser, D., *Jewish Sources in Early Christianity* (New York: Adama Books, 1987).

_____, *Judaism and the Origins of Christianity* (Jerusalem: Magnes Press, 1988).

Golb, N., *Who Wrote the Dead Sea Scrolls: The Search for the Secret of Qumran* (New York: Scribner, 1995).

Gordis, R., *The Book of God and Man: A Study of Job* (Chicago: Univ. of Chicago Press, 1965).

Gottstein, M.H., "Anti-Essene Traits in the Dead Sea Scrolls," *VT* 4.2 (1954): 141-7.

Grant, F.C., *The Gospels: Their Origin and Growth* (New York: Octagon Books, 1957).

Grant, M., *The Jews in the Roman World* (New York: Macmillan, 1973).

Green, W.S, "Palestinian Holy Men: Charismatic Leadership and Rabbinic Tradition," *ANRW* 19.2 (1979): 619-47.

Harnack, A., *The Mission and Expansion* II, 79 ff.; Arnold A. A. T. Ehrhardt, "The Birth of the Synagogue and R. Akiba," *The Framework of the New Testament Stories* (Manchester: Manchester University Press, 1964).

Haydin, H.M., "Three Conceptions of the Christian Life, A Study in the Epistles of James, 1 Peter, and 1 John," *BW* 23.1 (1904): 18, 20.

Hornblower, S. and Spawforth, A., eds., *Oxford Classical Dictionary*, 3rd ed. (Oxford; New York: Oxford University Press, 1996).

Jocz, J., *The Jewish People and Jesus Christ* (London: SPCK, 1954; reprint, Grand Rapids: Baker, 1980), 165.

Kampen, J., *The Hasideans and the Origin of Pharisaism: A Study in 1 and 2 Maccabees* (Atlanta: Scholars Press, 1980).

Knohl, I., *The Messiah Before Jesus* (Berkeley: University of California Press, 2000).

LaCocque, A., *Daniel in His Time* (Columbia, SC: University of South Carolina Press, 1988).

Larson, E.W., "Qumran and the Dead Sea Scrolls: Discoveries, Debates, the Scrolls and the Bible," *NEA* 63.3 (2000): 168-71.

Libermann, S., *Tosefta ki-fshutah, Order Zera'im*, Part I (New York: Jewish Theological Seminary, 1955), 124.

Licht, J., *Thanksgiving Scroll: A Scroll from the Wilderness of Judaea* (Eilat, Israel: Bialik Institute, 1957).

Lietzmann, H., *A History of the Early Church*. B.L. Woolf, trans. (reprinted; London: Lutterworth Press, 1961), I.

Martin, M., *The Decline and Fall of the Roman Church* (New York: Bantam, 1983).

Massebieau, L., "*L'Eptre de Jacques. Est-elle l'oeuvre d'un Chretien?*," *RHR* 32 (1895): 249-83.

Pines, S., "Judaeo-Christian Materials in an Arabic Jewish Treatise," *AAJRP* 35 (1967): 187-217.

Porter, J.R., *The Lost Bible* (Chicago: University of Chicago Press, 2001).

Pritz, R.A., *Nazarene Jewish Christianity from the End of the New Testament Period until its Disappearance in the Fourth Century* (Jerusalem: Magnes Press, 1992).

Qimron, E., "The Damascus Covenant 15.1-2," *JQR* 81.102 (1990): 115-18.

_____, "Further Observations on the Laws of Oaths in the Damascus Document 15," *JQR* 85.1-2 (1994): 251-7.

Rast, W.E., "Developments in Postexilic Judaism," *JOR* 50.1 (1970).

Ropes, J.H., *A Critical and Exegetical Commentary on the Epistle of St. James* (Edinburgh: T&T Clark, 1916).

Safrai, S. and Stern, M., *The Jewish People in the First Century*, Vol. 2 (Philadelphia: Fortress Press, 1987).

Scarborough, W.J., "James the Just," *JOBR* 9.4 (1941): 234-8.

Schiffman, L., *Reclaiming the Dead Sea Scrolls: Their True Meaning for Judaism and Christianity* (New York, Doubleday, 1995), 299.

Schoeps, H.J., *Theologie und Geschichte des Judenchristentums* (Tuebingen: J.C.B. Mohr, 1949).

_____, *Paul: The Theology of the Apostle in the Light of Jewish Religious History* (Philadelphia: Fortress Press, 1961).

Schubert, K., *The Dead Sea Community: the Background to the Dead Sea Scrolls* (New York: Greenwood Press, 1959).

Schumacher, G., *"Pella" in Abila Pella and Northern 'Ajlun* (London: Palestine Exploration Fund, 1885-90).

Schurer, E., *History of the Jewish People in the Age of Jesus Christ*, Vol. 2 (Edinburgh: T&T Clark, 1986).

Schwartz, D.R., Review of Kampen 1988, *JQR* 80.½ (1989): 187-9.

Scott, J.J., *Jewish Backgrounds of the New Testament*, (Grand Rapids: Baker, 2000).

Seitz, O.J.F., "Relationship of the Shepherd of Hermas to the Epistle of James," *JBL* 63:2 (1944), 131-40.

Spitta, F., *Zur Geschichte und Literatur des Urchristentums* (Gottingen:Vandenhoeck un Ruprecht, 1893).

Stark, R., *The Rise of Christianity: How the Obscure, Marginal Jesus Movement Became the Dominant Religious Force in the Western World in a Few Centuries*, (Princeton: Princeton University Press, 1997).

Starratt, F.A., "Ethical and Mystical Religion," *BW* 46.6 (1915): 363.

Stegemann, H., *The Library of Qumran* (New York: Brill, 1993).

Tabor, J., *The Jesus Dynasty: The Hidden History of Jesus, His Royal Family, and the Birth of Christianity* (New York: Simon & Schuster, 2007).

Taylor, J.E., "The Phenomenon of Early Jewish-Christianity: Reality or Scholarly Invention?," *VC* 44.4 (1990): 313-34.

Telfer, W., "Was Hegesippus a Jew," *HTR* 53.2 (1960): 143-53.

Torrey, C.C., "James the Just, and His Name 'Oblias'," *JBL* 63.2 (1944): 93-98.

Trever, J.C., "The Book of Daniel and the Origin of the Qumran Community," *BA* 48.2 (1985): 89-102.

VanderKam, J., *The Dead Sea Scrolls Today* (Grand Rapids: Eerdmans, 1994).

_____, Review of Eisenman (1983), *JAOS* 105.4 (1985): 798-9.

Verheyden, J., *De Vlucht van de Christenen naar Pella. Onderzoek van het Getuigenis van Eusebius en Epiphanius* (Brussels: Paleis der Academien, 1988).

Vermes, G., *The Dead Sea Scrolls in English* (New York: Penguin Books, 1997).

Wilken, R., "John Chrysostom," *Encyclopedia of Early Christianity*, E. Ferguson, ed. (New York: Garland, 1997).

Wilson, Marvin, *Our Father Abraham: Jewish Roots of the Christian Faith* (Grand Rapids: Eerdmans, 1989), 64-9.

Yadin, Y., *The Scroll of the War of the Sons of Light against the Sons of Darkness* (Oxford: Oxford University Press, 1962).

Zeitlin, S., "The Propaganda of the Hebrew Scrolls and the Falsification of History," *JQR* 46.3 (1956): 209-58.

_____, "The Titles High Priest and the Nasi of the Sanhedrin," *JQR* 48.1 (1957): 1-5.

Index